Campus Sexual Assault

Books in the **Contemporary World Issues** series address vital issues in today's society, such as genetic engineering, pollution, and biodiversity. Written by professional writers, scholars, and nonacademic experts, these books are authoritative, clearly written, up-to-date, and objective. They provide a good starting point for research by high school and college students, scholars, and general readers as well as by legislators, businesspeople, activists, and others.

Each book, carefully organized and easy to use, contains an overview of the subject, a detailed chronology, biographical sketches, facts and data and/or documents and other primary source material, a forum of authoritative perspective essays, annotated lists of print and nonprint resources, and an index.

Readers of books in the Contemporary World Issues series will find the information they need in order to have a better understanding of the social, political, environmental, and economic issues facing the world today.

Campus Sexual Assault

A REFERENCE HANDBOOK

Alison E. Hatch

ABC-CLIO™

An Imprint of ABC-CLIO, LLC
Santa Barbara, California • Denver, Colorado

Library of Congress Cataloging-in-Publication Data

Names: Hatch, Alison E., author.
Title: Campus sexual assault : a reference handbook / Alison E. Hatch.
Description: Santa Barbara, California : ABC-CLIO, 2017. | Series: Contemporary world issues | Includes bibliographical references and index.
Identifiers: LCCN 2016059521 (print) | LCCN 2017004423 (ebook) | ISBN 9781440841392 (alk. paper) | ISBN 9781440841408 (ebook)
Subjects: LCSH: Rape in universities and colleges—United States. | Rape victims—Services for—United States. | Sexual abuse victims—Services for—United States.
Classification: LCC LB2345.3.R37 H37 2017 (print) | LCC LB2345.3.R37 (ebook) | DDC 371.7/82—dc23
LC record available at https://lccn.loc.gov/2016059521

ISBN: 978-1-4408-4139-2
EISBN: 978-1-4408-4140-8

21 20 19 18 17   1 2 3 4 5

This book is also available as an eBook.

ABC-CLIO
An Imprint of ABC-CLIO, LLC

ABC-CLIO, LLC
130 Cremona Drive, P.O. Box 1911
Santa Barbara, California 93116–1911
www.abc-clio.com

This book is printed on acid-free paper ∞

Manufactured in the United States of America

Contents

Preface

As a professor of sociology and gender studies, the most emotionally difficult and disheartening aspect of my job has been hearing students disclose their experiences with sexual assault. Some come to my office to talk about their incidents; others discuss it in their course papers. Some survivors wish to pursue disciplinary measures against their perpetrators; others do not. Some have turned to therapists, friends, family, or others for help and support; others simply are not ready to talk about it. Despite these differences, what all survivors of sexual violence have in common is that they have experienced something terrible. They were violated, often at the hands of someone they knew, at a location they thought they could trust.

Campus sexual assault is a difficult topic to address. The reality is that sexual assault occurs on college campuses with alarming frequency. As a professor, and as a parent of children who will attend college someday, this fact is frightening. It is easy to get disheartened with statistics that estimate 1 out of every 5 women, and 1 out of every 20 men, experience sexual assault on campus. Our culture is saturated with images of violence against women as entertainment in movies, television, video games, and music. Survivors of sexual violence are often blamed for their assaults, rape myths abound, and perpetrators are often served minor punishments or not brought to justice at all. Unfortunately, many colleges and universities have been failing to address sexual assault on their campuses adequately.

It seems like every few weeks there is another story making media rounds about a sexual assault on a college or university campus, and we know that for every story we hear about, there are so many that we do not. What ultimately gives me hope are the brave voices of survivors who insist on justice, the campus antirape and antiviolence activists across the country, and the organizations and nonprofits that work to end sexual violence. We have come to a point in our culture's history when sexual violence is not something assumed to be "natural," or swept under the rug. We are demanding change.

Sexual assault, and campus sexual assault specifically, is not a new phenomenon. However, campus sexual assault has received a great deal more attention lately. Within the last several years, we have seen high-profile cases of campus sexual assault, new campus policies, new legislation, antirape and antiviolence activism, government interest and involvement in combating the problem, and documentaries and other forms of media raising awareness about the issue. With so much going on recently, the intent of this book is to gather information on this topic in a concise and easy-to-navigate format. The book provides relevant history on campus sexual assault, statistics, and key documents and discusses prevalent controversies. Additionally, it outlines key cases and people, includes the voices of various individuals who either have survived campus sexual assault or work to combat it, and provides a timeline of key dates. Also, it includes suggestions for additional resources, ideas for campus activism, and a list of organizations and nonprofits that work diligently to eradicate campus sexual violence.

Additionally, the scope of this text is limited to an overview of sexual assault that occurs to college students. By no means does this indicate that college students are the only ones at risk. Sexual assault in our elementary, middle, and high schools is also a serious, often hidden, issue. There are signs that this problem is receiving more attention, and I recommend readers who are interested in learning about school sexual assault to stay abreast of the relevant scholarship on the topic.

If you have, or a friend or loved one has, experienced sexual assault:

If you have experienced campus sexual violence, there are a variety of resources available to you. If you are in immediate danger or wish to report the assault to the police, you can call 911 and/or your campus police department. You may desire to seek medical treatment for injuries and disease, pregnancy tests, and a rape kit. If possible, avoid showering or cleaning your body beforehand. Additional sources include your college or university's victim's resource center, health clinic, and/or counseling center. It is likely your local community has a rape crisis center with a hotline, therapists, and advocates who can provide support and accompany you to medical treatment. The National Sexual Assault Hotline at 800–656-HOPE (4673) can offer guidance and assistance. Additionally, see Chapter 6: Resources for a list of organizations that provide resources and support.

Most important, remember that if you have experienced something sexual against your will, regardless of the type of sexual activity; regardless of your sex, gender, or sexual orientation; regardless of the sex, gender, or sexual orientation of the perpetrator; regardless of whether or not you knew the perpetrator; and regardless of whether or not you were intoxicated, *you are not to blame.* Seek out supportive friends, family, and/or medical or campus officials. With Title IX, you have the legal right to assistance and protection from your school, including changing dorms or classes if necessary. If you are concerned about confidentiality when talking to campus officials, remember to ask about their obligation to disclose information before you speak with them. If you feel as though your campus does not respond appropriately to your assault, you can file a complaint with the U.S. Department of Education and the U.S. Department of Justice.

If you have been told by a friend, loved one, student, coworker, or acquaintance that they have been sexually assaulted, your reaction is important. Listen, believe, do not place blame, and offer to help. They may just want you to provide them with a patient and supportive ear, and/or they may want you to accompany them to the hospital, the police, a campus official's office, or a counselor. Consider it an honor that the survivor trusted you with this information. Do not take that honor lightly.

Actions you can take on your campus:

Statistically speaking, it is highly likely that you know some-one who has survived sexual assault. It is to everyone's benefit that we create campuses that are free from sexual violence. If you are a college student or a parent of a college student, be sure to research the college or university's sexual assault policies, victim resources, prevention education, and safety measures. In general, be wary of data that indicates no reported instances of sexual assault, as this indicates there are likely difficulties or roadblocks to reporting. Research whether the school is under investigation by the Department of Education for Title IX vio-lations, and if so, determine if they are making positive strides in rectifying inadequacies. Look for sexual assault prevention education programs that include bystander intervention tech-niques and violence prevention. Be wary of education programs that put the onus of preventing assault on the potential victims themselves (e.g., telling women what to do in order to prevent assault). If you are a student on campus, join or start a campus antiviolence group to raise awareness about the issue. Demand that your school have ample resources in addition to providing support and education on violence prevention. As a peer and a friend, do not victim blame, and do your best to be supportive and helpful to survivors who seek your assistance.

It is my hope that someday my students will not have such terrible stories of sexual assault to share and that colleges and universities will be doing a better job preventing sexual vio-lence and supporting those who have survived it. Until then, I dedicate this book to anyone who has experienced sexual vio-lence. You are not alone and you are not to blame.

Acknowledgments

I am appreciative of the folks at ABC-CLIO for giving me the opportunity to write about such an important, and relevant, topic. Robin Tutt deserves extra gratitude for her patience and support. Thank you also to Gordon Matchado and Sivakumar Vijayaraghavan for their assistance with the editing process.

I am grateful to the College of Liberal Arts at Armstrong State University for providing me with summer research stipends that allowed me to concentrate on conducting the research necessary to write this book. Dr. Dan Skidmore-Hess, Chair of the Criminal Justice, Social and Political Science Department, provided me with support, encouragement, and departmental funding to attend a writing retreat. For those who are interested in a beautiful location conducive to concentrating on your craft, I highly recommend an artist retreat at the Lillian E. Smith Center in Clayton, Georgia. Thank you to Dr. Mary Barr for the recommendation.

This book would not have been possible without the assistance of several undergraduate research assistants, including Leena Ali, Kayla Berns, and Tracy Le. My mother, Caren Smith, also served as a dutiful research assistant. All four of these ladies helped me find the most useful and up-to-date information, and they did so with patience and good humor. I'm also thankful to Michael Tiemeyer for answering questions about statistics. Numbers are not my strong suit. Additionally, I am appreciative of my parents, Scott and Lisa Hatch and Caren Smith, and my siblings, Zach and Zoe Hatch, for their lifelong support and encouragement.

I am also thankful to those who contributed to this book. Your work in the field of sexual violence makes a positive difference in the lives of many. Additionally, I am appreciative of the survivor contributors and the many students I have had over the years who have confided their experiences with me. Telling your story takes great courage.

Last, I am very grateful to my husband, Dan, and my children, Paige and Ryan. They were very patient and understanding with me throughout this process. My family remains my motivation for wanting to make the world a better place.

Campus Sexual Assault

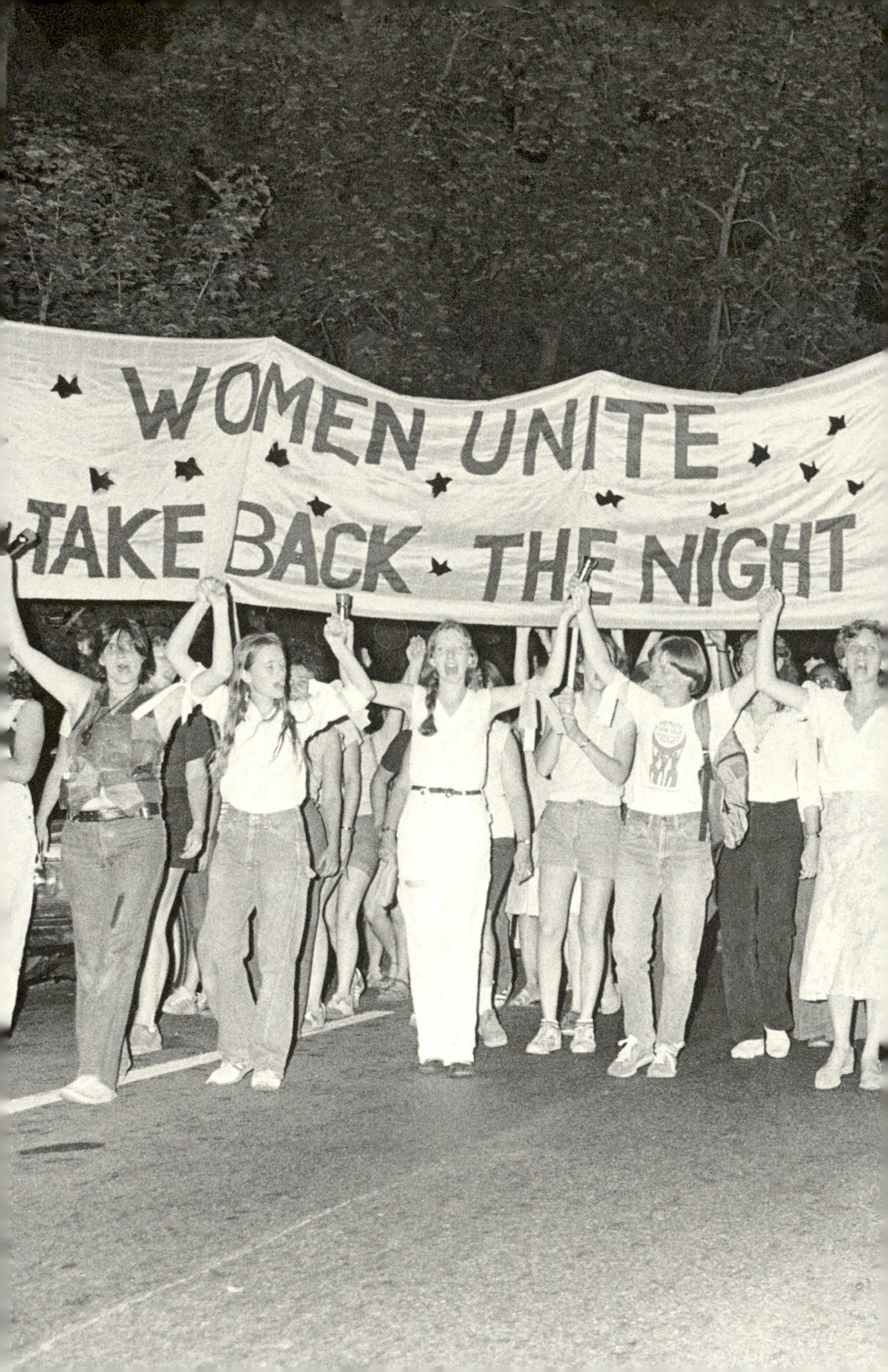
WOMEN UNITE
TAKE BACK THE NIGHT

Introduction

Attending a college or university is an important milestone in the lives of many young adults. It is an opportunity to further one's knowledge on an array of different topics, to meet and learn from peers who have varying life experiences and opinions, and to improve communication skills, build networks, and gain independence. While postsecondary education is often expensive, research indicates that overall financial and social benefits outweigh the costs. When students embark on the journey of attending college, they likely have many dreams and expectations for their experience. They do not envision, however, that their time in college will be marred by something as tragic as sexual assault. For an alarming number of students, facing sexual assault, or knowing someone who did, will be part of the college experience.

Sexual assault on college campuses is not a new phenomenon. And unfortunately, statistics indicate it happens with alarming frequency. The privilege of attending an institution of higher learning should not, but regrettably does, come with a 1 in 5 chance a woman, or 1 in 20 chance a man, will be sexually assaulted while in pursuit of a degree. Naturally, in light

A "Take Back the Night" protest in Boston in 1978. Since the 1970s, "Take Back the Night" events raise awareness about, and protest against, violence against women. Held in cities and campuses across the nation and world, they have become a staple of campus antirape activism. (Spencer Grant/ Getty Images) of such statistics, many people are outraged. Contemporary student activists, taking a page out of history from antirape activists in the 1970 and 1980s, are fighting for change. They are educating others on the reality of campus sexual assault and rape culture, they are fighting for their schools to be held accountable for their all-too-often poor treatment of survivors, and they are fighting for their schools to take sexual assault seriously and hold perpetrators responsible for their actions. Some contemporary politicians have entered the dialogue, fighting for tougher legislation and demanding that schools cease to turn a blind eye to the assaults occurring on their campuses. Many assert that this nation is in a watershed moment in its history in terms of combating sexual assault on college campuses. Simply put, people want college to be the experience it promises to be—one in which students experience personal growth and develop skills and knowledge without fearing for their safety.

This chapter will give an overview of the background to the topic of campus sexual assault. Following a brief discussion about the language used in this text, there is a synopsis of pertinent sexual assault statistics and research findings. Additionally, this chapter includes an overview of factors that contribute to making colleges and universities risky for sexual assault and a summary of the most salient aspects to the topic, including past and present campus activism, notable cases, and relevant legislation.

A Note about Language

In common parlance, the terms *sexual assault* and *rape* are often used interchangeably, despite having different definitions. In general, *sexual assault* refers to any type of sexual contact or behavior that occurs without consent, including penetration, attempted rape, forcing a victim to perform sexual acts, incest, child molestation, fondling, or unwanted sexual touching. *Rape* refers to sexual penetration of a vagina, anus, or mouth with any body part or object without consent of the victim. Rape is achieved by physical force, emotional or psychological coercion, deception, and threat or against a person incapable of giving consent. The legal definitions of both *sexual assault* and *rape* vary by state, and some states have more narrow definitions of *rape*. RAINN (Rape, Abuse, & Incest National Network) maintains an updated list of sexual assault and rape definitions by state on their website (www.rainn.org).

The term *campus sexual assault* is used throughout this book to refer to sexual assault that occurs to a student attending a postsecondary institute of higher learning, such as a college or university. This includes assaults that occur both on and off campus. Despite the term, research indicates many, if not most, assaults occur off campus property.

The text uses both *survivor* and *victim* to refer to someone who has experienced sexual assault. There are pros and cons to each word. Many anti–sexual violence advocates prefer the use of the word *survivor* because it recognizes personal strength and agency. *Survivor* is a word that invokes reclamation and taking back one's life after a traumatic event. However, it is important to remember that in the most tragic of cases, there are those who do not survive the violence perpetrated against them. The term *victim* is perhaps more commonplace; however, it comes with baggage, conjuring up images of helplessness and contributing to feelings of powerlessness. On the other hand, the use of the word *victim* also recognizes the enormity of the problem. Those who experience sexual violence are victims to a crime, and using the word *victim* reminds us there was a perpetrator who broke the law. Ultimately, those who have experienced violence of any kind have the right to choose whichever terminology they feel the most comfortable with for themselves.

There is debate about the use of the word *alleged* when used to describe an incident of sexual assault, a perpetrator, or a victim. The word *alleged* is commonly used when discussing sexual assault when there has not been a final resolution in the criminal justice system. Likewise, in cases of campus sexual assault, *alleged* is often used when there has not been a resolution by the university or college. This is consistent with the presumption that the accused are innocent until proven guilty. However, *alleged victim* and *alleged assault* not only cast doubts on the victim's accounts, but are both insensitive, and likely inaccurate, as most accounts of sexual assault are credible. The reality is that only a small percentage of campus sexual assault cases make their way through the entire criminal justice system. Very few cases of campus sexual assault even make their way through the disciplinary proceedings at a college or university. And, as will be discussed further in this book, schools sometimes mishandle these cases and perpetrators are not brought to justice. In other words, it seems inappropriate to refer to such cases as "alleged." It is also worth noting that the practice of using *alleged* is generally not applied to a discussion of any other crime. While this text uses *alleged* to refer to cases that have not yet been proven in a court of law or by a school disciplinary proceeding, readers should be aware of the pitfalls in doing so.

Relevant Research Findings

Prevalence

Over the last several years, the topic of sexual assault on college campuses has received a great deal of attention. With so many high-profile cases, legislative initiatives, and courageous activists in the news, it is easy to assume the crisis of campus sexual assault is only a recent phenomenon. In reality, feminists, anti–sexual assault activists, and students raised this issue decades ago. Today, there is hope that our society is beginning to finally listen. Thanks to research that has evidenced the existence and prevalence of rape on college campuses, and to brave individuals willing to discuss their cases and fight the institutions that wronged them, many are hopeful that the tide is turning.

Research today on campus sexual assault is plentiful, but that has not always been the case. In 1957, sociologists Clifford

Kirkpatrick and Eugene Kanin published "Male Sex Aggression on a University Campus" in the journal *American Sociological Review*. At the time, when the possibility that one could be raped by an acquaintance was neither acknowledged nor discussed, this groundbreaking article introduced the idea of "attempted intercourse with violence" within dating relationships on college campuses. The authors found that 291 women on one campus had experienced over a thousand "offensive episodes."

The work of Kirkpatrick and Kanin was followed in the 1980s by that of clinical psychologist Mary P. Koss. Koss is recognized as the pioneer of campus sexual assault research. In 1987, Koss, and her colleagues Christine Gidycz and Nadine Wisniewski, published the results of their national study of over 6,000 students from 32 colleges and universities. They found that one in four women in college have experienced rape or attempted rape since the age of 14 and that most sexual assaults are perpetrated by acquaintances (often referred to in sexual assault literature as *date rape* and/or *acquaintance rape*). Their research continues to be widely cited and replicated. Additionally, the measure they developed, the Sexual Experiences Survey, has become a frequently used tool to study unwanted sexual encounters. Koss's work is notable for drawing attention to the existence and prevalence of date rape.

Koss laid the groundwork for our knowledge of campus sexual assault. Following her work, numerous studies have been conducted on the topic. In order to grasp the contemporary gravity of the situation, accurate and up-to-date statistics on prevalence are integral. Statistics are necessary in order to raise public awareness and concern and, in turn, appropriate resource allocation. Yet, statistics on sexual assault can be complex and controversial. Not only are rape and sexual assault vastly underreported crimes, but there is dispute as to what studies yield the most accurate numbers. With different statistics originating from different sources, *dueling data* creates confusion and debate.

According to data gathered by RAINN, about two out of every three sexual assaults committed in the United States go unreported to the police. There are many reasons why survivors of sexual assault do not report the crime. Feelings of shame, denial, and fear may keep survivors from coming forward. Additionally, in a culture that often engages in victim blaming, survivors may feel as though they deserved the assault or fear that they will be blamed if they do come forward. Some choose not to report their assaults because they have previous experience of, or have witnessed, authorities not taking sexual assault reports seriously. Survivors may fear the re-traumatization that can occur in the process of pursuing a charge of sexual assault. Others may not report because the assault does not fit common stereotypes of what rape is "supposed" to look like, for example, if it was perpetrated by someone they knew as opposed to by a stranger. Male survivors of sexual assault may have additional hurdles to reporting based on our problematic cultural norms of masculinity. Specifically, there exists a misguided notion that men "can't be raped" because they are too strong to be physically overpowered and/or are too hypersexual to not want sex in the first place. Additionally, in a heteronormative society, male survivors may fear that others would make assumptions about their sexual orientation. Those from marginalized communities, such as lesbian, gay, bisexual, and transgender (LGBT) survivors, also face unique challenges in reporting their assaults. The discrimination they face surrounding their identity may make them reluctant to seek help from police, hospitals, or crisis centers. The same can be said of survivors of color, who may be hesitant to seek help for fear of a biased criminal justice system. Also, undocumented survivors may fear deportation or find language barriers insurmountable.

More specifically speaking, while many campus sexual assault survivors disclose to friends, few report their assaults to campus officials or law enforcement. Research indicates, for example, that only 12 percent of sexual assaults against women are reported to police or university officials (Kilpatrick et al.

2007; Washington Post-Kaiser Family Foundation Poll 2015). Another study found that fewer than 5 percent of completed or attempted rapes of women in college were reported to law officials (Fisher et al. 2000). Those who experience rape or sexual assault on campus face the same hurdles to reporting as discussed earlier. Additionally, college student survivors of sexual assault may choose not to report because they do not know how to report or to whom, they find a lack of support from friends and peers, they suffer from feelings of shame or self-blame, they fear they will not be believed, alcohol was involved, they fear ruined reputations, they believed it was unimportant, they did not want the perpetrator punished, and/or unsympathetic school officials encouraged them not to report. Additionally, the prospect of going up against a school administration may be especially daunting to students of color or members of the LGBT community who perceive their campuses to be insensitive to issues of race or sexual orientation or who feel the larger anti–sexual assault movement speaks mostly to, and about, white heterosexual women. Also, graduate students potentially have a lot to lose if they report instances of sexual misconduct, especially if the perpetrators are faculty members that graduate students are dependent upon for their training, mentoring, and a successful career trajectory.

Given that sexual assault is so underreported in general, many argue statistics gleaned from data on assaults reported to law enforcement or campus personnel (e.g., FBI Uniform Crime Statistics, campus crime statistics) are best treated as underestimates of the actual prevalence of sexual assault. For example, according to the American Association of University Women, nine out of ten colleges and universities in 2014 reported zero instances of sexual assault on their campuses in their annual crime data. That zero sexual assaults occurred on a campus in any given year is highly unlikely. Instead, such a statistic, which is based on *reported* sexual assaults, may reflect an institution that does not encourage reporting in the first place or that fails to provide accurate reports to the government.

Alternatively, many argue a better indication of the prevalence of sexual assault can be obtained from research in which respondents are asked to disclose their experiences. Surveys allow respondents to disclose sexual assault incidents without mandating they make any formal reports to officials. There are a variety of surveys on campus sexual assault. Some are government funded, like the National Crime Victimization Survey (NCVS) conducted by the Bureau of Justice Statistics and the College Sexual Assault (CSA) study funded by the Department of Justice. Studies are also conducted by other organizations, like the survey on college sexual assault administered by the Washington Post-Kaiser Family Foundation Poll or the survey on campus sexual assault conducted by the Association of American Universities. And some studies are conducted by researchers at various universities. While there is a fair amount of consistency among prominent research regarding the prevalence of campus sexual assault, there are also some stark differences. When analyzing statistics on campus sexual assault, careful consideration of the design of the survey is important. Arguably, the strongest surveys take into consideration the best practices in both the language used in the questions and the methods employed in administering the survey.

The debate about the NCVS, an annual crime report conducted through household surveys administered by the U.S. Census Bureau for the Bureau of Justice Statistics, is illustrative of the difficulty in creating the best measures to achieve accurate statistics. The survey comes from a criminal justice perspective, asks about *point-in-time* events that constitute criminal behavior, and has long been viewed as a reliable source of statistics on all types of crime victimization. However, the NCVS has been criticized for its methods in counting sexual assault and rape, including in a review by the National Research Council, part of the National Academies, which found that the survey failed to employ best methods and likely undercounts the prevalence of sexual assault. Some of the concerns include the fact that privacy is not stressed for the administration of the NCVS surveys as questions are asked in person or over the phone. Given that most victims of sexual assault are assaulted by someone they know, if the abuser is within earshot they may be unlikely to report. Also, the NCVS does not include alcohol or drug use in its definition of rape or sexual assault, whereas other surveys, like the CSA study, take into account the inability to consent if the victim was intoxicated from alcohol or drugs.

Additionally, the NCVS survey includes questions that ask directly about rape as opposed to using behavioral cues or describing events that would constitute rape, like those utilized in the CSA study. In the 1980s, Mary P. Koss was one of the first to contend that asking directly about rape fails to measure instances of rape that the victim does not acknowledge, or wish acknowledge, as such. Studies like the CSA study and National Intimate Partner and Sexual Violence survey published by the Centers for Disease Control and Prevention take a public health approach, which means respondents may report instances of sexual assault even if they do not view it as a crime, whereas respondents to the NCVS may be less likely to report sexual assault if they do not personally view the assault as a crime. On the other hand, critics of surveys that use broader definitions, such as the CSA, argue they risk over-reporting sexual assault. Additionally, some contend that the statistics gleaned from the CSA study are not representative of all schools or all students, since the study was conducted at two large universities using a web-based survey. The NCVS is a compilation of data from 160,000 adults and teens across the nation and uses an expansive definition of *student* that counts respondents as students regardless of whether they live on campus or whether they are at home taking online classes around their work schedules. While there is much to be said of the value of a larger, nationally representative data set, critics maintain the smaller sample in the CSA study reflects the population usually referred to in the context of the *campus rape crisis*.

Ultimately, the difference in numbers between studies can be significant. For example, the NCVS indicates that

0.6 percent (or 6.1 in 1,000) female students experienced rape or sexual assault over 1995–2013. That statistic is vastly different from the oft-cited *one in five* (or 200 in 1,000) statistic that corresponds to the finding that approximately 20 percent of female students experience rape or sexual assault while at college. The one in five statistic originates from several studies that typically incorporate broader definitions of sexual assault, including prompts for situations in which a victim would be unable to consent (if the victim had passed out or was drunk, drugged, incapacitated, or asleep). A difference in methodologies can explain, at least in part, the difference in findings.

While criticized as being misleading and too high by some, the reality is that the commonly cited one in five statistic reflects the findings of various research studies that ask respondents to self-report instances of sexual assault. For example, the National College Women Sexual Victimization Study (Fisher et al. 2000) estimated the percentage of completed or attempted rape victimization among women in college or universities to be between 20 percent and 25 percent over the course of a college career. A survey by the Association of American Universities administered at 27 universities and with over 150,000 student responses found that 23 percent of female undergraduates reported they were victims of non-consensual sexual contact. The National Institute of Justice's Campus Climate Survey (Krebs et al. 2016), based on data from 23,000 students in nine schools, found the average sexual assault prevalence rate for women since they entered college to be 21 percent and the prevalence rate for fourth-year female undergraduates to be 25 percent. This study also illustrated how the prevalence of sexual violence varies depending on the school, with the rates ranging from an alarming one in two at some schools to one in eight in others. And the results of the CSA survey (Krebs et al. 2007), which estimates that 19 percent of college women are victims of sexual assault, were used as the basis of the 1 in 5 statistic put forth by the Obama administration in their White House initiative to combat campus sexual assault.

Importantly, research indicates that women between the ages of 18 and 24 are at elevated risk for sexual assault. While past research suggests women in that age bracket who attend college to be at greater risk than women who do not attend college, the recent NCVS data indicate that 18- to 24-year-olds who do not attend college to be at even greater risk than 18- to 24-year-olds who do attend college. This finding was heralded by some as debunking a "myth" and that the occurrence of sexual assault on campuses is not as frequent as advocates declare. While the debate on research studies and statistics will likely continue, arguably what is most important is recognizing an age category in which women are at increased risk, whether they attend school or not, and working to combat the problem.

There is more variability in the statistics on male survivors of campus sexual assault. This is possibly due to the hurdles men face in reporting and the taboo nature that surrounds male victimization in our culture. Typically, the most cited finding, that 1 in 20 men (or 5%) experience sexual assault while in college, is based on research including the AAU Campus Climate Survey on Sexual Assault and Sexual Misconduct (2015) and the Washington Post–Kaiser Family Foundation Poll (2015). The Campus Sexual Assault Survey (Krebs et al. 2007) found 1 in 16 men (6.1%) experienced completed or attempted sexual assault since entering college. The Campus Climate Survey (2016) found that among undergraduate males the average prevalence rate for sexual assault since entering college was 7 percent. Additional research on prevalence indicates that transgender students are at higher risk than non-transgender students for sexual violence in college (Association of American Universities, 2015).

Statistics are complicated and can be both confusing and divisive. But debates about specific numbers are likely missing the larger point. Research makes it clear that women between the ages of 18 and 24 are at elevated risk for sexual assault. Additionally, most evidence points to a high prevalence of sexual assault occurring on college campuses. And while accurate statistics are necessary in terms of fueling a constructive public discourse, when it comes down to it, even one sexual assault is too many.

There is a lot of interest in campus "climate surveys" as a potential solution to the debate about statistics. In climate surveys, campuses can gather and analyze their own survey data to determine how to best understand the scope of the problem and how to work to solve it. The Obama administration's White House Task Force to Protect Students from Sexual Assault recommended the use of anonymous campus climate surveys and released a guide on how to best phrase questions and generate responses. Critics contend that the survey should not be left up to the schools to create and that Education Department officials should take the reign. Others argue that the problem of underreporting is likely not solved by campus climate surveys. However, in terms of campuses taking a proactive approach to helping the people whom they serve, administering climate surveys may be a good first step. At the very least, it keeps schools from having to, or wanting to, rely on the artificially low statistics that are released by their disciplinary offices.

The "Red Zone"

In football lingo, the "red zone" describes the area on the field between the 20-yard line and the goal line. The "red zone" has another, more ominous meaning for female college freshmen. First coined by Robin Warshaw in her classic text *I Never Called It Rape* (1988/1994), which was based on the research of Mary P. Koss, the "red zone of danger" refers to the period of time when college women are the most susceptible to sexual assault and rape. Warshaw defined the red zone as beginning when a first-year female steps on campus and ending at the Thanksgiving break. While many agree that the risk for sexual assault is increased at the beginning of the school year, there is some debate about the most accurate parameters of the red zone.

At first, the notion that women were at increased risk for sexual assault in their first few weeks at college was largely based on anecdote. However, several studies have since found evidence for the existence of an especially perilous time period. For example, the CSA study (Krebs et al. 2007) found more than 50 percent of college sexual assaults occur in August, September, October, or November. Additionally, the CSA findings indicate "that women who are victimized during college are most likely to be victimized early on in their college tenure"(p. 68). Another study that cites support for the notion of a red zone found that first-year women were at higher risk for unwanted sexual behavior, especially in the fall semester (Kimble et al., 2008).

This period of vulnerability for first-year women is attributable to several factors. Unfortunately, new female students make good targets: they may be insecure, be unsure of campus geography, have poorly established friendship networks, and feel considerable social pressure to "fit in." Additionally, there are lots of parties, with a lot of access to alcohol and drugs, and students may be testing the limits of their newfound freedom and lack of parental supervision. Moreover, upperclassmen may be especially motivated to "score" with newcomers. While female first-year students may be at increased risk when they first get to campus, this does not negate the reality that the sexual assault can occur at any stage in a female's or male's college career.

Perpetrators

Researching perpetrators of sexual assault is difficult for numerous reasons, including the fact that identified offenders constitute a very small percentage of the number of aggressors. Undetected rapists, those who are neither reported nor prosecuted, make up the largest percentage of perpetrators. While there is not one "typical" profile of a perpetrator of campus sexual assault, research indicates there are some commonalities.

Perpetrators are overwhelmingly male regardless of the gender of their victim(s); research indicates that 98 percent of female victims and 93 percent of male victims identify a male assailant. The vast majority, approximately 90 percent, of campus sexual assaults are perpetrated by someone a victim knows. Typically, assailants are boyfriends, ex-boyfriends, classmates, acquaintances, coworkers, or friends. For some survivors, knowing their perpetrator complicates their decisions to report the assault to officials and likely plays a role in the overall low report rates. Other possible risk factors for assailants include men who hold negative attitudes toward women, accept rape myths, consume violent/degrading pornography, are controlling, lack empathy, and/or perceive a lack of sanctions for abusive behavior. Additional risk factors include men who belong to all-male peer groups like fraternities and sports teams and/or men who connect sexual prowess, dominance, and aggression to masculinity. Also, campus rapists are adept at identifying "likely" victims, often plan and premeditate their attacks, use psychological weapons like manipulation and threats, and use alcohol and isolation to deliberately render victims vulnerable.

Clinical psychologist and campus sexual assault expert David Lisak published his landmark study with Paul M. Miller in 2002 on "undetected rapists." In a sample of 1,882 college men, 120 (6.4%) respondents self-reported acts that met the legal definitions of rape or attempted rape, and among those men, 63 percent admitted to doing so multiple times, averaging 5.8 rapes each. The findings counter the assumption that campus sexual assaults boil down to one-time mistakes and confusion about consent. Instead, Lisak argues that the overwhelming majority, 91 percent, of sexual crimes on campuses are perpetrated by serial rapists.

As with much research in this field, Lisak's research is not immune to criticism. He has been called to defend his research, and his methods, on multiple occasions. For example, another study in 2015 published in *JAMA Pediatrics* found a higher proportion of college men who would be considered rapists but a smaller percentage who were repeat offenders (Swartout et al. 2015). The debate about Lisak's findings, similar to debates over other studies, underscores the continued need for research in this field. Ultimately, it is always best practice to consider multiple sources of research in order to be best informed.

Victim Impacts

Sexual violence impacts victims in varied ways. Some survivors of sexual assault suffer from physical injuries. However, not all acts of sexual assault result in physical injuries per se. Instead, the assault often takes an emotional and psychological toll, which may manifest in physical ailments. Survivors report suffering from nightmares, sleeplessness, depression, fear, hyper-vigilance, denial, panic attacks, and suicidal thoughts. They may withdraw from activities that usually brought them joy, their grades may suffer due to lack of attendance or inability to concentrate, and they may fail or drop out of school. Some survivors engage in harmful coping mechanisms, like alcohol or drug abuse. Others suffer from symptoms of Posttraumatic Stress Disorder (PTSD), struggle to feel safe, and/or feel as though they cannot trust anyone. Many rape survivors suffer from RAPE trauma syndrome, a specific type of PTSD, which includes common emotional, behavioral, and physical reactions to sexual assault exhibited in the months or years afterward. Such reactions include fear, anxiety, depression, sexual dysfunction, and social maladjustment. Sexual assault may also lead to sexually transmitted diseases and pregnancy.

In her recent research on college sexual assault survivors, Lauren Germain (2016) found that many felt as though they did not fit the "perfect victim icon." This so-called perfect victim is a cultural construct, a conglomeration of media images and pictures put forth by campus crime prevention campaigns. The "perfect victim" of sexual assault is a successful student who was not drinking at the time of her assault, who was attacked by a stranger, who attempted to fight off her assailant, who suffered physical injuries, and who promptly went to the hospital afterward. In reality, few campus sexual assaults, and victims, fit that model. However, the respondents in Germain's study found fault in their behaviors, and feared others would not believe them if their responses did not fit the "perfect victim" icon. If, for example, they were drinking at the time of their assault, did not scream, or did not immediately go the hospital or police, the respondents felt they would not be believed.

In reality, Germain found that many survivors seem naturally inclined to engage in self-care after an assault. They often shower and sleep. These are behaviors that victims are told *not* to do, as showering washes away the perpetrator's DNA evidence and time elapsed reduces likelihood of finding evidence. For some, their failure to do things the "correct way" caused guilt and influenced their decision to not report. Comparing themselves to a fictional "perfect victim" had negative ramifications for their well-being.

As discussed previously, male survivors may face additional hurdles in making the decision to report or not report their assaults. Many male survivors face difficulties reconciling their assault with cultural assumptions about masculinity that falsely render men incapable of experiencing sexual assault. Ultimately, male survivors may face a lack of sympathy and understanding, which can further add to their trauma.

As will be discussed at greater length later, many survivors of campus sexual assault feel betrayed by their colleges or universities. Some were re-traumatized by the treatment they received from school officials or peers. Some survivors have even described the treatment they received from their schools as more traumatic than the assault itself. Living in or near where the assault occurred, suffering blame or judgment from peers, seeing the assailant walk on campus, suffering harassment from the assailant, and knowing an assailant has not been punished by the school can all compound feelings of anger and depression. If a student feels as though the institution is failing to believe, let alone protect, them, the campus climate can be very difficult to endure.

Taken all together, rape and sexual assault is clearly a serious public health concern for college and university campuses.

While preventing sexual assault from occurring is essential, so is providing encouragement and opportunities for victims to heal. Recovering from sexual assault comes in many forms and may take weeks, months, or years. For many survivors, talking to trusted friends, family, and/or therapists or counselors is essential. Some find becoming a resource for others who experience sexual assault to be personally gratifying. While some are more comfortable not talking about their experiences, others turn their anger and frustration, against their perpetrator or against the school they perceive mishandled their case, into student activism. Participating in organizations, attending rallies, raising awareness, fighting for change, and even filing Title IX complaints or lawsuits can be cathartic for survivors. Ultimately, survivors of sexual assault will never forget what happened, but it is essential that they be supported in their journey toward recovery.

False Reporting

Unfortunately, many survivors of sexual assault face scrutiny when they come forward to report the crime. This is despite the reality that false reporting of sexual violence is low. A review of relevant research by David Lisak and colleagues (2010) indicate the rate of false reporting to be between 2 and 10 percent. Lisak's data includes only one study at a college or university. In the study conducted at a university, of rape allegations that were investigated by the university police department over the course of ten years, 5.9 percent were determined to be false. Ultimately, to date, there is not much research on false reporting specifically on college campuses.

According to guidelines by the International Association of Chiefs of Police, a determination of a false allegation should be made only after a thorough investigation turns up evidence that supports an assault did not occur. However, research on false reports is complicated by the reality that police departments may use different guidelines in determining if a case is false. What also complicates matters is the assumption that if an alleged assailant is not brought forth to a campus disciplinary hearing, or receives little or no punishment, then that is indicative of their lack of culpability. College and university disciplinary procedures are not the same as cases tried in the criminal justice system, and many argue they are ill equipped to make determinations of guilt.

There have been two high-profile campus sexual assault cases that were based on false information. In 2006, three members of the Duke Lacrosse team were found to be innocent of the charges of sexual assault and kidnapping of an exotic dancer they had hired to perform at a party. The racially charged case garnered a great deal of media interest and ultimately led to the resignation and disbarment of the district attorney who served as the lead prosecutor. In 2014, *Rolling Stone* magazine published an article about an alleged gang rape at a fraternity house at the University of Virginia. The alleged victim's story turned out to be unverifiable and the article was retracted after it was determined to be poorly fact checked. Both scandals created a great deal of controversy.

Arguably, one of the greatest tragedies of false allegations is the potential for them to divert attention away from the vast majority of cases that are factual. Cases of false reporting may lead people to assume "crying rape" is a common occurrence. Sexual assault allegations need to be thoroughly investigated without bias, and any preconceived notion that the allegation is false has the potential to cause immeasurable damage. The assumption that false reporting occurs often, which it does not, harms sexual assault survivors.

Risk Factors on College Campuses

Sexual assault, of course, is not the only crime that occurs on college campuses. On an average college or university campus, students engage in a long list of criminal behavior, ranging from burglary to illegal drug use. This is not to mention the host of academic violations that occur on campuses everywhere, such as plagiarism, or even the most deadly and tragic of campus crimes: mass shootings. While all types of crimes occur on college campuses, it is worth considering why sexual assault is as prevalent as it is. What is it about college—the climate and the students themselves—that creates such a seemingly fertile ground for sexual assault? There is not one clear answer to this question. But there are many variables worth considering. Typically, as researchers Elizabeth Armstrong and her colleagues (2006) suggest, explanations for the high rate of sexual assault on college campuses fall under three broad categories. First is a psychological approach that focuses on perpetrator or victim characteristics. A second approach focuses on a "rape culture" that exists on campuses, and a third approach concentrates on especially dangerous contexts or settings, like fraternities or bars. Since victims and perpetrators were discussed earlier, what follows is an overview of additional possible risk factors, including campus culture and all-male peer groups.

Rape Culture

In the 1970s, second-wave feminists raised public awareness about the issue of rape and sexual assault. Previously believed to be uncommon, or at least something that should not be discussed, the issue of sexual violence was brought to the forefront by feminists. In 1975, Susan Brownmiller published *Against Our Will: Men, Women and Rape*. The book comprehensively revealed the common historical and contemporary acceptance of rape as a conscious process of male intimidation, violence, and power. Her text, which became a best-selling classic, forced readers to examine how rape impacts women's lives and how common an occurrence it has and continues to be. The book has been attributed with changing public outlooks on the issue, and Brownmiller is credited as the first to use the term *date rape*. Scholars also credit Brownmiller's term *rape-supportive culture* as likely influencing the concept of a *rape culture*.

The documentary *Rape Culture* (1975) was produced by Cambridge Documentary Films in association with the DC

Rape Crisis Center and the organization Prisoners against Rape. The documentary, later revised in 1983, is recognized for being among the first to fully define and popularize the concept of rape culture. The concept has since been defined and elaborated upon by many feminists and anti–sexual violence advocates. Emile Buchwald, one of the editors to the text *Transforming a Rape Culture* (1993/2005), defined a rape culture as

> a complex of beliefs that encourages male sexual aggression and supports violence against women. It is a society where violence is seen as sexy and sexuality as violent. In a rape culture, women perceive a continuum of threatened violence that ranges from sexual remarks to sexual touching to rape itself. A rape culture condones physical and emotional terrorism against women and presents it as the norm. (p. xi)

In sum, a rape culture is one in which cultural practices excuse, or tolerate, sexual violence. A rape culture is one in which rape is an everyday occurrence and sexual violence is ignored, trivialized, or thought to be humorous. In a rape culture, victims are blamed for their assaults, and myths about rape abound. Rape myths are beliefs that both deny and justify male sexual aggression against women, for example, the belief that women are asking to be raped if they dress "provocatively" or that women who say "no" to sexual advances really mean "yes." A rape culture leads women to be fearful and assumes men to be violent. Women in a rape culture live by a daily "rape schedule," which is the assumption that they could be sexually assaulted and consequently alter their lifestyle and behavior in attempts to try to prevent rape. Based on these definitions, feminists argue that the United States has a rape culture. By extent, then, it is argued that our college campuses are infused with rape culture. For some, the existence of rape culture on college campuses is evidenced in the high rates of campus sexual assault and the trivial, or nonexistent, disciplinary measures taken against perpetrators. It is also evidenced in the attitudes and behaviors surrounding sexual violence on college campuses. For example, students may joke about rape or actively encourage it, such as the 2010 incident at Yale where fraternity pledges surrounded a women's dorm and chanted "no means yes, yes means anal." Victims of campus sexual violence are blamed for their assaults, peppered with accusations about the amount of alcohol they consume, blamed for the outfit they wore, or blamed for the location they visited or the company they kept. College campuses center their prevention programming on telling women to "be safe," as opposed to telling men not to rape and about the necessity of consent. And campus sexual assault victims who have the courage to come forward are often derided as liars by their peers and sometimes school officials. As potential further indication of a rape-supportive culture on campus, nearly one in three college men admit they would act on "intentions to force a woman to sexual intercourse" if they were confident they would not face any consequences (Edwards et al. 2014).

Some dispute the existence of a rape culture in the United States, claiming it to be overblown or that the focus on rape culture on college campuses is tantamount to "hysteria," as is argued by Caroline Kitchens in a 2014 *Time* magazine article. The influential organization RAINN recommended to the White House Task Force to Protect Students from Sexual Assault that the emphasis on "rape culture" may lead people to "lose sight of the fact" that "rape is caused not by cultural factors but by the conscious decisions, of a small percentage of the community, to commit a violent crime" (Berkowitz & O'Connor 2014, p. 2). In turn, RAIIN's position was criticized by many other anti–sexual violence advocates. It thus remains a debate as to whether college campuses are synonymous with rape culture or if rape culture is a contributing factor to the prevalence of campus sexual assault.

Hook-Up Culture

Unlike generations past, college students today rarely date in the traditional sense of the term. Instead, many students "hook-up," or in other words, engage in short-term, uncommitted, sexual encounters ranging from kissing to intercourse. Kathleen Bogle's research on hook-ups argues there were several significant changes in American culture that altered the contemporary sexual script for college students. Starting in the 1960s, the United States witnessed the liberalization of attitudes about sexuality, the advent of the pill and second-wave feminism, an increase of women on campus, less pressure to marry young, and a fundamental shift in thinking about intercourse before marriage as no longer taboo. All of these changes helped usher in a new dominant sexual script on college campuses: instead of dating, college students "hook-up." For college students, hooking-up is often a casual sexual encounter, but it also sometimes serves as the beginning of more long-term romantic relationships.

Some argue that contemporary hook-up culture should shoulder much of the blame for campus sexual assault, or at the very least it should be considered as going hand in hand with rape culture. One concern is the role of alcohol in the contemporary sexual script. While drinking did not play a big role in the dating era, hooking-up and drinking often go hand in hand, as hooking-up often occurs during or after a night of partying. And, as discussed later in this chapter, alcohol is often considered a risk factor for sexual assault. Another concern is that hooking-up reduces sex to emotionless recreation without consequences. In other words, students are motivated to have sex, regardless of any negative repercussions. In an atmosphere in which hooking-up is commonplace, well-meaning bystanders may not be able to differentiate between typical hooking-up behavior and problematic assault situations. Additionally, the contemporary dating script has a distinct sexual double standard. Not only is women's sexuality more closely scrutinized and judged, but men may feel entitled to sex. A sense of entitlement to sex has risky implications for sexual assault. In a study on college hook-up culture, Jennifer Katz and her colleagues (2012) found that while similar proportions of men and women hooked up, women disproportionately faced negative social reputations and unwanted, possibly coercive, sex.

With all of this being said, the reality is that sexual assault occurred on college campuses long before hook-up culture entered the scene. Some anti–sexual assault advocates worry that a narrow focus on hook-up culture may too easily remove blame from the perpetrators for their actions. Brock Turner, a student found guilty of sexual assault at Yale, placed blame for his actions on a "party culture" surrounded by "binge drinking" and "sexual promiscuity." To many, including his victim, his apology failed to recognize that regardless of campus culture, he was to blame for his own actions. Additionally, critics contend that a focus on combating hook-up culture may be motivated by moralistic concerns and wistfulness for the dating model of the past. Regardless, given the multitude of cultural changes that ushered in a hook-up culture, it seems unlikely that college campuses will return to the more traditional dating culture of generations past.

Alcohol Consumption

Alcohol use is prevalent on college campuses and in many ways drinking is central to college culture. Students with their newfound freedom and lack of parental supervision find plenty of opportunities to consume alcohol, from house parties to fraternity parties to pub crawls. Ultimately, most college students drink alcohol, and many sometimes binge drink (the consumption of a lot of alcohol in a short period of time, defined by the CDC as when men consume five or more drinks and women consume four or more drinks in about two hours). While alcohol consumption may be viewed by some as a positive lubricant for social life, it is also highly correlated with sexual assault.

Campus sexual assault can be classified into one of three categories. Forcible sexual assault includes unwanted sexual contact or intercourse that occurs due to force or threat of force. Alcohol- or drug-facilitated sexual assault refers to unwanted sexual contact or intercourse that occurs when an assailant deliberately slips an intoxicating substance, like a "date rape drug," into the victim's drink, which renders the victim physically and/or cognitively impaired. Incapacitated sexual assault refers to unwanted sexual contact or intercourse that occurs when a victim willingly consumes alcohol or drugs, or a combination of both, that renders the victim physically and/or cognitively impaired.

In situations of sexual assault involving voluntary or involuntary incapacitation, the victim may have difficulty making decisions, have decreased ability in recognizing dangerous situations, may lose consciousness, may struggle to resist a perpetrator, and may suffer from impaired memory after consumption. In short, a victim lacks the ability to consent while incapacitated. It is worth noting that consent is also impossible in situations in which a victim is asleep, unconscious, or physically/mentally disabled or impaired.

Of the three, forcible sexual assault occurs the least often among campus sexual assaults. Among forcible sexual assaults, weapons are used only in a minority cases; instead, perpetrators typically use tactics such as holding a victim down or twisting an arm. Among campus sexual assaults, incapacitated sexual assaults occur the most often. Research published in 2010 in the *Journal of American College Health* found that 30 percent of surveyed college women reported experiencing a drug- or alcohol-related sexual assault or rape, and 5 percent reported experiencing forcible rape. Of the cases involving drug- or alcohol-related rape, the majority (85%) were preceded by voluntary incapacitation, mostly due to alcohol consumption. Involuntary incapacitation preceded the smaller, remaining percentage (15%) of sexual assaults. Additional research finds that female victims of incapacitated rape are at substantial risk of being victimized again.

In some situations in which victims are rendered involuntarily incapacitated, perpetrators use "party" or "club" drugs to facilitate sexual assault. Odorless, colorless, and tasteless, there are numerous date rape drugs that can be consumed in an alcoholic beverage without the user's knowledge. Some of the most common include gamma-hydroxybutyric acid (GHB), which is a central nervous system depressant. Victims who have consumed GHB (street names include Liquid X, Liquid Ecstasy, Georgia Home Boy) become incapacitated and are unable to resist assault; some suffer amnesia. Rohypnol (street names include Roofies, Roach, Ruffles) is a strong sedative that causes partial amnesia. Katamine (street names include Special K, Kitkat, Cat Valium) is a dissociative anesthetic that creates a dreamlike state and makes it difficult for the user to move. Other more general drugs have been reported to be used as well, including painkillers, sedatives, and anti-anxiety medications.

It is worth noting that while the majority of sexual assaults are preceded by voluntary consumption of alcohol, victims may not be aware of the presence of date rape drugs in their drinks. Also, alcohol is considered the biggest date rape drug, more prevalent than any other intoxicant. Sexual predators use alcohol as a weapon to purposely make a victim impaired or seek out victims who are already intoxicated. Perpetrators may also drink alcohol as an excuse for their actions.

Clearly, alcohol plays a significant role in campus sexual assaults. In fact, alcohol use plays a role in a myriad of problems on campuses, including injuries, fatalities from alcohol poisoning, or driving under the influence. However, from the perspective of many anti–sexual assault advocates, there is a danger in focusing on alcohol consumption as the core to sexual assault prevention efforts. The presence or absence of alcohol does not change cultural norms that allow or encourage sexual assault to occur. In other words, alcohol is not the root of the problem. Additionally, a focus on alcohol consumption may be used to excuse "bad decisions" made by assailants while under the influence. And, importantly, a focus on alcohol consumption may result in making victims feel as though they are to blame for the assault if they were drinking and may keep them from seeking help. While it is important to understand the role alcohol can play in campus sexual assault, victims should never be blamed for consuming alcohol; instead, the responsibility rests solely with the perpetrator.

"Men's Clubs"—Fraternities and Athletics

All male peer groups, such as fraternities and athletic teams, are considered high risk for rape-supportive attitudes and behaviors. In such groups, many men hold themselves, and each other, to a code of masculinity that encourages sexual prowess and aggression.

Fraternities have a long, and varied, history in the United States. Contemporary fraternity residences are uniquely situated to house a good number of college and university men and yet, as private dwellings, do not operate under the scrutiny of campus oversight. Unlike sororities, which are forbidden by their governing body, the National Panhellenic Conference, from throwing parties, most fraternities are not dry and many have a reputation for hosting alcohol-laden parties. As one attorney quipped, fraternities are basically "unregulated bars." Fraternities have come under fire for having a disproportionate number of injuries, ranging from hazing incidents, to assault, to harm and even death fueled by alcohol consumption. Additionally, the potential problems inherent with easy access to alcohol are compounded with a fraternity culture of "brotherhood" that sometimes encourages the sexual coercion of women. Common fraternity party themes, such as Pimps and Hos and Playboy Mansion, in which female attendees are asked to arrive scantily clad, create a sexually charged and objectifying atmosphere. Research on fraternity parties by Elizabeth Armstrong and her colleagues (2006) found that fraternity parties are dangerous for women because the men "control party resources and work together to constrain women's behavior." Unfortunately, there are many cases of college women who were intoxicated and then isolated and eventually sexually assaulted at a fraternity party by a member(s) or nonmember(s). The sexual prowess of fraternity men is rewarded by their peers, and female students and fraternity and ex-fraternity members have recounted the existence of "conquest" tallies, explicit picture walls, and ratings of women that are displayed and discussed among the group. For example, in 2011, a fraternity member from Kappa Sigma at the University of Southern California circulated an email to his fraternity brothers asking for help in creating a "gullet report" that includes information about the women they've had sexual activity with, in order to "strengthen brotherhood and help pin-point sorostitutes more inclined to put out." The email continues to explain that women will be referred to as "targets" as they are "not actual people like us men."

According to John D. Foubert, rape prevention advocate and founder of the nonprofit One in Four, fraternity men are three times more likely as other male students to rape. However, before college, sexual assault perpetration rates for fraternity and non-fraternity members are the same. In fact, according to research by a fraternity insurer, sexual assault is the second most common insurance claim for fraternities after assault and battery. Arguably, this indicates that there is something about the culture of fraternities that influences sexual assault. In 1990, anthropologist Peggy Reeves Sanday published the classic text *Fraternity Gang Rape: Sex, Brotherhood, and Privilege on Campus*. Her research on rape perpetrated by fraternity men outlines how male bonding, pornography, cultural messages about sex, and a "boys will be boys" attitude of authorities all contribute to an environment that leads to sexual harassment, date rape, and gang rape. Specifically, Sanday argues that multiple perpetrator rape by fraternity brothers promotes group cohesiveness and resolves doubts about heterosexuality in close-knit intimate groups of men.

Colleges and universities face an uphill battle in attempting to regulate fraternities. For one, fraternities are private societies with long histories. They tie alumni strongly to the university, as fraternity alumni provide millions in much needed and appreciated donations. Some universities have contractual relations by which they cannot disclose the risk of the fraternity to the general public, or they face backlash when they attempt to warn students, as Wesleyan did recently when they attempted to keep students from visiting the unrecognized Beta Theta Pi house. Additionally, the Greek system helps to woo potential students and provides housing for roughly one in eight, thereby easing the burden on university and college housing. Also, fraternity men often take oaths of lifelong loyalty, which can result in silence and covering for the criminal activities of one's "brothers," thus making punishing perpetrators especially difficult.

Fraternities are defensive of any allegation that they pose a greater risk than any other group on campus and decry that they have become "target defendants." Investigative reporter Caitlin Flanagan conducted a year-long investigation of fraternities for *The Atlantic* and found that fraternities did indeed pose significant risks. However, fraternities should not be treated as a homogenous group. While there are some fraternities that have certain reputations for being risky places for women (e.g., those with nicknames like "Rape Factory" or "Sexual Assault Expected"), some fraternities emphasize scholastic achievement and/or community service and distance themselves from an alcohol-infused and sexually charged, if not misogynist, atmosphere. Fraternity houses that are considered the "highest risk" are those that throw parties with skewed gender ratios, gender segregation, and an environment that is less conducive to conversation (e.g., parties with especially loud music). While fraternities are high risk for rape-supportive attitudes and behaviors, it is unclear whether the fraternity atmosphere itself increases levels of sexual aggression or whether those with high levels of hostility toward women seek out groups with members like themselves.

In addition to fraternities, male athletic teams are highly correlated with holding rape-supportive attitudes. Researchers first began to look at the connection between sexual assault and student athletes in the mid-1990s. These first studies found that male student athletes are disproportionately involved in sexual assault or attempted sexual assault. For example, oft-cited research by Todd Crosset and colleagues (1996) found that male student athletes comprised of less than 4 percent of the total male population yet represented 19 percent of the perpetrators reported for sexual assault. In a more recent research, 54 percent of male student athletes (including both intercollegiate and intramural) admitted to coercing a partner into sex. The same study found that student athletes were more likely than their nonathletic peers to both endorse negative attitudes toward women and believe common rape myths, such as the belief that women often allege rape to get back at men and that rape is not legitimate if a woman does not physically struggle (Young et al., 2016).

Much like fraternity culture, male athletic culture emphasizes hyper-masculinity, sexual aggression, and excessive alcohol consumption. Additional factors may compound these risks for athletes, including the reality that many male sports are sex segregated, male dominated, and violent by design. According to sociologist Laura L. Finley (Siers-Poisson 2014), "power and performance" sports, like football, hockey, wrestling, boxing, and basketball, have a disproportionate number of athletes involved in sexual assault cases. However, student athletes in individual sports like swimming, tennis, and running do not commit rape and sexual assault in disproportionate numbers. While it is unclear why some sports are more highly represented in sexual assault cases than others, there are some potential factors to consider. For example, if athletes conform to the norms of the team, and those norms include hyper-masculinity, male superiority, and the need to prove sexual proficiency, this may lead to sexually aggressive attitudes and behaviors. Athletes involved in team sports may find themselves motivated by groupthink, where they make decisions as a group in a way that discourages individual responsibility. This may shed some light on the research that finds student athletes to be almost three times more likely to engage in multiple perpetrator assault.

Additionally, on many campuses, male athletes, typically from team sports, are given celebrity status. Their status on campus may provide them with incentives, like financial support and academic leniency, in addition to public adulation from students, faculty, and administrators. What follows from such prominence, oftentimes, is a sense of entitlement, clout, and impunity. Student athletes may operate under the assumption that their misbehavior will go unpunished. On the other hand, some argue that student athletes may not be any more involved in sexual assault than non-athletes but that they are under intensified scrutiny. As campus "stars," their behaviors are more closely watched, and this may lead the public to be much more aware of the transgressions of athletes as opposed to those of non-athletes.

What has come to light in recent years, in many high-profile sexual assault scandals in campus athletic programs, is that communities rally behind their athletes and that coaches and athletic programs often shield alleged perpetrators while disbelieving and/or maligning victims. In the rare cases in which athletic perpetrators are punished, the penalties are often lenient. Athletics, especially the team sports, bring in money for colleges and universities. Bad publicity about student athletes is a public relations problem for the school in terms of ticket sales, donor dollars, and recruitment. Thus, school athletic programs, and college administrations, have worked hard to protect their athletes. In fact, up until recently, many athletic departments oversaw the cases involving sexual assault allegations against their athletes. This conflict of interest prompted the National Collegiate Athletic Association to issue a resolution that athletic departments cannot lead sexual assault investigations but can only participate.

Recent high-profile sexual assault cases involving student athletes have, to name just a few, occurred at the Air Force Academy, Baylor University, Florida State University, Hobart & William Smith College, Pennsylvania State University, University of Colorado, University of Connecticut, University of Michigan, University of Missouri, University of Montana, University of Notre Dame, University of Oregon, University of Tennessee, and Vanderbilt University. The University of Minnesota football team drew a lot of attention for their boycott of all football-related activities due to the suspension of ten players over an alleged sexual assault. Additionally, there have been cases at the high school level, such as the sexual assault scandal at Steubenville High in Ohio. In many of these cases, the university or athletic departments have been accused of protecting the perpetrators and condoning a rape culture. However, in the wake of some serious scandals, such as the sexual abuse of boys over the course of decades by assistant football coach Jerry Sandusky at Pennsylvania State University, and the finding that Baylor University's head football coach Art Briles continuously ignored or minimized allegations of sexual assault committed by football players, there is increased attention and condemnation of "cover ups," motivating schools to move more swiftly to show they are taking sexual assault allegations seriously.

Ultimately, there are a lot of factors to consider and there is a good deal of debate as to why sexual assault occurs on college campuses at the frequency in which it does. That dispute, in turn, fuels the arguments about what can or should be done to minimize, if not eradicate, campus sexual assault. The next chapter, on controversies, summarizes some of the most prevalent debates on this issue. What follows here is a brief overview of the history of campus sexual assault activism, including the student-led movements of the present and relevant legislation.

Selected Activism: Past and Present

Campus sexual assault has recently moved to the forefront of our national consciousness, but that is not because it is only newly occurring. Unfortunately, sexual assault on college campuses has, arguably, always existed. It has moved to the top of our national agenda today largely because of a wave of student activism. And today's activists have the hard work of scholars and advocates of the previous decades to thank for laying the groundwork for their contemporary success in raising awareness. Arguably, some of the earliest anti–sexual assault activism occurred after the Civil War, when African American women were organizing and fighting against the long-held practice of white men raping women of color. In truth, it would take volumes to discuss the full history of anti–sexual assault organizing. Instead, what follows are some notable examples of anti–sexual assault activism on college and university campuses, from the past to the present.

While it is commonly understood today that one can be sexually assaulted by an acquaintance, this was a reality that was neither acknowledged nor discussed in the past. As mentioned previously, early scholarship by sociologists Clifford Kirkpatrick and Eugene Kanin brought to light the reality of campus rape. While their groundbreaking article "Male Sex Aggression on a University Campus" published in 1957 did not use the words *date rape* or *acquaintance rape*, it did demonstrate the existence of "attempted intercourse with violence" within dating relationships on college campuses. It was shortly thereafter that the second wave of the feminist movement became a key force in raising awareness about rape and sexual assault. In the 1960s and 1970s, feminists involved in the women's movement worked to break down gender barriers and fight gender-based discrimination. Popularizing the idea that the *personal is political*, feminists raised collective consciousness on issues ranging from relationships, to health, to sexuality, to women's roles in the family and the workplace. Feminists challenged the conventional thinking of the time that rape was a sexual act committed by deviants and instead argued that sexual assault was a direct outcome of patriarchy and was much more commonplace than assumed. Feminists maintained that sexual assault and rape were symptomatic of a rape culture, one in which sexual violence is trivialized, ignored, and encouraged. In 1971, Susan Griffin's essay "Rape: The All American Crime" appeared in *Ramparts* magazine. Griffin discussed rape in terms of domination, thereby departing from the commonly held assumption that rape was a crime of passion. In 1975, Susan Brownmiller published the classic text *Against Our Will: Men, Women and Rape*. As discussed previously, Brownmiller's best-selling book revealed the common historical and contemporary acceptance of rape and discussed it in terms of a pressing political problem. Brownmiller is credited with bringing the feminist antirape movement into the mainstream.

The women's movement organized some of the first rape crisis centers—community-based organizations that helped victims of sexual assault by providing hotlines, counseling, and legal and medical assistance, in addition to educational outreach. Some of the first rape crisis centers opened in the early 1970s in San Francisco, Washington, D.C., and other large politically active cities. In 1975, after the murder of a Philadelphia woman who was walking home at night, the first Take Back the Night marches were held, motivated by the desire to make the streets a safe place for women. Since then, Take Back the Night marches and candlelight vigils protest against, and raise awareness about, violence against women. Take Back the Night events have become a staple of campus antirape activism, as have Clothesline Projects, which date to the early 1990s. The Clothesline Project is a display of shirts that have been decorated with emotions, experiences, and sentiments about gender violence.

College campuses in the 1960s and 1970s were bustling hubs of activism of all kinds. Students protested against the Vietnam War in addition to organizing and demonstrating for civil rights, gay rights, women's rights, the student movement, and the environmental movement. Student activists engaged in direct action, which included public marches, sit-ins, strikes, and rallies. There were numerous examples of student-led activism against campus sexual assault during the 1970s, including students at the University of Maryland successfully lobbying for one of the first campus-based rape crisis centers in response to a series of gang rapes and abductions. Students led a four-day sit-in in reaction to rapes at the University of Pennsylvania, which led to the development of campus rape crisis services, a women's studies program, and increased campus security. Following a rape at the University of California–Berkeley, the school led the way for a campus-wide sexual assault program to be adopted by all schools in the University of California system.

The momentum for campus antirape activism continued beyond the politically active 1970s. In the early 1980s, therapist Claire Walsh created the Sexual Assault Recovery Service and Campus Organized against Rape (COAR) at the University of Florida. COAR was a peer education group that became one of the earliest nationally recognized antirape education programs. Walsh spoke on national television shows and supplied information to hundreds of schools, leading COAR to become a model for similar programs across the country. In 1985, prompted by perceived insensitive comments about sexual assault made by an administrator, students led a sit-in at the University of Michigan. On April 5, 1986, Jeanne Clery, a student at Lehigh University, was raped and murdered in her dorm room. Outrage over her tragic death spurred the Jeanne Clery Disclosure of Campus Security Policy and Campus Crime Statistics Act of 1990, which requires colleges and universities to disclose crime on or near their campus. In 1990, students at Brown University created "rape lists" naming "men who won't take no for an answer" on bathroom walls. The lists, and the controversy surrounding them, received national attention. In 1991, four student sexual assault survivors filed a landmark lawsuit against Carleton College for failing to protect them against known assailants and mishandling their complaints. The plaintiffs and the college reached an agreement that brought about changes to Carleton's policies and practices. The same year, both Speak-Out: The North American Student Coalition against Campus Sexual Violence and the Coalition of Campuses against Rape (CCOAR) were formed. Over the years, SpeakOut held national conferences and CCOAR maintained a network committed to advocacy and resource development. Also the same year, Katie Koestner called local newspapers about her experience being raped by a date at the College of William and Mary. *Time* magazine featured *Koestner*, a docudrama loosely based on the incident, and her assault resulted in the first sexual misconduct hearing at a university. In 1992, spurred by feminist student activism, progressive Antioch College adopted a Sexual Offense Prevention Policy that required ongoing verbal consent at every step of a sexual encounter. Nationally, the precedent-setting policy was ridiculed for being too prescriptive. In 1998, hundreds of students at Bates College staged a protest over the college's mishandling of sexual assaults, which spurred changes to campus policy.

Meanwhile, several cases drew widespread attention, fueling the student-led activism. For example, in 1974, six University of Notre Dame football players were accused of the gang rape of a local woman. A top school administrator referred to her as "a queen of the slums with a mattress tied to her back." The men were suspended for one year for violating campus rules, and no criminal charges were filed. On October 5, 1984, Liz Seccuro was gang raped at the Phi Kappa Psi fraternity house at the University of Virginia. Campus authorities took no action and over 20 years later, after receiving an apology from one of her attackers, Seccuro successfully pursued justice and chronicled her story in a 2011 memoir. In March 1989, a mentally challenged girl was gang raped by football players at Glen Ridge High School in New Jersey. The case drew national attention, sharply split residents of the town, and was adapted into a book and movie. In 1991, three white St. John's lacrosse players charged with the gang rape of an African American woman were acquitted. The case involved six men accused of raping the intoxicated student after she had been pressured to drink. In June 1998, Brenda Tracy asserted she was gang raped by four men, two of whom were Oregon State football players. The players were suspended for one game and the coach said they made "a bad choice." Tracy came public with her experience in 2014 and met with the coach, Mike Riley, in 2016.

In the backdrop of highly publicized cases and student-led activism, researchers and journalists were investigating the issue of campus sexual assault and contributing scholarship that soon became classics in the field. In 1982, *Ms.* magazine published the article "Date Rape: A Campus Epidemic" by Karen Barret (1982) that documented the campus rape problem. A couple of years later, the magazine published "Date Rape: The Story of an Epidemic and Those Who Deny It," based on early findings from the research of clinical psychologist Mary Koss. Koss conducted a three-year study at 35 schools, including more than 7,000 students. The ultimate results of her research, later published with colleagues in *The Journal of Consulting and Clinical Psychology*, found that sexual assault on college campuses was common and was typically perpetrated by someone known to the victim. Also noteworthy is *I Never Called It Rape*, written by journalist Robin Warshaw and published in 1988. Based on personal accounts, scholarly studies, and Koss's research findings on campus sexual assault, Warshaw's seminal text discussed the hidden topic of date rape. Additionally, in 1990, cultural anthropologist Peggy Reeves Sanday's *Fraternity Gang Rape: Sex, Brotherhood, and Privilege on Campus* drew on interviews with victims and fraternity members to analyze the existence of rape culture in all-male groups.

This increased awareness about, and attention to, campus sexual assault was not without criticism. Campus antirape activism was sometimes then, and still is today, met with backlash. For example, fraternity members responded with misogynistic threats during the first Take Back the Night vigil at Princeton University in 1987. More famously was the reaction of journalist Katie Roiphe. In 1993, she published a book chronicling her personal thoughts on date rape and contemporary feminism, entitled *The Morning After: Sex, Fear, and Feminism on Campus*. In it, she argued that campus feminism had taken a wrong turn and focused on women's victimization, stripping women of power and autonomy. Roiphe questioned the notion of an epidemic of campus sexual assault and argued that in cases of campus date rape, women are at least partially responsible for their actions. Her book was met with mixed results; some found her arguments brave and insightful, and others found them problematic and shortsighted. The book remains Roiphe's best-known work.

The antirape activism, both on campus and off, coupled with groundbreaking scholarship on acquaintance rape, created a strong foundation for a wave of contemporary activism in the new millennium. In the last couple of decades, there has been an increase in research on campus sexual assault, in addition to proactive governmental involvement and successful student-led activism. Taken together, there is now increased awareness on all fronts. As a society, we now know more about the prevalence of sexual assault on college and university campuses and the all-too-common institutional mishandling of such cases. Most promising is the change brought about by students who not only wish to raise awareness and combat sexual violence but who are also bravely standing up to their educational institutions and demanding accountability and change.

Many significant research studies have added to our contemporary understanding of the prevalence of campus sexual assault. This includes the National College Women Sexual Victimization Survey funded by the Bureau of Justice Statistics and the National Institute of Justice (Fisher and Turner 2000), the Campus Sexual Assault Survey funded by the National Institute of Justice (Krebs et al. 2007), the American Association of Universities' Campus Climate Survey on Sexual Assault and Sexual Misconduct (2015), the Washington Post-Kaiser Family Foundation Poll's Survey on Current and Recent College Students on Sexual Assault (2015), and the Campus Climate Survey released by the National Institute of Justice (2016). Additional groundbreaking research includes that of David Lisak and Paul M. Miller (2002), who report that most campus rapes are committed by a small number of undetected and repeat offenders, and the investigative series conducted by the Center for Public Integrity (2010), in collaboration with National Public Radio, that demonstrated, among other things, the inadequate response of colleges and universities to reports of sexual assault. Along the same vein, *The New York Times* published the story "Reporting Rape and Wishing She Hadn't" (2014), which chronicled a woman's experience being gang raped by football players at Hobart and William Smith College and illustrated the inadequacies of the school's adjudication system. In 2014, a controversial article in *Rolling Stone* magazine about an alleged gang rape at a fraternity at the University of Virginia was released and later retracted after the main informant's story was found to be fabricated. And bestselling author Jon Krakauer released *Missoula: Rape and the Justice System in a College Town* (2015), an exposé of several sexual assaults that occurred at the University of Montana and the difficulties the survivors endured afterward from the community, the university, and the justice system.

Notably, the release of two documentaries on campus sexual assault helped bring awareness of the issue to the mainstream. *It Happened Here* (2014) chronicled the personal struggles of a handful of survivors of campus sexual assault and illustrated institutional callousness and cover-ups. Similarly, *The Hunting Ground* (2015) documented the prevalence of campus sexual assault and the failure of college administrations to handle these cases properly. This critically acclaimed documentary profiled many survivors, including Andrea Pino and Annie E. Clark, two student activists from the University of North Carolina–Chapel Hill. Pino and Clark filed a Title IX complaint against their school and paved the way for students at other campuses to do the same. The documentary has since been screened on hundreds of campuses, and an edited version was shown on CNN. Lady Gaga, herself a survivor of sexual assault, co-wrote a song for the film entitled *'Til It Happens to You*. The song was nominated for an Oscar at the 88th Academy Awards. In an emotional and touching performance of the song at the awards ceremony, Lady Gaga was joined on stage by 50 sexual assault survivors after an introduction by Vice President Joe

Biden. Biden urged people to take the "It's on Us" pledge to intervene in potentially dangerous situations. One of the most significant contemporary changes is the more active role the media has taken in reporting and discussing campus sexual assault. In the past, incidents of sexual assault and rape at colleges and universities did not typically make the headlines of the daily newspaper. However, now the media is interested in covering campus sexual assault, and that is arguably reflective of society's changing attitudes on the matter. Sexual assault is no longer understood as a taken-for-granted assumption about college dating life that can be ignored or trivialized. However, the increased role of the media in covering and discussing campus sexual assault, be it social or news media, is a double-edged sword. On one hand, the media is responsible for raising awareness about the all-too-common occurrence of campus sexual assault. Additionally, survivors often learn, and are inspired by, the experiences and activism of other survivors via media outlets. On the other hand, the media often focuses on the most scandalous, extreme, or shocking stories. This is a distortion of what most campus assaults actually look like. Also, many survivors of sexual assault are loath to have their lives, and traumatic experiences, picked apart by the public eye. Whether the media's involvement does more harm than good is debatable. What we do have, thanks to journalists who report for news media or students who report on social media, are concrete examples of rape-supportive actions on college campuses, including, to name just a few, the following recent examples: pledges to the Yale University Delta Kappa Epsilon chanted "no means yes, yes means anal" and other similar phrases through an area of campus with dorms; flyers that listed "Top Ten Ways to Get Away with Rape" were found at Miami University of Ohio; the Sigma Phi Epsilon fraternity at the University of Vermont sent out a questionnaire asking "who would you rape?"; a member of the Phi Kappa Tau fraternity at Georgia Tech sent an instructional email to members titled "Luring Your Rapebait" that encouraged members to ply women with a lot of alcohol; a Dartmouth student-run website published a student's "rape guide" that encouraged the rape of a freshman student (the named student was sexually assaulted weeks later at a fraternity); the Phi Delta Theta fraternity at Texas Tech held a party with a banner that read "no means yes, yes means anal," sparking campus protests.

Additionally, the media has reported on many cases that have consequently become "high-profile" because of the controversial nature of the circumstances or because of the status of the students involved. Some of the most high-profile cases have been those that exemplify college and university callousness or mismanagement, have especially tragic outcomes, and/or those involve perceived "public figures," like college athletes. What follows are some contemporary cases that were reported, sometimes extensively, in the media. Students Lisa Simpson and Anne Gilmore alleged they were gang raped by University of Colorado–Boulder football players and high school recruits on December 7, 2001. The incident set off a long-running scandal that cost many university officials their jobs and called into question recruiting tactics. On January 25, 2005, *Sports Illustrated* published a story breaking the silence of Katie Hnida, the first female placekicker on the University of Colorado football team. Hnida disclosed that in 2000, she was raped by a football player and sexually harassed by fellow teammates. In 2006, Megan Wright reported being gang raped at Dominican College. Allegedly, the school did little in response; she dropped out and later committed suicide. The same year, Laura Dickinson was raped and murdered in her dorm room at Eastern Michigan University. The school claimed that there was no foul play, but school authorities were later found to have withheld information and deceived the public. In 2007, the North Carolina Attorney General's office dropped charges against three Duke University lacrosse players who were charged with first-degree sexual offense and kidnapping of an exotic dancer they had hired to perform. What was later believed to be based on a false allegation, this scandal resulted in the firing of the lacrosse coach, the disbarring of the district attorney, and civil suits lodged against the school and the city by the lacrosse players.

In 2008, a sophomore high school student at Richmond High in California left her homecoming dance and was robbed, beaten, and gang raped by multiple men and boys over the span of two hours. The case drew national attention and outrage over the "mob mentality" of the attackers and for the presence of ten or more bystanders who failed to intervene. In 2010, Elizabeth "Lizzy" Seeberg, a freshman at St. Mary's College, committed suicide ten days after accusing a Notre Dame football player of sexual assault. After the alleged assault, she had received an intimidating text from a friend of the accused and found little support from university administrators or police. In 2012, a 16-year-old girl attended parties with Steubenville High School students in Ohio. She was sexually assaulted by two football players over the course of several hours, and her assault were captured and widely disseminated on social media. Later that same year, Florida State University student Erica Kinsman reported being raped. Her alleged perpetrator was later identified as football player Jameis Winston. The scandal received a lot of media attention, with accusations that both the Tallahassee Police Department and the university botched the investigations. Also in 2012, a jury found former Pennsylvania State assistant football coach Jerry Sandusky guilty on 45 out of 48 counts of sexual abuse, stemming from the sexual assault of ten young boys, culled from a charity he created, over the course of over a decade. The scandal resulted in the termination of the school president and head football coach. Sandusky was later sentenced to at least 30 years in prison. In June 2012, Thomas Francis "Trey" Malone III, committed suicide nine months after he reported sexual assault at Amherst College. His suicide note alleged institutional callousness and plead for the better treatment of sexual assault victims.

In 2013, Brandon Vandenburg, a Vanderbilt football player, organized some of his teammates to sexually assault a woman he had been dating, and after protracted legal proceedings, many argued the sentences the perpetrators received were too lenient. The same year, Lena Sclove, a student at Brown University, was choked and sexually assaulted by fellow student Daniel Kopin. Kopin was suspended but able to return to school while Sclove was still a student. In 2014, James Madison University punished three fraternity members found guilty of sexual assault and sexual harassment with "expulsion after graduation." In a very highly publicized case in 2015, Brock Turner, a Stanford freshman, sexually assaulted an unconscious woman behind a dumpster. Turner later received a punishment of six months in county jail (of which he served three) sparking national outrage for the leniency in punishment. On November 22, 2015, Cherelle Locklear committed suicide less than two months, after she maintained she was raped at the Sigma Pi fraternity house at William Paterson University; her mother asserted that the university failed to adequately investigate the assault. In 2016, Jesse Matthew accepted a plea deal for the murder and kidnapping of University of Virginia student Hannah Graham and Virginia Tech student Morgan Harrington. Matthew was also accused of raping students at Liberty University and Christopher Newport University in previous years. Also in 2016, Baylor campus president Kenneth Starr was removed from his position in the wake of a campus scandal about sexual assault committed by football players. Additionally, former Indiana University student and fraternity member John P. Enochs accepted a plea deal dismissing two felony charges of sexual assault. He was sentenced to a year's probation with no prison time, and his punishment was widely criticized for being too lenient.

Many more pages can be devoted to the reports of campus sexual assaults over the last couple of decades, and that is not including the majority of campus sexual assaults that do not make it to the news. The scores of reports paint a pretty bleak picture—sexual assault occurs on college and university campuses, and in many cases it seems as though the schools (and police departments) fail the victims by not adequately investigating alleged incidents or not adequately punishing known perpetrators. These unfortunate realities have inspired a new generation of student activists. Sexual assault survivors and allies have worked tirelessly to raise awareness, to combat violence, and to fight for justice. Through protests, the creation of organizations, powerful first-person editorials, and lawsuits, anti–sexual assault student activists are responsible for making significant changes to campus culture. The following are some notable examples of campus activism. In 2000, Columbia University students started SAFER (Students Active for Ending Rape) with the goal to empower student-led campaigns to reform campus sexual assault policies. In April 2004, Laura Dunn, a student at the University of Wisconsin–Madison, alleged she was sexually assaulted by two men from her crew team. Dunn is now a victim's rights attorney, and the founder and executive director of the nonprofit SurvJustice. In 2011, Grace Brown, a freshman at the School of Visual Arts, inspired by the experience of a friend, created Project UnBreakable, a photography project on Tumblr that captured images of survivors of sexual assault, domestic violence, and child abuse holding posters with quotes from their abusers. The project grew to include over 4,000 pictures from around the world.

In October 2012, *The Amherst Student*, a student newspaper at Amherst College, published an essay by Angie Epifano that discussed her sexual assault by a male acquaintance and subsequent institutional callousness. Her widely read essay provoked changes in the school's handling of sexual assault. In 2013, a group of students, survivors, and professors cofound the advocacy group End Rape on Campus to formalize and centralize work around campus sexual assault. Three of the original student survivor cofounders (Annie Clark, Andrea Pino, and Sofie Karasek) are predominately featured in the film *The Hunting Ground*. The same year, Know Your IX was cofounded by sexual assault survivors Dana Bolger and Alexandra Brodsky with the goals of empowering students to end sexual violence at their schools and to inform students of their rights under

Title IX. In April 2013, 37 former and current Occidental College sexual assault survivors filed two federal complaints against the college for violation of the Clery Act and Title IX. They held a press conference to provide testimonials and voice concerns about the school's policies and mishandling of their reports, including allegations that the school retaliated against those who spoke out against sexual assault. Later that month, Carolyn Luby, a University of Connecticut student, published an open letter to the campus president drawing attention to violence on campus. Luby is one of five women who filed a federal lawsuit saying University of Connecticut responded to their sexual assault complaints with indifference, and her story is featured in the film *It Happened Here*. In the summer of 2013, activists from the Know Your IX, ED ACT NOW campaign traveled to Washington, D.C., to protest outside the Department of Education and delivered a petition calling on the Office for Civil Rights (OCR) to conduct timely and transparent investigations and issue meaningful sanctions for schools found to be in violation of Title IX.

In 2014, male students at North Carolina State University created Undercover Colors, a nail polish that detected the presence of date-rape drugs in a drink, which sparked debate about whose responsibility it is to prevent sexual violence. On March 31, 2014, *The Harvard Crimson*, Harvard's school newspaper, published an anonymous editorial entitled "Dear Harvard: You Win," chronicling a student's sexual assault and failure of the institution to take action. The column went viral and spurred campus change. In a follow-up essay after her graduation, the author identified herself as Ariane Litalien. The same year, Faculty against Rape was formed to get faculty more involved in preventing campus sexual assault and improving campus responses.

At the beginning of the fall semester in 2014, Columbia University art student and survivor Emma Sulkowicz began carrying around a 50-pound dorm mattress as part of her senior art thesis entitled "Carry that Weight." Sulkowicz vowed to cease carrying the mattress only when her alleged perpetrator was expelled or left the university. Her activism inspired similar protests across the nation and the globe, and she ended up carrying the mattress across the stage with her on graduation. The same month, nearly 200 students at the University of Chicago marched in protest of a campus hacking group that threatened sexual assault. The threat was made in retaliation for a list posted to Tumblr with names of students accused of varying degrees of sexual assault. In October 2014, California Institute of the Arts students walked out of their classes and held a peaceful occupation of the school's administrative offices to protest the handling of rape allegations. The same month, students at Ohio's Miami University protested conservative political pundit George Will's campus speech due to his editorial for *The Washington Post* that argued victims of campus sexual assault have a "coveted status that confers privileges."

On October 9, 2015, Harvard's school newspaper, *The Harvard Crimson*, published Vivian Maymi's essay chronicling her rape by a date in her sophomore year. In February 2016, eight female students filed a Title IX civil suit against the University of Tennessee, stating that the university created a hostile environment for women by ignoring sexual assaults committed by athletes, in addition to condoning an athletic culture that encouraged underage drinking, drug use, and sexual violence. A month later, students accused Brigham Young University, operated by the Church of Jesus Christ of Latter-day Saints, of charging sexual assault victims who come forward with breaking the rigid student honor code that prohibits premarital sex. The accusations resulted in the filing of a Title IX complaint and the creation of an online petition calling for Brigham Young University to give immunity to sexual assault victims so that they can come forward without fear. The activism paid off, and BYU changed its policy and no longer pursues honor code investigations of sexual assault victims. On April 2, 2016, *The Harvard Law Record* published an editorial written by Kamilah Willingham, in which she defended her rape allegation to 19 faculty of the law school who published an open letter discrediting her account. The story of her assault, and Harvard's reaction to it, is predominately featured in the film *The Hunting Ground.* And on June 2, 2016, the victim in the Stanford Brock Turner sexual assault case read a powerful 12-page letter outlining the profound impact the assault had on her life during Turner's sentencing hearing. The letter was widely circulated and read on the floor by members of Congress.

The preceding examples of student-led activism just barely skim the surface. At campuses across the nation, there are student organizations working to fight campus sexual assault, including, to name a few, chapters of the Feminist Majority Leadership Alliance, End Rape on Campus, Students Active for Ending Rape (SAFER), and groups for men like One in Four and Campus Men of Strength. Ultimately, there are hundreds of activists unnamed here, and they all deserve recognition for fighting rape culture in a myriad of ways, ranging from hosting awareness events, to protests, to filing Title IX complaints and lawsuits. Change is happening, and student activists are leading the charge.

Relevant Legislation and Government Initiatives

Activists and survivors have relied upon key pieces of legislation to assist them in fighting for, and understanding, their rights. Arguably, Title IX is one of the most, if not the most, important pieces of legislation in the context of campus sexual assault. President Nixon signed into law Title IX of the Education Amendments of 1972. This landmark federal law prohibits discrimination on the basis of sex in any federally funded education program or activity. If found in violation of Title IX, any federally funded school, education program, or activity could lose federal funding. Title IX, later renamed the Patsy Mink Equal Opportunity Act in 2002 in honor of the late coauthor and sponsor Representative Pasty Mink, has impacted education in numerous ways since its inception. Most notably,

Title IX has been employed in efforts to level the playing field between women's and men's athletics. The origins of applying Title IX to sexual harassment and assault date to the 1970s; however, it took decades for this approach to be commonplace.

In the 1970s, Catharine MacKinnon was attending law school at Yale University. While there, she made the realization, radical at the time, that sexual harassment was a form of sexual discrimination that interfered with women's equal access to education. She drafted her legal theory and put the idea to test in 1977 when she advised a group of female Yale students who had been sexually harassed to file a lawsuit. In *Alexander v. Yale*, the women alleged they had been sexually propositioned by male faculty in return for better grades and that there was no legal recourse available to them. The plaintiffs sought a grievance procedure for sexual harassment claims. In 1980, the suit was dismissed on the basis that the students had graduated and thus did not have legal standing. However, the court upheld the argument that sexual harassment constitutes discrimination. Additionally, Yale developed a harassment grievance board that became a model for universities and colleges across the nation. MacKinnon's framework paved the way for future student survivors of sexual harassment and sexual assault to take legal action when they felt their schools failed them. In the decades that followed, students filed Title IX complaints against their schools for mishandling sexual assault allegations, a practice that eventually became widespread.

The use of Title IX for sexual assault cases was clarified in a letter released by the U.S. Department of Education's OCR on April 4, 2011. This Dear Colleague Letter sent to colleges, universities, and schools across the nation reiterated that Title IX covered sexual violence and included requirements and obligations that schools have to address sexual assault and harassment. Under Title IX, schools are legally required to both respond to and remedy hostile environments. If a student has experienced sexual harassment, schools must stop the discrimination. They must also proactively work to prevent its recurrence and address its effects, including providing the survivor with resources and necessary accommodations (e.g., a change in housing or class schedule). Failure to do so could mean the loss of federal funding. The Dear Colleague letter included controversial disciplinary guidelines, which will be discussed further in the following chapter. In April 2014, largely in response to the need for further clarification, the OCR released a 53-page FAQ to address the 2011 Dear Colleague letter. Again in April 2015, the OCR released another Dear Colleague letter that reminded school districts, colleges, and universities that they must have a designated Title IX coordinator to ensure the school complies with the legal obligations outlined by Title IX.

Today, campus survivors of sexual harassment or sexual assault (which is considered to be an extreme form of harassment) have two options if they believe their school failed to follow Title IX guidelines. One option is to file a Title IX complaint with the OCR to initiate an investigation into the school's procedures and practices. Another option is to file a civil lawsuit against their school under Title IX. The two are not mutually exclusive, so it is possible to do both. However, the OCR will not conduct an investigation while a lawsuit is in progress. Two cases at Yale University illustrate the application of Title IX in cases of sexual assault. In 2003, in one of the earliest Title IX lawsuits of this nature, Kathryn Kelly brought a civil action under Title IX against Yale alleging that after her sexual assault the university failed to respond to concerns and that the dean publicly defamed her. In this first case to confront student-on-student sexual assault at the university level, the Connecticut District Court said universities are responsible for responding to allegations of that nature. In 2011, 16 Yale students and alumni filed a Title IX complaint with the OCR alleging a sexually hostile environment. After the investigation, the OCR entered into a voluntary resolution agreement with the university.

Thanks in large part to student activists, like Andrea Pino and Annie E. Clark, who filed a Title IX complaint against their college and taught and inspired others to do the same, filing Title IX complaints against colleges and universities is commonplace today. There is currently a growing backlog of approximately 300 OCR Title IX investigations at over 200 schools. Additionally, numerous Title IX civil lawsuits have been filed against colleges and universities directly. Filing lawsuits, submitting Title IX complaints, and engaging in student activism is fueled by student frustration. Many campus sexual assault survivors believe that their college or university failed to take their sexual assault seriously. Survivors have reported all kinds of institutional mismanagement, at a range of different colleges and universities across the nation, including experiencing the following from campus officials: callousness, disbelief, defamation, retribution for reporting, failure to provide support and protection, failure to hold perpetrators responsible, and efforts to cover up allegations. Many survivors and experts argue that universities and colleges approach campus sexual assault as a public relations problem and that concerns about donors, athletic programs, and enrollment often take precedence. Student survivors consequently report feeling revictimized by the reporting and investigative and disciplinary processes at their schools, leading to negative academic and health repercussions.

The existing research on school responses largely supports the criticisms that universities and colleges are not holding perpetrators accountable. For example, the Center for Public Integrity's nine-month investigation, which resulted in the project "Sexual Assault on Campus: A Frustrating Search for Justice" (2010), reported that students found responsible for sexual assault often received little or no punishment from the school system. Of the 33 student survivors interviewed, over half said they were unsuccessful in seeking criminal charges, essentially because district attorneys declined to prosecute. This led to the students having to seek justice in school-run proceedings that resulted in either light punishments or no punishments for the assailants. The investigation found that many of the informal proceedings at the schools were essentially mediations—a practice frowned upon by the Department of Education for use in sexual assault cases. Similarly, a *Washington Post* investigation (Anderson 2014) found that of 478 sanctions for sexual assault at about 100 schools in 2012 and 2013, 12 percent of students were expelled, 237 sexual assault cases were dismissed for lack of evidence, and 44 cases ended in acquittal. In 2014, the *Huffington Post* reviewed data from nearly three dozen colleges and universities and found that in less than 30 percent of the cases, students found responsible were expelled, and they were suspended in only 47 percent of the cases (Kingkade 2014). Additionally, the documentary *The Hunting Ground* reported on a variety of lenient punishments meted out by schools to students found responsible for sexual assault, including a paper assignment, community service, nominal fines, and expulsion after graduation (2015). As a result, students across the nation have responded to the failure of many colleges and universities to take sexual assault seriously, and failing to abide by Title IX, by demanding change and accountability.

Not everyone is on board with the flurry of contemporary legal action bolstered by the Dear Colleague Letter. Some fear that schools are now "over complying" and certain organizations, like the Foundation for Individual Rights in Education (FIRE), argue that the Dear Colleague Letter eliminates due process for individuals and institutions. A number of accused students have also sued their schools under Title IX arguing, generally speaking, that their school failed to provide due process in the haste to combat campus sexual assault. Additionally, mothers of young men who they say were unjustly found responsible of sexual assault cofounded Families Advocating Campus Equality (FACE) in 2013 to advocate for "equal treatment and due process by those affected by sexual misconduct allegations on campus." The debate over the OCR guidelines, and what role schools and universities should have in investigating campus sexual assault, is discussed further in the following chapter.

There are additional pieces of legislation, besides Title IX, that play a key role in the subject of campus sexual assault. In 1974, President Gerald Ford signed into law the Family Education Rights and Privacy Act (FERPA), also known as the Buckley Amendment. FERPA protects the privacy of student education records at any school receiving federal funding. Essentially, FERPA restricts schools from releasing anything from a student's education records without that person's permission. However, what constitutes an "education record" is controversial, as it was not clearly defined by Congress. Anti–sexual assault advocates say schools use FERPA too often as justification for not sharing information about a student's misconduct or disciplinary case.

In November 1990, President George H.W. Bush signed into law the Crime Awareness and Campus Security Act, later renamed the Jeanne Clery Disclosure of Campus Security Policy and Campus Crime Statistics Act (the Clery Act), after Jeanne Clery. As mentioned previously, Clery was a college student who was raped and murdered in her dorm at Lehigh University in 1986. This federal statute requires schools that participate in federal financial aid programs to publicly disclose, on an annual basis, their campus security policies and crime statistics over the past three years. Additionally, the act requires schools to give timely warnings of crimes that represent a threat to the campus community and imposes certain basic requirements on handling cases of sexual assault, stalking, and domestic and dating violence. The act has been amended and expanded several times, including the 1992 Federal Campus Sexual Assault Victims Bill of Rights, also referred to as the Ramstad Act. The bill exists as part of the Clery Act and affords sexual assault victims certain basic rights, including their options to notify law enforcement and to be informed of counseling services. In 2013, the Campus Sexual Violence Elimination (SaVE) Act, an amendment to the Violence against Women Reauthorization Act, was signed into law by President Barack Obama. The SaVE Act expands upon Clery and encourages greater transparency by requiring campus crime statistics to also include and report instances of dating violence, domestic violence, and stalking. Additionally, this Clery expansion requires that campuses guarantee victims enhanced rights, have protocol and standards for disciplinary hearings, and have campus-wide prevention education programs.

Students can file a Clery Act complaint if they feel as though their college or university has violated the law. The complaint is forwarded to and handled by the appropriate regional office of the U.S. Department of Education, and a school may be fined up to $35,000 per Clery Act violation. Taken together, the Clery Act and Title IX are powerful tools in combating campus sexual assault that are available to most students. However, military schools (the Air Force Academy, the Coast Guard Academy, the Merchant Marine Academy, the Naval Academy, and the Military Academy) are exempt from both Title IX and the Clery Act. The motivation for Congress to exempt the service academies from Title IX is unclear; perhaps the need was not understood because the academies did not allow women at the time Title IX went into effect, or perhaps it was believed the uniform code of military justice was sufficient. The result, according to victims' advocates, is that there is no viable option at these schools to challenge discriminatory academy polices or inadequate procedures for reporting sexual assault or sexual harassment.

In 1994, Congress enacted the Violence against Women Act (VAWA) written by then senator Joseph Biden. The act improved federal, state, and local responses to sexual assault, domestic violence, and stalking and provided various grants, including those for campus sexual violence. VAWA was reauthorized in 2000, 2005, and 2013 with modifications and additions. The 2013 reauthorization included the Campus SaVE Act, discussed previously. Additionally, there are numerous Title IX court cases, on the state and federal levels, which have bolstered efforts to combat campus sexual assault. For example, in February 1992, the U.S. Supreme Court established that students who suffer from sexual harassment in schools that receive federal financial assistance may sue for monetary damages under Title IX. In this case, *Franklin v. Gwinnett County Public Schools*, a male coach/teacher continually sexually harassed and abused a female high school sophomore. In *Gebser v. Lago Vista Independent School District* (1998), the Supreme Court argued that there was no liability under Title IX for school administrators if they did not know about sexual discrimination. In this case, a male teacher engaged in sexual relations with a ninth-grade student. The student never informed the school district, but the police ultimately arrested the teacher after discovering the two had engaged in sexual intercourse. The student and the mother sued the school under Title IX. Ultimately, the Supreme Court found that monetary damages cannot be awarded if the institution is unaware of the discrimination.

The landmark Supreme Court ruling in *Davis v. Monroe County Board of Education* (1999) said schools can be held liable under Title IX for failing to address known student-on-student harassment, including assault. This case stems from the experience of a fifth grader who was harassed by a classmate. Both the victim and her mother reported the harassment, yet no timely actions were taken. The victim's mother sued the school board and several school officials under Title IX for failing to take action. Thus, between the *Gebser* and *Davis* rulings, the Supreme Court has determined that if administrators have notice of sexual misconduct and respond with deliberate indifference, institutions are potentially liable for civil damages.

Additional Title IX cases were identified by the National Center for Higher Education Risk Management as litigation "game changers" for school sexual misconduct. While a thorough discussion of these cases is beyond the scope of this book, they include *Jackson v. Birmingham Board of Education* (2005), *Lisa Simpson et al. v. University of Colorado* (2007) (discussed in Profiles chapter), *Tiffany Williams v. Board of Regents of the University System of Georgia* (2007), *Melissa Jennings & Debbie*

Keller v. The University of North Carolina-Chapel Hill (2007), and *Fitzgerald v. Barnstable School Committee* (2009). In recent years, Title IX court cases for sexual assault are becoming commonplace, ranging from students alleging their schools mishandled their sexual assaults to cases alleging campus overreach and/or failure to provide due process to the accused.

The Obama administration made combating campus sexual assault a primary policy initiative, due in part to Vice President Biden's legislative experience and interest in combating violence against women. In 2009, President Obama declared April the Sexual Assault Awareness Month. In 2011, in an effort to reduce dating violence and sexual assault among teens and young adults, Biden launched the 1is2Many initiative. The Dear Colleague letter, written by Obama appointee Assistant Secretary of Civil Rights Russlynn Ali, signaled the administration's intent to take campus sexual assault seriously. In January 2014, the Office of the Vice President and the White House Council on Women and Girls published a report on sexual violence entitled Rape and Sexual Assault: A Renewed Call to Action. The report analyzed data on sexual assault and noted that it was a particular problem on college campuses. Afterward, Obama established the White House Task Force to Protect Students from Sexual Assault and charged the task force with providing resources, improving transparency, and raising awareness. Three months later, based on conversations with thousands of people related to the issue, the task force released a report entitled Not Alone that addressed the problem of sexual assault on college and university campuses. Not Alone provided recommendations and action steps for best practices. Additionally, a corresponding public awareness campaign and pledge, called It's on Us, encouraged people to be active bystanders and to intervene in problematic scenarios. The efforts of the Obama administration transformed the way colleges and universities respond to allegations of sexual misconduct; as *The Washington Post* wrote, Obama and Biden "re-wrote the rulebook" on campus sexual assaults. The Trump administration may take a different perspective on the issue of campus sexual assault, and Secretary of Education Betsy DeVos may choose not to uphold the guidance in the "Dear Colleague Letter."

States legislatures have also been grappling with the issue, and some have focused on the nature of *consent*. In September 2014, Governor Jerry Brown signed a bill that made California the first state to enact legislation with an affirmative consent standard for colleges and universities. New York, Illinois, and Connecticut followed suit and have similar affirmative consent standards for college students. The debate about consent, and specifically *affirmative* consent policies, is discussed in the following chapter. Moreover, the issue of campus sexual assault has caught the attention of members of Congress. Congress members have proposed and fought for a range of different bills, some that aim at providing increased protections for victims, others that attempt to bolster the rights of the accused.

Conclusion

This chapter gave an overview of the background and history of campus sexual assault, including a discussion of research findings, risk factors, and the history of campus activism, notable cases, and relevant legislation. It has been said that the nation is experiencing a watershed moment for campus sexual assault. Today, due to decades of scholarship, legislation, and student activism, campus sexual assault is no longer an issue that can so easily be brushed under the rug. Students and activists are fighting against campus rape culture and for institutional accountability. Also, the nation as a whole is grappling with the issue of sexual violence in its various iterations. It is clear there are no easy answers. While students do have mechanisms to fight against rape-supportive campus cultures and inadequate handling of sexual assault allegations, the burden for change, unfairly, continues to remain mostly on the shoulders of victims. And unfortunately, until sexual assaults cease to occur on college campuses, this work will never be done. Ideally, the future is one in which women and men, survivors and allies, students and administrators all work together to combat sexual assault at our nation's schools.

References

Abbey, A. (2002). Alcohol-Related Sexual Assault: A Common Problem among College Students. *Journal of Studies on Alcohol 14*: 118–128.

American Association of University Women. (2015, November 23). Newly Released Campus Sexual Violence Data Raise Red Flags. Retrieved November 21, 2016, from: http://www.aauw.org/article/campus-sexual-violence-data/

Anderson, N. (2014, December 15). Colleges Often Reluctant to Expel for Sexual Violence—with U -V.A. a Prime Example. Retrieved February 16, 2017, from: https://www.washingtonpost.com/local/education/colleges-often-reluctant-to-expel-for-sexual-violence--with-u-va-a-prime-example/2014/12/15/307c5648-7b4e-11e4-b821-503cc7efed9e_story.html?utm_term=.95fb9826b386

Anonymous. (2014, March 31). Dear Harvard: You Win. *The Harvard Crimson*. Retrieved November 21, 2016, from: https://www.thecrimson.com/article/2014/3/31/Harvard-sexual-assault/

Armstrong, E., L. Hamilton, and B. Sweeney. (2006). Sexual Assault on Campus: A Multilevel, Integrative Approach to Party Rape. *Social Problems 53*, 4: 483–499.

Association of American Universities. (2015). Campus Climate Survey on Sexual Assault and Sexual Misconduct. Retrieved November 21, 2016, from: https://www.aau.edu/Climate-Survey.aspx?id=16525

Barret, K. (1982). Date Rape: A Campus Epidemic? *Ms.* magazine.

Bekiempis, V. (2015, January 9). When Campus Rapists Don't Think They Are Rapists. *Newsweek*. Retrieved

November 22, 2016, from: http://www.newsweek.com/campus-rapists-and-semantics-297463

Berkowitz, S. and R. O'Connor. (2014, February 28). RAINN Recommendations for White House Task Force to Protect Students from Sexual Assault. Retrieved February 16, 2017, from: https://www.rainn.org/images/03-2014/WH-Task-Force-RAINN-Recommendations.pdf

Black, M. C., K. C. Basile, M. J. Breiding, S. G. Smith, M. L. Walters, M. T. Merrick, J. Chen, and M. R. Stevens. (2011). The National Intimate Partner and Sexual Violence Survey (NISVS): 2010 Summary Report. Atlanta, GA: National Center for Injury Prevention and Control, Centers for Disease Control and Prevention.

Bogdanich, W. (2014, July 12). Reporting Rape and Wishing She Hadn't: How One College Handled a Sexual Assault Complaint. *New York Times*. Retrieved November 21, 2016, from: http://www.nytimes.com/2014/07/13/us/how-one-college-handled-a-sexual-assault-complaint.html?_r=0

Bogle, K. A. (2008). *Hooking Up: Sex, Dating, and Relationships on Campus*. New York: New York University Press.

Bohmer, C., and A. Parrot. (1993). *Sexual Assault on Campus: The Problem and the Solution*. New York: Lexington Books.

Brownmiller, S. (1975). *Against Our Will: Men, Women and Rape*. New York: Fawcett Books.

Buchwald, E., P. Fletcher, and M. Roth (eds.). (1993/2005). *Transforming a Rape Culture*. Minneapolis, MN: Milkweed Editions.

Cantor, D., B. Fisher, S. Chibnall, C. Bruce, R. Townsend, G. Thomas, and H. Lee. (2015, September 21). Report on the AAU Campus Climate Survey on Sexual Assault and Sexual Misconduct. Retrieved November 21, 2016, from: http://www.upenn.edu/ir/surveys/AAU/Report%20and%20Tables%20on%20AAU%20Campus%20Climate%20Survey.pdf

Carey, K., S. Durney, R. L. Shepardson, and M. Carey. (2015). Precollege Predictors of Incapacitated Rape among Female Students in Their First Year of College. *Journal of Studies on Alcohol and Drugs 76*, 6: 829–837.

Center for Public Integrity. (2010). Sexual Assault on Campus: A Frustrating Search for Justice. Retrieved November 21, 2016, from: https://cloudfront-files-1.publicintegrity.org/documents/pdfs/Sexual%20Assault%20on%20Campus.pdf

Civic Research Institute. (2011). Training Bulletin: Words Matter. Suggested Guidelines on Language Use for Sexual Assault. *Sexual Assault Report 15*, 2: 17–31.

Crosset, T., J. Ptacek, M. McDonald, and J. Benedict. (1996). "Male Student-Athletes and Violence against Women: A Survey of Campus Judicial Affairs Offices." *Violence against Women 2*, 2:163–179.

DeMitchell, T. (2016, March 18). Davis v. Monroe County Board of Education. *Encyclopedia Britannica*. Retrieved November 20, 2016, from: https://www.britannica.com/topic/Davis-v-Monroe-County-Board-of-Education

Dick, K., and A. Ziering. (2016). *The Hunting Ground: The Inside Story of Sexual Assault on American College Campuses*. New York: Hot Books.

Edwards, S. K. Bradshaw, and V. Hinsz. (2014). Denying Rape but Endorsing Forceful Intercourse: Exploring Difference among Responders. *Violence and Gender 1*, 4: 188–193.

Eilperin, J. (2016, July 3). Biden and Obama Rewrite the Rulebook on College Sexual Assaults. *Washington Post*. Retrieved November 21, 2016, from: https://www.washingtonpost.com/politics/biden-and-obama-rewrite-the-rulebook-on-college-sexual-assaults/2016/07/03/0773302e-3654–11e6-a254–2b336e293a3c_story.html

Epifano, A. (2012, October 17). An Account of Sexual Assault at Amherst College. *The Amherst Student*. Retrieved February 16, 2017, from: http://amherststudent.amherst.edu/?q=article/2012/10/17/account-sexual-assault-amherst-college.

Fisher, B., F. Cullen, and M. Turner. (2000). The Sexual Victimization of College Women Research Report. National Institute of Justice, Bureau of Justice Statistics. Washington, DC. Retrieved November 21, 2016, from: https://www.ncjrs.gov/pdffiles1/nij/182369.pdf

Fisher, B., L. Daigle, and F. Cullen. (2010). *Unsafe in the Ivory Tower: The Sexual Victimization of College Women*. Thousand Oaks, CA: Sage Publications.

Flanagan, C. (2014, March). The Dark Power of Fraternities. *The Atlantic*. Retrieved November 21, 2016, from: http://www.theatlantic.com/magazine/archive/2014/03/the-dark-power-of-fraternities/357580/

Foubert, J. (2007). Creating Lasting Attitude and Behavior Change in Fraternity Members and Male Student Athletes: The Qualitative Impact of an Empathy-Based Rape Prevention Program. *Violence against Women 13*, 1: 70–86.

Foubert, J., J. Newberry, and J. Tatum. (2007). Behavior Differences Seven Months Later: Effects of a Rape Prevention Program. *NASPA Journal 44*, 4: 728–749.

Frintner, M. P., and L. Rubinson. (1993). Acquaintance Rape: The Influence of Alcohol, Fraternity Membership, and Sports Team Membership. *Journal of Sex Education and Therapy 19*, 4: 272–282.

Germain, L. J. (2016). *Campus Sexual Assault: College Women Respond*. Baltimore, MD: Johns Hopkins Press.

Griffin, S. 1971. Rape: The All American Crime. *Ramparts*. Retrieved November 21, 2016, from: http://www.unz.org/Pub/Ramparts-1971sep-00026

Hartmann, M. (2011, March 8). Frat Email Explains Women Are "Targets," Not "Actual People". *Jezebel*. Retrieved November 26, 2016, from: http://jezebel.com/5779905/ usc-frat-guys-email-explains-women-are-targets-not-actual-people-like-us-men

Humphrey, S. (2000). Fraternities, Athletic Teams, and Rape. *Journal of Interpersonal Violence 15*, 12: 1313–1323.

The Hunting Ground. (2015). [Motion Picture, Chain Camera Pictures]. Retrieved October 16, 2016, from: http://thehuntinggroundfilm.com/

It Happened Here. (2014). [Motion Picture, Neponsit Pictures]. Retrieved October 16, 2016, from: http://www .ithappenedhere.org/

Katz, J., V. Tirone, and E. van der Kloet. (2012, March 31). Moving In and Hooking Up: Women's and Men's Casual Sexual Experiences during the First Two Months of College. *Electronic Journal of Human Sexuality*. Retrieved November 21, 2016, from: http://www.ejhs.org/volume15/ Hookingup.html

Kilpatrick, D., H. Resnick, K. Ruggiero, L. Conoscenti, and J. McCauley. (2007). Drug-Facilitated, Incapacitated, and Forcible Rape: A National Study. Prepared for the U.S. Department of Justice by the National Crime Victims Research & Treatment Center. Charleston, SC. Retrieved November 21, 2016, from: https://www.ncjrs.gov/ pdffiles1/nij/grants/219181.pdf

Kimble, M., A. Neacsiu., W. Flack, Jr., and J. Horner. (2008). Risk of Unwanted Sex for College Women: Evidence for a Red Zone. *Journal of American College Health 57*, 3: 331–337.

Kingkade, T. (2014, June 10). How a Title IX Harassment Case at Yale in 1980 Set the Stage for Today's Sexual Assault Activism. *The Huffington Post*. Retrieved November 21, 2016, from: http://www.huffingtonpost.com/2014/06/10/ title-ix-yale-catherine-mackinnon_n_5462140.html

Kingkade, T. (2014, September 29). Fewer Than One-Third of Campus Sexual Assault Cases Result in Expulsion. *The Huffington Post*. Retrieved November 21, 2016, from: http://www.huffingtonpost.com/2014/09/29/campus-sexual-assault_n_5888742.html

Kingkade, T. (2016, February 1). Why Colleges Hide behind This One Privacy Law All the Time. *The Huffington Post*. Retrieved November 21, 2016, from: http://www.huffingtonpost.com/entry/colleges-hide-behind-ferpa_us_56a7dd34e4b0b87beec65dda

Kingkade, T. (2016, July 6). Why It's Harder for Graduate Students to Report Sexual Harassment. *The Huffington Post*. Retrieved November 22, 2016, from: http://www.huffingtonpost.com/entry/grad-students-sexual-harassment_us_57714bc6e4b0dbb1bbbb37c7

Kingkade, T. (2016, November 15). What a Trump Presidency Could Mean for Combating Campus Rape. *Buzzfeed News*. Retrieved November 23, 2016, from: https://www.buzzfeed.com/tylerkingkade/trump-campus-rape-title-ix?utm_term=.nhxG7ayAV#.gxGkmw54a

Kirkpatrick, C., and E. Kanin. (1957). Male Sex Aggression on a University Campus. *American Sociological Review 22*, 1: 52–58.

Kitchens, C. (2014, March 20). It's Time to End "Rape Culture" Hysteria. *Time*. Retrieved November 21, 2016, from: http://time.com/30545/its-time-to-end-rape-culture-hysteria/

Koestner K. (2016, June 2) How I Convinced the World You Can Be Raped by Your Date. BBC News. Retrieved February 16, 2017, from: http://www.bbc.com/news/magazine-36434191

Koss, M. P., C. A. Gidycz, and N. Wisniewski. (1987). The Scope of Rape: Incidence and Prevalence of Sexual Aggression and Victimization in a National Sample of Higher Education Students. *Journal of*

Consulting and Clinical Psychology 55, 2: 162–170. doi:10.1037/0022–006x.55.2.162.

Krakauer J. (2015). *Missoula: Rape and the Justice System in a College Town*. New York: Doubleday.

Krebs, C., C. Lindquist, M. Berzofsky, B. Shook-Sa, and K. Peterson. (2016). Campus Climate Survey Validation Study Final Technical Report. National Institute of Justice, Bureau of Justice Statistics. Washington, DC. Retrieved November 21, 2016, from: http://www.bjs.gov/content/pub/pdf/ccsvsftr.pdf

Krebs, C., C. Lindquist, T. Warner, B. Fisher, and S. Martin. (2007). The Campus Sexual Assault Study. National Institute of Justice. Washington, DC. Retrieved November 21, 2016, from: https://www.ncjrs.gov/pdffiles1/nij/grants/221153.pdf

Lawyer, S.H., V. Bakanic Resnick, T. Burkett, and D. Kilpatrick. (2010). Forcible, Drug-Facilitated, and Incapacitated Rape and Sexual Assault among Undergraduate Women. *Journal of American College Health 38*, 5: 453–460.

Lewis, S., S. Schuster, and B. Sokolow. (2010). Gamechangers: Reshaping Campus Sexual Misconduct through Litigation. NCHERM Whitepaper. Retrieved November 21, 2016, from: https://www.ncherm.org/documents/2010NCHERMWhitepaperFinal.pdf

Lisak, D., S. Nicksa Gardineier, and A. Cote. (2010). False Allegations of Sexual Assault: An Analysis of Ten Years of Reported Cases. *Violence against Women 16*, 12: 1318–1334.

Lisak, D., and P. M. Miller. (2002). Repeat Rape and Multiple Offending among Undetected Rapists. *Violence & Victims 17*, 1: 73–84.

Lombardi, K. (2010, February 24). A Lack of Consequences for Sexual Assault. The Center for Public Integrity. Retrieved November 21, 2016, from:

https://www.publicintegrity.org/2010/02/24/4360/
lack-consequences-sexual-assault

Maymi, V. (2015, October 9). Here's How I Was Raped. *The Harvard Crimson*. Retrieved November 21, 2016, from: https://www.thecrimson.com/article/2015/10/9/assault-no-grey-area/

New, J. (2015, April 28). Obama Urged to Add Sex Assault Protections at Military Academies. *Inside Higher Ed*. Retrieved November 21, 2016, from: https://www.insidehighered.com/quicktakes/2015/04/28/obama-urged-add-sex-assault-protections-military-academies

RAINN. (n.d.). About Sexual Assault. Retrieved November 21, 2016, from: https://www.rainn.org/about-sexual-assault

RAINN. (n.d.). Rape and Sexual Assault Crime Definitions. Retrieved November 26, 2016, from: https://apps.rainn.org/policy/compare/crimes.cfm

Reilly, R. (2005, January 20). Another Victim at Colorado. *Sports Illustrated*. Retrieved February 16, 2017, from: http://www.si.com/more-sports/2010/01/01/hnida

Roiphe, K. 1993. *The Morning After: Sex, Fear, and Feminism on Campus*. Boston, MA: Little Brown.

Sanday, P. R. (1990). *Fraternity Gang Rape: Sex, Brotherhood, and Privilege on Campus*. New York: New York University Press.

Seccuro, L. (2011). *Crash into Me: A Survivor's Search for Justice*. New York: Bloomsbury.

Siers-Poisson, J. (2014, January 2). Student-Athletes Commit Rape, Sexual Assaults More Often Than Peers. The Kathleen Dunn Show, National Public Radio. Retrieved November 21, 2016, from: http://www.wpr.org/student-athletes-commit-rape-sexual-assaults-more-often-peers

Sinozich, S., and L. Langton. (2014). Rape and Sexual Assault Victimization among College-Age Females, 1995–2013. U.S. Department of Justice, Office of Justice Programs,

Bureau of Justice Programs. Washington, DC. Retrieved November 21, 2016, from: http://www.bjs.gov/content/pub/pdf/rsavcaf9513.pdf

Swartout, K., M. Koss, J. White, M. Thompson, A. Abbey, and A. Bellis. (2015). Trajectory Analysis of the Campus Serial Rapist Assumption. *JAMA Pediatrics 169*, 12: 1148–1154.

Sweet, E. (1985). Date Rape: The Story of an Epidemic and Those Who Deny It. *Ms.* magazine.

Taylor, H. (2014). To Curb Sexual Assault on Campuses, Surveys Become a Priority. *Chronicle of Higher Education 60*, 35: A6–A8.

Warshaw, Robin. (1998/1994). *I Never Called It Rape: The Ms. Report on Recognizing, Fighting and Surviving Date and Acquaintance Rape.* New York: Harper & Row.

Washington Post-Kaiser Family Foundation Poll. (2015). Survey on Current and Recent College Students on Sexual Assault. Retrieved November 21, 2016, from: http://kff.org/other/poll-finding/survey-of-current-and-recent-college-students-on-sexual-assault/

White House Council on Women and Girls. (2014). Rape and Sexual Assault: A Renewed Call to Action. Washington, DC: Office of the Vice President. Retrieved November 21, 2016, from: https://www.whitehouse.gov/sites/default/files/docs/sexual_assault_report_1–21–14.pdf

White House Task Force to Protect Students from Sexual Assault. (2014). Not Alone: Together against Sexual Assault. Retrieved June 5, 2016, from: www.notalone.gov.

Willingham, K. (2016, April 2). To the Harvard Law 19: Do Better. *The Harvard Law Record.* Retrieved November 21, 2016, from: http://hlrecord.org/2016/04/page/4/

Young, B.-R., S. Desmarais, J. Baldwin, and R. Chandler. (2016). Sexual Coercion Practices among Undergraduate Male Recreational Athletes, Intercollegiate Athletes, and Non-Athletes. *Violence against Women* : 1–18. doi: 10.1177/1077801216651339.

Zhang, R. (2014, September 23). Franklin v. Gwinnett County Public Schools. Encyclopedia Britannica. Retrieved November 20, 2016, from: https://www.britannica.com/topic/Franklin-v-Gwinnett-County-Public-Schools

2 Problems, Controversies, and Solutions

Introduction

Campus sexual assault is a problem that needs urgent attention. This is clear from the multitude of research that indicates a high rate of sexual assault at our nation's universities and colleges, from the backlog of investigations the Office for Civil Rights is conducting of schools for alleged mishandling of sexual assault cases, from the scores of Title IX and Clery Act lawsuits and federal complaints filed by students, and from the pleading of hundreds of college survivor-activists asking for change. That there *is* a problem is not controversial. However, there are many controversial elements to the issue of campus sexual assault. The previous chapter discussed some of these debates, including how to best measure and study the prevalence of campus sexual assault, and what risk factors might play a role in explaining the occurrence of sexual assault. This chapter provides an overview of some additional concerns, including disputes about the best practices for investigation and adjudication of campus sexual misconduct. Additionally, a summary of debates about what role college and university

Bringham Young University (BYU) student Katie Townsley stands in solidarity with sexual assault victims during a campus demonstration in April 2016. When BYU students reported sexual assault, it triggered the Mormon-owned school to investigate the victims for possible honor code violations, including those against premarital sex and alcohol use. The practice drew widespread condemnation, and BYU changed its policy to no longer conduct honor code reviews of sexual assault victims. (AP Photo/ Rick Bowmer) faculty should play is followed by a critical discussion about the controversies surrounding consent. Last, this chapter will cover various proposals aimed at stemming the tide of campus sexual assault.

Disciplinary Processes

Until the 1960s, colleges and universities operated under a doctrine referred to as in loco parentis, Latin for "in the place of a parent." Derived from British and American common law, the doctrine of in loco parentis meant that university and college faculty and administrators had the ability to enact strict behavior policies and regulate students' personal lives, including dress codes and curfews. The doctrine did not survive the social movements in the 1960s, which included the fight for the increased rights of students. A change in social values, coupled with court cases that afforded constitutional protections to students, ushered in the demise of in loco parentis. By the 1970s, responsibility for safety was shifted away from school officials and onto the students themselves. In a review of the legal history of the relationship between universities and their students, Philip Lee (2011) argues that there have been various ensuing schools of thought since the doctrine of in loco parentis. Universities have ranged from being merely "bystanders" to the activities of their students, to attempting to strike a balance between universities and students for a shared responsibility in ensuring student safety. Contemporarily, while the era of curfews is long over, some believe that the pendulum is swinging back, and that parents and students expect universities to protect their students from harm.

The demise of in loco parentis has raised doubts about what role the university plays in the discipline of its students. Many argue the disciplinary system that exists in colleges and universities is best equipped for issues like plagiarism, but woefully inadequate to deal with serious crimes like sexual assault. However, Title IX mandates that schools that receive federal funds must investigate, fairly and equitably, sexual assault complaints. Thus, federal law directs universities and colleges to investigate and determine whether an accused student is "responsible" for sexual misconduct. Contemporarily, likely due to increased pressure from student survivors and the federal government to take campus sexual assault seriously, the role of universities and colleges in investigating, finding responsibility, and meting out punishments for campus sexual assault is a contentious topic. What follows is a discussion about the merits of sexual assault cases handled by colleges and universities in comparison to the criminal justice system, the debate about the current standard of punishment used by schools for cases of sexual misconduct, and various proposals for punishment of students found responsible for sexual misconduct.

School versus Criminal Justice System

Most survivors of campus sexual assault do not report their attacks. The reasons for choosing not to report, as discussed previously, are numerous. Survivors who do wish to report have several options. They can inform their college or university, they can file a police report, or they can do both. While it may be to the benefit of survivors that they have multiple reporting choices, the reality is that campus sexual assault is especially complex because of the dual jurisdiction between law enforcement and campus administration. Sexual assault is both a crime defined by state law and a violation of a college or university's misconduct policy. As such, there is debate about whether campus sexual assault is a matter best left in the hands of campus officials or if the criminal justice system is better suited to handle such allegations.

In 2011, the U.S. Education Department's Office for Civil Rights issued a Dear Colleague letter as a reminder to colleges and universities as to their responsibilities in handling allegations of sexual assault, including the requirement that schools "take immediate and effective steps to end . . . sexual violence." Additionally, the letter reiterated the obligation that schools develop and publish a sexual assault policy and grievance procedures, in addition to designating a Title IX coordinator. Schools must also advise students of their rights to file a criminal complaint and, if the student desires, assist the student in contacting law enforcement. If an incident of sexual misconduct is reported to a campus official, Title IX mandates that the school investigate the allegation in a prompt and equitable manner. A disciplinary board typically determines whether sexual harassment, which includes sexual assault, has occurred. If someone is found to have committed sexual assault, they are held "responsible" (as opposed to a finding of "guilty" in a criminal proceeding) for violating the sexual misconduct code. Often, that same disciplinary board also decides what sanction will be imposed, with expulsion being the maximum penalty possible.

Some argue that the investigation and adjudication of campus sexual assault should be left to law enforcement and propose that colleges send sexual assault complaints to the police. Arguing that campus adjudication procedures are set up for issues like plagiarism and under-age drinking, critics contend that universities and colleges are ill equipped to handle cases of sexual assault. For example, the members of the disciplinary board, typically faculty, administrators, and sometimes students, do not have official training or background in investigation procedures. Nor do faculty or administers typically have an understanding of the intricacies of handling sexual assault cases, like the need for conducting sensitive interviews, or the knowledge necessary to determine incapacitation from alcohol. As such, woefully inadequate disciplinary boards may be likely to give the same minor punishment to someone responsible for sexual misconduct as they would to someone responsible for cheating. Even the most extreme punishment, expulsion, seems too minor. As journalist Zoë Heller (2015) argues, "Indeed, the fact that college rapists only face expulsion would seem to be a good reason why colleges ought not to be trying rape cases at all. If the aim is to address sexual assault with the seriousness it deserves, why leave it to panels made up of minimally trained professors, administrators, and in some instances students to deal with such cases? Why treat rape as a Title IX issue, rather than as a felony?"

Numerous organizations, including the Rape, Abuse & Incest National Network (RAINN), have stated opposition to college and universities adjudicating sexual assault cases. RAINN argues that school disciplinary measures, often led by amateurs, trivializes sexual assault. Another concern is that campus disciplinary boards may be more concerned in protecting the school's reputation and image than they are in actually seeking justice. Additionally, the Foundation for Individual Rights in Education (FIRE) argues that campus disciplinary procedures, under increased pressure to take sexual assault seriously, may rush to judgment and fail to provide due process rights to the accused. Many accused students have, in fact, made that argument and have sued their universities or filed Title IX complaints for gender discrimination. For example, a student accused of sexual assault at the University of Cincinnati argued in his lawsuit that the university failed to provide him with fair treatment. A student twice investigated for sexual assault at the University of Chicago sued the school, alleging a "gender biased, hostile environment against males."

FIRE proposes amending federal law to require colleges to send sexual assault complaints to local law enforcement; however, in the meantime, they argue for additional protections for the accused. For example, while the accused and the accuser are both able to have an advisor of their choice, including a lawyer, FIRE believes those advisors should be able to be actively involved, including having the ability to cross-examine the accuser. The Office for Civil Rights (OCR), on the other hand, discourages the cross-examination of an accuser because of the potential to intimidate and traumatize.

On the other hand, many antirape advocates believe campus sexual assault should be handled by the college or university and are wary of the involvement of law enforcement. They argue that most survivors are unlikely to report to the police. Additionally, they argue that the criminal justice system is failing victims of sexual assault. For example, officers and investigators react to sexual assault allegations with callousness or disbelief, District Attorney's offices often turn down sexual assault cases, investigations take years, and there is a lack of specially trained investigators and a backlog of untested rape kits. Most rape cases end in acquittals, and perpetrators who are found guilty are often given minor punishments. In sum, the criminal justice system has the potential to not only re-traumatize the victim, but fail to hold the perpetrator responsible. Advocates of campus adjudication procedures argue that the campus proceedings can do a better job than the criminal justice system. According to Occidental Professor Danielle Dirks (2014), "College campuses, which are supposed to be the bastions of cutting-edge knowledge and a chance to shape the rest of the country, actually can do right." Thus, the best approach is to demand that universities and colleges do what is required of them by law and handle allegations of sexual assault fairly and equitably. From this perspective, any mandated criminal justice involvement would have a chilling effect that would keep survivors from reporting.

In the meantime, as the debate over whether campus sexual assault should be handled by the criminal justice system or by the college disciplinary system carries on, several schools are experimenting with a hybrid approach. For example, some colleges and universities are beginning to hire experienced investigators to assist in the investigation process or, like the University of Pennsylvania, are hiring investigators to preside over sexual misconduct cases.

Standard of Proof

As discussed above, the 2011 Dear Colleague letter issued by the Office for Civil Rights served as a wake-up call for colleges and universities with regards to their responsibilities in handling sexual misconduct. An especially controversial element of the letter stated that in order to be in compliance with Title IX, schools must use a "preponderance of evidence" standard to resolve complaints. The standard requires that a university or college hearing a sexual misconduct case determine discrimination is "more likely than not" to have occurred. In other words, a disciplinary board must find an alleged assailant was more than 50.1 percent likely to be responsible. Before this fairly pointed reminder, the OCR estimated 80 percent of colleges were already using the preponderance standard. However, some schools, including many of the Ivy Leagues, were using a "clear and convincing" standard instead. "Clear and convincing" is a higher standard of proof, which requires that a hearing determine that discrimination is more substantially likely to have occurred than not. In other words, the clear and convincing standard requires a roughly 70 percent chance that the accused is responsible for sexual misconduct. The 2011 Dear Colleague letter, confirmed again in correspondence in 2014, said that colleges and universities must use the preponderance standard of proof and that the clear and convincing standard was in violation of Title IX. Since running afoul of Title IX means the potential loss of federal funds, the Dear Colleague letter prompted many schools, including Duke and Stanford, to revisit their policies and procedures.

Critics of the use of the preponderance standard for campus sexual misconduct argue that it fails to protect students who are falsely accused of sexual assault. They argue that a student's right to due process—the student's right to fair and unbiased procedures—is compromised under the lower standard of proof. From their perspective, the OCR requirement that there must be equitable treatment of both the complainant and the respondent is undermined by the preponderance standard. Various organizations, including the civil liberties group FIRE, the American Association of University Professors, and fraternity groups, all argue the standard is too low. Some also contend that the OCR violated the Administrative Procedure Act by creating a new regulation without notifying the public and seeking response beforehand. That concern is the basis of several federal lawsuits against the U.S. Department of Education, including *Doe v. Lhamon* filed by a former University of Virginia law student and the organization FIRE.

On the other hand, proponents of the use of the preponderance standard for campus sexual misconduct point out that it is the same standard that is used in civil court. Since the maximum punishment a school can give for sexual assault is expulsion, which happens rarely, proponents contend these cases are not about a loss of liberty. In other words, they argue the higher standard of proof is not necessary because unlike criminal proceedings, schools are determining if a school policy was violated, not whether someone should be imprisoned. From this perspective, it is argued that students found responsible for sexual misconduct are often able to attend other schools with ease and do not suffer life-long repercussions. Additionally, while some law professors are critical of the lower standard, at least 90 law professors from 50 universities signed a white paper in support of the preponderance standard. The paper argued that sexual harassment was a civil rights issue and pointed to the use of the preponderance standard to adjudicate all other discrimination claims, like racial harassment.

The lower standard of proof for sexual misconduct is not necessarily new, as there were cases dating back to the early 1990s where the Department of Education used the preponderance of evidence standard. However, schools were only notified on a case-by-case basis of this expectation. Now that the Dear Colleague letter made the standard of proof clear, however, it remains contentious. Is the OCR's preponderance standard of proof requirement an example of "over-reach" that violates due process or a sorely needed directive that holds aggressors and universities accountable? The debate about the appropriate standard of proof for campus sexual assault wages on.

Type of Punishment
Many survivors of campus sexual assault report a myriad of problematic ways their universities or colleges responded to

their allegations. The responses of some campus officials are misguided at best. For example, a University of North Carolina administrator responded to Annie E. Clark's report of sexual assault by saying that "rape is like a football, if you look back on the game, and you're the quarterback . . . is there anything you would have done differently?" Such a response essentially blames the victim for the assault. Additionally, survivors at various universities and colleges across the nation recount that campus officials have responded to their reports of sexual assault by encouraging them to drop out or take time off from school, dissuading them from making formal reports with law enforcement or the university, and/or failing to provide appropriate protections or accommodations. There are many likely motivations for this kind of response from administrators. Campus sexual assault is a potential public relations problem that can result in the loss of donor dollars and future applicants. In this regard, some administrators may be motivated to sweep such allegations under the rug. Additionally, some campus officials may lack official training in appropriate institutional responses to campus sexual assault allegations.

Among students who are found responsible for sexual misconduct, few are disciplined by the school. Results from the Campus Sexual Assault Study found that only 1 percent of perpetrators of sexual assault were disciplined by their schools (2007). Additionally, an investigation by the Center for Public Integrity found that most perpetrators of campus sexual assault receive little or no punishment if they are found responsible for sexual misconduct (2009). In an analysis of data from nearly three dozen colleges and universities by *The Huffington Post*, students found responsible of sexual assault were expelled in only 30 percent of the cases (2014). In the cases in which penalties are enforced, advocates and survivors say the punishment rarely fits the crime. In reality, the expulsion or suspension of a student found responsible for sexual misconduct is rare. Instead, many colleges and universities assign lenient punishments, including community service, fines, papers, and attendance in training/education seminars. Schools may be influenced by the recommendation of the Association for Student Conduct Administration that counsels universities to not be "punitive" when handling campus rape. However, from the perspective of anti–sexual assault advocates, some punishments are especially egregious, like the punishment meted out by James Madison University, which punished three fraternity members found responsible for sexual misconduct with expulsion after graduation. The callous response of campus officials, coupled with inadequate or non-existent punishments, lead some survivors to feel betrayed by their universities. As one survivor of campus sexual assault at the University Alabama put it, "The assault was bad, but the way my school has treated me has created more trauma than the original assault did."

In many ways, the punishments handed down by campus proceedings mirror the lenient punishments meted out by the criminal justice system. In an analysis of Department of Justice data, RAINN found about one in four reported rapes lead to an arrest, and one in four arrests lead to a felony conviction and incarceration. Further, pursuing a rape case in the criminal justice system can take years, and there is a backlog of hundreds of thousands of rape kits with DNA evidence that remain untested. In other words, it remains controversial as to whether sexual assault assailants are more or less likely to receive appropriate punishments through a criminal proceeding or by a school disciplinary board.

Out of frustration for the perceived inadequate punishments dispensed by colleges and universities, advocates have proposed a variety of different approaches to punishment for those found in violation of sexual misconduct, including transcript notations, mandatory minimum punishment policies, and the use of restorative justice to assign reparations.

One controversial approach to campus punishment is to put a mark on the permanent record of students found responsible for sexual misconduct, or who left the school while an investigation was ongoing. Nicknamed "scarlet letter" policies after the famous novel of the same name, a transcript notation would follow students found responsible for sexual assault to new schools, graduate programs, and potentially the workforce. No federal law requires such a sanction, and schools do not have any legal responsibility to ask applicants if they have been found responsible for sexual misconduct. As a result, many anti–sexual assault advocates argue that it is too easy for students who are found responsible for sexual misconduct to simply transfer to another school. The case of Jesse Matthew provides a high-profile example. Matthew was named a suspect in a rape allegation at Liberty University. He left Liberty and attended Christopher Newport University, leaving there after he was named in another sexual assault allegation. He was later charged with the murder and kidnapping of a University of Virginia student and a Virginia Tech student. Inspired by Matthew's troubling history, the state of Virginia passed a law that requires colleges and universities to note on transcripts if a student was suspended or expelled for sexual assault. New York has passed a similar law, and similar legislation is being considered elsewhere, including Washington, D.C.

Advocates of transcript notation policies argue that they protect students from perpetrators of sexual assault. Transfer schools or graduate programs can clearly see the student was responsible for a conduct violation and can take that into consideration in their admissions process. On the other hand, critics argue that it would keep students from being able to pursue their education and, moreover, branding a student for life is too severe a punishment. Additionally, critics contend that the campus adjudication process is not the same as a court of law, and as a result, innocent people may be permanently maligned. Some anti–sexual assault advocates are also wary, concerned that such a "high-stakes" punishment would result in schools becoming more reluctant to penalize in general.

While colleges and universities have cited the Federal Education Rights and Privacy Act as preventing them from denoting sexual assault on transcripts, this is widely understood as an incorrect interpretation of the law. The trade organization,

Association for Student Conduct Administration, called for schools to begin adding notations about sexual assault sanctions on transcripts. Additionally, the American Association of Collegiate Registrars and Admission Officers switched from opposing such policies to suggesting that schools consider it. As such, more schools and states may adopt scarlet letter policies.

Another consideration by some state legislatures is punishment policies that establish minimum sanctions for colleges to assign to students found responsible of sexual misconduct. Critics of minimum sanction policies argue that legislators should not determine what appropriate punishments should be and that administrators are better suited to determine sanctions because they can review the specific circumstances of the case. Considered by a handful of states, minimum sanction policies for colleges and universities have not gained any legislative traction. However, California passed a bill for mandatory prison sentences for those found guilty of certain sexual assaults. The bill was motivated by the lenient six-month sentence given to Brock Turner, the Stanford swimmer who was found guilty on three felony counts for the sexual assault of an unconscious woman.

While neither state nor federal law yet requires colleges and universities to have minimum sanctions for students found responsible for campus sexual assault, some schools have adopted their own minimum sanction policies. For example, Dartmouth requires mandatory expulsion for students found responsible of certain types of sexual assault. Other schools have placed more emphasis on expulsion in cases of sexual misconduct, and Duke comes close to Dartmouth's policy by referring to expulsion as the "preferred sanction" for such cases. Critics of mandatory expulsion policies are concerned that a one-size-fits-all model may discourage victims from reporting if they do not wish for their assailant to receive such a severe punishment. Additionally, critics fear that the college adjudication process is too flawed, and innocent students could be erroneously expelled for crimes they did not commit. However, advocates argue that mandatory expulsion policies ensure that students found responsible for sexual assault receive a severe punishment for their crime.

Some advocates argue that survivors of campus sexual assault are poorly served by the adversarial procedure used by most colleges and universities and argue that schools need to handle sexual assault in a different manner altogether. Mary P. Koss, psychologist and pioneer of campus sexual assault research, proposes the use of a restorative justice model. Restorative justice is used occasionally in the criminal justice system for a variety of offenses, influenced in part by practices traditionally used in tribal courts that allow any stakeholders to make a statement to the court and the defendant. Koss launched the first restorative justice program for perpetrators of sex crimes with prosecutors in Pima County, Arizona. The program, RESTORE, was developed with the goal of holding perpetrators accountable to the people and communities they violated. The program and restorative justice method showed promise, and Koss believes restorative justice also has the potential to be useful in campus sexual assault cases (2014). Generally speaking, a restorative justice approach requires that the offender listen to the victim and accept responsibility and that the two work with a trained facilitator to create a mutually agreed upon resolution. Koss argues that restorative justice can have profound implications for the perpetrator, including realizing the impact of their actions on the victim, the influence of bad peer groups, and/or the extent of alcohol problems. For victims, restorative justice allows for their voice to be heard and the ability to witness offender remorse, and it allows for involvement in defining the terms of reparation—which could include anything from therapy to expulsion. Given the propensity for the adversarial process to result in lenient punishments, over which victims have no control, the restorative justice model gives victims the opportunity to work toward an outcome they desire.

While some college or university campuses have restorative justice options for offenses like disorderly conduct or vandalism, there are no known universities or colleges that utilize the approach for sexual assault. The University of Michigan is an example of a school that comes close—allowing the use of restorative justice in cases of sexual misconduct (e.g., harassment, emotional/verbal abuse)—but not in cases of sexual misconduct that includes assault. For many, restorative justice is not viewed as appropriate for sexual assault cases. Critics argue that asking a victim to confront her assailant would be re-traumatizing, and some fear the option would provide schools with (another) way to avoid issuing punishments. Further, some critics fear that social pressure would lead female survivors to choose restorative processes, even if they would prefer adversarial, because of the cultural norm that dictates that women are "supposed to forgive." Moreover, as clarified by the 2011 Dear Colleague letter, Title IX guidelines prohibit mediation for cases of sexual assault. Some interpret restorative justice as a form of mediation and thereby believe it cannot be used for cases of campus sexual assault. However, Koss maintains mediation and restorative justice are not the same thing: mediation is based on neutrality, whereas restorative justice is only pursued when a perpetrator accepts responsibility. Proponents of providing the option of restorative justice argue that it empowers survivors and gives them more options and control. At this point, there is no evidence that this approach stops student assailants from re-offending or makes student survivors feel more empowered. However, given the widespread concern about existing approaches to punishment, more schools may consider incorporating the techniques of restorative justice.

As survivors demand better treatment, and as the accused demand increased rights, the controversies about the school adjudication process for campus sexual assault will likely live on.

Faculty Responsibility

College students look to faculty members for more than classroom instruction. Students often share with trusted professors and instructors personal information, and faculty are often the first to notice troubling change in a student's behavior, indicating something is amiss. This frequently results in faculty serving in the role of *first responder* for survivors of campus sexual assault. In these situations, faculty can provide essential support and guidance. However, faculty are typically not trained therapists, and not all schools equip faculty with the skills necessary to serve as appropriate first responders. Mis-information, a lack of support, or victim blaming on the part of a professor (or administrator) could be further traumatizing for a student survivor.

While many faculty are deeply invested in their student's well-being and success, it is debatable what role they should play in the issue of campus sexual assault. Typically, sexual assault prevention programs and disciplinary procedures fall to administrators and other non-faculty staff. However, sexual violence impacts the classroom. Sometimes, survivors of sexual assault do poorly in school, including withdrawing from or failing classes. Additionally, survivors may struggle with classroom topics, such as rape, because it may elicit painful memories and/or cause psychological distress. Ultimately, faculty are accustomed to serving as mentors for their students, but the relationship between faculty and the issue of campus sexual assault is multifaceted. There is debate over classroom content and whether or not instructors should include trigger warnings for potentially problematic material. There is dispute about whether faculty should be mandated to officially report accounts of sexual assault, even if it is against the student's wishes. Additionally, faculty are often in a difficult position with regards to the role they play in campus dialogue about sexual assault policy and whether they can or should be vocally critical of their institution.

Faculty Activism

Should faculty be considered advocates for their students or primarily employees that represent the colleges and universities that employ them? Many faculty believe it is their role, if not responsibility, to assist students in demanding campus change with regards to sexual assault. For example, Professors Danielle Dirks and Caroline Heldman at Occidental College advised student survivors of their rights under Title IX, helped launch an organization with survivors called End Rape on Campus, and joined survivors in filing a Title IX complaint against Occidental, alleging the mishandling of sexual assault cases and retaliation against those who spoke out against the school's alleged inadequate response to the issue.

While there are plenty of faculty who have taken an activist role on campuses across the nation, many others are fearful of speaking out against their institution, even if they feel as though the school's procedures and practices are inadequate. Several examples of faculty losing their jobs after speaking out against their institutions seem to justify these fears. For example, Heather Turcotte, a professor in the Women, Gender, and Sexuality Studies department at the University of Connecticut believes her outspoken criticism of the university president's poor response to threats of rape and violence against a female student cost her job. Kimberly Theidon, a highly regarded anthropology professor at Harvard, believes her outspoken support of campus sexual assault victims resulted in her being terminated and denied tenure. Jennifer Freyd, a psychology professor at the University of Oregon, was critical of the school's handling of a gang rape case involving basketball players. Freyd believes the school chose not to use the campus climate survey she developed and paid for an outside source to create one, in retaliation for her vocal criticism. There are other examples of retaliation against faculty activists at schools across the nation. A list of some additional faculty experiences with retaliation can be found on the website of the group Faculty against Rape (www.facultyagainstrape.net).

Alleged retaliation against faculty for their public criticism of their institutions raises questions about academic freedom. Academic freedom refers to the conviction that faculty and students should be able to express their views without fear of sanction and it protects faculty and students from reprisals for disagreeing with administrative policies. In other words, in theory, academic freedom allows faculty to critique their institutions. However, in practice, this can be risky for one's career. Outspoken criticism may result in negative ramifications for job security, and it may result in backlash from the community at large. For example, the Occidental professors and student activists discussed above were subjected to online harassment from trolls.

Not all professors are interested in taking an active role against campus sexual assault, and many may not even know the scope of the problem. However, arguably, tenured professors especially have the ability to call attention to issues surrounding campus sexual assault and serve as a force for positive change. The American Association of University Women advises faculty and staff to fight campus sexual violence by, for example, encouraging prevention programs, participating in training programs, organizing public awareness campaigns, and ensuring the school has a Title IX coordinator. Additionally, Professor Simona Sharoni at the State University of New York–Plattsburgh and Professor Caroline Heldman from Occidental College, cofounded the group Faculty against Rape, an organization for faculty members who wish to have a greater role in the struggle to confront campus sexual assault.

In addition to whether faculty can, if they desire, be active in a role to combat campus sexual assault without fear of repercussions, further questions about academic freedom are raised in the debate about trigger warnings and mandatory reporting.

Trigger Warnings

The use of trigger warnings in general is nothing new, though the use of trigger warnings in college classrooms has recently gained traction and attracted a fair amount of controversy. Trigger warnings originated in Internet communities, primarily for the benefit of people with posttraumatic stress disorder.

For survivors of various forms of violence, including combat violence, incest, child abuse, and sexual abuse, there are certain sounds, smells, or sights that can "trigger" an intense emotional and sometimes physical response. Thus, trigger warnings are commonly used online and in the media to warn readers/viewers that the content is graphically violent or deals with subject matter in a way that could cause a recurrence of past trauma. With a trigger warning, people are given knowledge about the content that can help them choose whether or not they wish to view or engage with the material.

In classrooms, trigger warnings are written on syllabi or made at the outset of a lecture, film viewing, or reading assignment on potentially difficult material. In a poll conducted by National Public Radio (NPR), 54 percent of instructors of undergraduates at over 800 universities report using a trigger warning, most likely in reference to sexual or violent material. The instructors typically used trigger warnings of their own volition, not because of any student requests or institutional policies. Additionally, the NPR study found fewer than 2 percent of schools had any official policies about their use. While the poll indicated that the majority of faculty respondents used trigger warnings in their classrooms, the use of such warnings is controversial.

Those in favor of trigger warnings argue that they allow students who are struggling with trauma to prepare for, and manage, their reactions to the material. Someone who is triggered by classroom material may suffer from a variety of responses, including anxiety, panic attacks, and intellectual disengagement from the material. Advocates of trigger warnings argue that if students are given a heads up on what to expect, they can plan accordingly, which perhaps includes contacting a therapist, asking for an alternative assignment, or stepping out of the room for a few minutes. With regards to campus sexual assault specifically, a lecture that includes a discussion of rape could be extraordinarily difficult for a survivor of sexual assault. Advocates of trigger warnings argue that their use not only is respectful recognition that the material may impact some people on a personal level but also serves as a reminder to everyone to be mindful of the fact that there are likely survivors in the room. Sofie Karasek, cofounder of End Rape on Campus, argues that the facilitation of respectful conversations and the use of trigger warnings allow survivors to delve into the material on their own terms and feel supported in doing so. In general, faculty who use trigger warnings do not see them as an excuse to allow students out of engaging with the material. Instead, many faculty who use trigger warnings do so in tangent with creating a safe space for dialogue on especially difficult topics. The idea is not to avoid the material but to be sensitive to the fact that the topic has personal meaning to some and to make a concerted effort not to blindside them.

On the other side of the argument are those who are critical of trigger warnings. Some view the demand for trigger warnings as led by overly "politically correct" students and consequently are wary of "coddling millennials" who are "oversensitive." Additionally, critics argue that if students are given an option out of class material, they will lose out on important learning experiences—based on the belief that students need to be challenged on difficult material in order to grow both intellectually and emotionally. The debate about trigger warnings was intensified by a welcome letter released by a dean at the University of Chicago in 2016. Addressing the Class of 2020, he made it clear that the college does not condone trigger warnings or "safe spaces" as a matter of commitment to "freedom of inquiry and expression." From his perspective and that of others, trigger warnings are an infringement of academic freedom. There is concern about the chilling effect such warnings may have on teaching, especially if faculty fear addressing difficult topics in their classes because they do not wish to be responsible for triggering students or angering superiors. Additionally, some fear that students will expect trigger warnings for material that simply is uncomfortable for them or that challenges their beliefs, not because they have had a significant traumatic experience.

In this regard, faculty are fearful of the implications trigger warnings may have on censorship.

Ultimately, some argue trigger warnings are a violation of academic freedom and a threat to students' intellectual growth. Others argue that the use of trigger warnings is a pedagogical best practice that signals concern and respect for student survivors of violence. The debate about trigger warnings is likely to continue, as campuses decide whether to create official policy about their use, including when and where to use them.

Mandatory Reporting

As mentioned previously, faculty are often first responders to students who have experienced sexual assault. What faculty choose to do once they are given that information is complex. Ideally, if a student discloses an incident of sexual assault, the faculty member is trained and well equipped to provide that student with resources on how to report and where to seek medical and emotional care, either on or off campus. But in addition to providing resources, should a faculty member also file an official report with the school or police supplying the details they have been told, regardless of the student's desires? What if a student discloses information about a sexual assault in a class paper? Should the instructor report that to authorities? This issue of faculty as "mandatory reporters" is a controversial one, raising concerns about the Clery Act, school responsibility, student welfare, and academic freedom.

There is historical precedence in mandatory reporting policies. The federal Child Abuse Prevention and Treatment Act, passed in 1974, requires states to implement mandatory reporting provisions or lose funding for crime programs; as a result, all states have enacted mandatory reporting for the treatment of children. Typically, professional groups that work with children, such as groups of teachers, social workers, and doctors, are mandatory reporters for child abuse, meaning they must report any suspicion of abuse to either law enforcement or a child protection agency. In some states, these reporting requirements extend to the suspicion of elder abuse and/or intimate partner violence. Mandatory reporting policies for campus sexual assault follow a similar logic as do the policies for child abuse, in that university students are young and vulnerable and may be unwilling to report sexual assault. Additionally, the Clery Act requires that schools tabulate and report the number of crimes on their campuses. However, campus sexual assault is vastly underreported. Some institutions look to mandatory reporting policies as a way to fulfill their reporting obligations. Notably, crimes that occur off campus are not included in official campus crime statistics. Thus, sexual assault (which often occurs at off-campus locations) may not be fully included in official tallies. As such, campus crime statistics may be influenced by the proportion of students who live on campus; if a campus has more students living in dorms, their crime statistics may indicate a higher rate of sexual assault in comparison to schools where most students live off campus.

Currently, there is a lot of variability in how mandatory reporting applies to campus sexual assault. In general, policies and/or legislation define certain individuals as mandatory reporters for campus sexual misconduct, meaning that if they become aware of an incident of sexual assault they must report it to the appropriate authorities. For some colleges and universities, mandatory reporting is a matter of campus policy. For some states, like Virginia, mandatory reporting for campus sexual assault is a matter of state law. There are two aspects of mandatory reporting policies that are especially controversial. The first is concern about the definition of all faculty and staff as mandatory reporters, which is the case at many schools. The second is concern with policies or legislation that mandates notification to law enforcement.

At the foundation of the debate about faculty as defined mandatory reporters are different interpretations of the Clery Act, Title IX, and the Dear Colleague letter. The Clery Act mandates that crime statistics (including sexual assault and rape) be gathered by campus police or security, local law enforcement, and other school officials who have "significant responsibility for student and campus activities." Until recently, the definition of school officials who have "significant responsibility" for "student and campus activities" has long been interpreted as excluding faculty. Similarly vague, the Dear Colleague letter, which elaborates on the application of Title IX to campus sexual harassment, says that "responsible employees" must report sexual assault to the school's Title IX coordinator. The term *responsible employees*, however, is not specifically defined beyond "someone who has authority to take action to redress sexual violence" or who has been given the duty to report. Responsible employees exclude pastoral and professional counselors; beyond that, the Office for Civil Rights has left the choice up to schools to define who constitutes a "responsible employee." In other words, the OCR left it up to each campus to define who must report all known incidents of sexual assault. Likely in response to increased scrutiny of how colleges and universities handle sexual assault, many campuses have recently adopted mandatory reporting policies that charge all faculty and staff to report student's declarations of sexual assault to school officials. To critics of such policies, this is a problematic overreaction to federal legislation. To advocates, this is a necessary step to help combat campus sexual assault.

If faculty members are defined as mandatory reporters, the process typically goes as follows. Professors or instructors are typically advised (or mandated) to put a statement on their syllabi that warns students that any declaration of sexual assault will be reported. Faculty are additionally advised to stop a student from speaking, if it looks as if the student is planning on sharing an experience of sexual assault, in order to warn the student of the faculty's reporting obligations. If a student does share details of a sexual assault, in the classroom, in an assignment, or in a professor's office, the faculty member is then required to report the assault, typically to the campus Title IX coordinator. The report must occur, even if the student does not wish to file an official complaint or even if the student was mistakenly under the impression that their admission would be held in confidence. After the faculty reports, the Title IX coordinator or designated campus official contacts the victim and then decides how to proceed, including whether the school can honor any wish for confidentiality.

Advocates of policies that define all faculty and staff as mandatory reporters argue that it will combat underreporting and ensure greater university accountability. If reports of sexual assault make it to the Title IX coordinator, the reasoning goes, then such incidents cannot be as easily swept under the rug. Additionally, such a policy sends the message that a college or university takes sexual misconduct seriously. Advocates also argue that defining faculty as mandatory reporters relieves them of some burden, especially as faculty are not typically trained therapists and may not know how best to advise survivors. By having to report the disclosures, they are involving campus officials, who may be better equipped to assist the victims. The Association of Title IX Administrators is in favor of defining all faculty and staff as mandatory reporters. They argue that such polices not only protect vulnerable populations and result in safer schools but that they also avoid "confusion" about who is responsible for reporting while simultaneously strengthening the school's ability to meet reporting obligations. Advocates also argue that mandatory reporting policies help to identify perpetrators who are serial offenders and/or pose other risks to the campus community at large.

On the other hand, critics of policies that define all faculty and staff as mandatory reporters have a variety of stated concerns. First is the recognition that it takes strength and bravery to discuss an experience of sexual assault. That a survivor chose to discuss their experience with a professor, for example, indicates the trust they hold in that particular teacher. For various reasons discussed in the first chapter, many survivors of campus sexual assault do not wish to file official reports with their school or with the police. Thus, some survivors may seek out faculty in order to privately discuss the assault—and critics contend that reporting the details of their disclosure is a breach of confidence and disrupts the teacher-student relationship. Additionally, critics argue that if students fear their professors or instructors must report, students will not disclose their experiences to anyone—resulting in a chilling effect on campus. Stopping a student mid-sentence, for example, is not only insensitive but may result in that student never telling anyone about their assault. Critics also argue that such policies take away personal agency from the survivor in a vulnerable time in which their autonomy was recently compromised. Further, asking a student to retell their stories to campus officials or law enforcement if they are unwilling, or not ready, can be re-traumatizing.

Faculty critics are also concerned about violations of academic freedom, especially as it applies to the disclosure of sexual assault in the classroom or in class assignments. For example, certain classroom material may trigger a survivor to reveal an experience of sexual assault in a class discussion or paper. Some faculty argue that such admissions are a natural part of the learning experience; warning students to not share those experiences due to the reporting obligations of the instructor is not only stifling, but threatens a "safe" classroom atmosphere that encourages and allows open dialogue. The American Association of University Professors argues that faculty do not fall under the category of mandatory reporters under the Clery Act and cites both concerns about the chilling effect such policies can have on a campus and concerns about academic freedom, especially for faculty members who teach courses that deal directly with these topics, like those in women, gender, and sexuality studies.

There is another layer to this debate in those states that have, or are considering, proposals that require colleges and universities to notify law enforcement of any known sexual assault, often referred to as "mandatory referral" legislation. For example, the state of Virginia passed a law in 2015 that requires campus mandatory reporters (all faculty and staff) to report known incidents of sexual assault to the Title IX coordinator, who then convenes a committee that includes a law enforcement representative. Additionally, several other states have also considered or are considering similar legislation. Advocates of mandatory referral measures argue that informing law enforcement gives victims access to criminal justice resources and victim assistance. Additionally, notifying police can provide an alternative to the much criticized campus adjudication process and is believed to ensure a more thorough investigation process that protects the rights of the accused and the accuser.

On the other hand, NASPA (Student Affairs Administrators in Higher Education) published an open letter, signed by over 15 other organizations and groups, petitioning, among other concerns, against the passage of bills that mandate campus employees to report sexual assault to the local police. One of their arguments is that such a requirement conflicts with an amendment to the Clery Act that states that schools that receive federal funds must inform student victims of sexual assault, dating violence, domestic violence, and stalking of their rights to "decline to notify" law enforcement. Laws that mandate the notification of law enforcement negate the student's right to decline to notify. Additionally, the organization Know Your IX is against mandatory referral legislation for a variety of reasons, including forcing victims into a broken system that often fails victims of sexual assault. Also, they argue that if campus officials go to the police without the survivor's consent it will keep victims from reporting to anyone, and thus they would lose out on being able to get assistance from Title IX–mandated services and accommodations.

Campuses and state legislatures will continue to debate mandatory reporting procedures and weigh whether such policies reduce campus violence or silence student survivors. Meanwhile, there are several proposed alternatives. One is simply having a sufficient number of confidential sources available to students. In fact, the Obama administration's White House Task Force to Protect Students from Sexual Assault emphasized the importance of having confidential advocates on campus, warning that schools in which almost every employee is a mandatory reporter "can mean a survivor quickly loses control over what happens next." Many schools have heeded this advice and hired additional personnel and created more resources for student survivors. Additionally, some schools have anonymous filing options, where a sexual assault can be reported without violating a student's privacy, but while still gathering enough data to fulfill Clery Act requirements. For example, some schools have adopted *Callisto*. Developed by survivor Jessica Ladd, *Callisto* is a confidential online sexual assault reporting system that gives students the opportunity to create a time-stamped record of their account and the option to submit a report that isn't sent to the school until they are "matched" with another victim of the same perpetrator.

Ultimately, professors and instructors have the potential to be impacted by campus sexual assault in a myriad of ways. Faculty could face policies about trigger warnings and mandatory reporting that they may or may not agree with. And some faculty may get involved in trying to change their institution's culture surrounding sexual assault. Additionally, many faculty feel strained when students report sexual assault. While most professors and instructors want what is best for their students, they are not trained as therapists or crisis interventionists. This emotional burden may be especially significant for female faculty. Due to cultural gender role assumptions, survivors of sexual assault often feel most comfortable speaking about their trauma with female professors. Female faculty are often assumed to be more empathetic to students' personal troubles, and survivors of violence at the hands of men may feel more comfortable sharing with women. Additionally, courses where these issues are more likely to come up are often instructed by women (for example, courses in women and gender studies). In the end, both female and male faculty can suffer from "vicarious trauma" due to the confidences of student survivors. Researchers argue that providing faculty with support and access to resources, like counseling, is important for their well-being.

Consent

Sexual consent is generally understood as permission, or an agreement, to engage in sexual activity. According to RAINN, while the legal definition of consent varies by state, typically, there are three main ways in which consent is analyzed in relation to sexual acts. Specifically, the law looks to determine the following: whether consent was freely given, without fraud, coercion, violence, or threat of violence; whether consent was affirmative, meaning there were clear indications of agreement; and whether the individual had capacity, or legal ability, to consent. The issue of consent is an important, albeit sometimes contentious, factor in the conversation about campus sexual assault. There is debate about *affirmative consent* policies cropping up on campuses across the nation, there is confusion about the nature of consent when someone is intoxicated, and there is uncertainty about the relationship between sexual coercion and consent.

Affirmative Consent

Affirmative consent, sometimes referred to as "yes means yes," is defined as a clear, unambiguous, conscious, and voluntary agreement by all participating individuals to engage in sexual activity. Replacing the common standard "no means no," affirmative consent requires an ongoing presence of "yes" throughout the progression of sexual activity. Typically, such policies state that affirmation must be given verbally or through the use of nonverbal cues. Silence, or lack of resistance, does not imply consent. Previous sexual relations do not indicate consent. Further, affirmative consent policies make it clear that an individual must be capable of giving continuous consent (in other words, one cannot be passed out from alcohol, asleep, or under age).

Affirmative consent changes the way sex is approached; as opposed to taking a lack of a "no" as a signal to proceed, such policies require a clear indication of a *desire* to proceed. Advocates have been fairly successful in arguing that an affirmative consent standard is an important tool in combating campus sexual assault. In 2014, California governor Jerry Brown signed affirmative consent into law, and New York followed shortly thereafter, making affirmative consent the mandated standard at campuses in those states. Additionally, affirmative consent policies exist at more than 800 schools across the nation, including at all of the Ivy Leagues except for Harvard. While the widespread adoption of such policies is relatively new, affirmative consent policies are not without precedent. Antioch College developed the first affirmative consent policy in 1992. Antioch's policy required verbal consent at each progressive level of sexual activity, and at the time, their concept was widely ridiculed. Today, Antioch's policy is understood as prophetic.

Despite the adoption of such policies at many schools and some states, some believe that affirmative consent rules are problematic. Critics argue that such policies are a result of widespread over-correcting for the historical failure of colleges and universities to properly handle campus sexual assault. They point to the difficulty in determining whether an appropriate level of consent was achieved. In their view, nonverbal consent is especially murky and difficult to prove. Another criticism is that the requirement to get continuous consent is awkward, could kill "the mood," and is not relevant to the actual nature of sexual experiences. Critics maintain that it infantilizes women and that it is more efficient to require one "no" then multiple "yeses." Additionally, critics like the organization FIRE argue that affirmative consent policies threaten due process, as it shifts the burden of proof to the accused. No longer does the victim have to prove they said "no"; the accused has to prove the one making the allegation said "yes."

On the other hand, advocates for affirmative consent rules believe it is an important step forward. Arguing that while the *no means no* standard created blurry lines, the *yes means yes* standard is more straightforward because it requires clear consent. Affirmative consent arguably reduces ambiguity, especially given research that indicates students are divided on what actions constitute consent. Advocates believe that affirmative consent can be helpful in increasing dialogue between partners, and that making sure one's partner is a willing participant every step of the way is just common sense. Consent advocates also argue that checking in with a partner can be done in a "sexy" manner and can lead to, as journalist Ann Friedman (2014) put it, "much hotter sex." Additionally, Jaclyn Friedman, coeditor of the book *Yes Means Yes! Visions of Female Sexual Power & a World without Rape* (2008), travels to campuses across the nation and argues that by and large college students embrace the idea of affirmative consent because it gives them more clarity in navigating sexual relations.

Currently, it is too soon to determine whether affirmative consent policies can make significant inroads in reducing rates of campus sexual assault. Until research can provide evidence to the success or failure of such policies, affirmative consent standards will likely continue to be adopted due to pressures from students and others who believe it is a step in the right direction. But the concept is far from being widely accepted, and there are concerns about whether the policies go too far, or if they go far enough, if they are too vague, or if they are too intrusive. Additionally, not even proponents of affirmative consent are always on the same page. Some argue that affirmative consent policies should be limited to only verbal agreement, such as Antioch's policy. Others argue that affirmative consent policies should include nonverbal cues or gestures, such as the California law. While the debate wages on, many campuses are adopting *consent education* programs that teach not only that gaining consent is important but, in an effort to combat negative connotations, that "consent is sexy."

Intoxication

As discussed in the previous chapter, alcohol plays a big role in the lives of many college students. Easy access to alcohol, coupled with social pressures and freedom from parental over-sight, means many students are drinking, often binge drinking, regularly. While perhaps in an ideal world all campus sexual encounters would occur between two sober people who clearly consented, this is not realistic. There are many situations in which students drink and engage in sexual activity, which has the potential to complicate the issue of consent. In general, state laws make it clear that consent is not possible if someone is intoxicated. However, laws vary by state on the definition of intoxication. According to law professor Cynthia Godsoe, in many states people are intoxicated to the point of being legally incapable of consent only if they are passed out or unconscious. Additionally, the laws in many states treat situations in which one is "voluntarily incapacitated" differently from situations in which someone was forcibly intoxicated (e.g., by being drugged).

Since the relevant federal legislation (e.g., Title IX and the Clery Act) and the subsequent guidelines do not clearly address alcohol, colleges and universities are left to their own devices to develop protocols on alcohol use as it relates to consent and the definition of intoxication. Many schools have crafted broadly worded sexual misconduct guidelines that prohibit any sex without consent, including sex when consent is not possible because the person is "under the influence" of alcohol or drugs. Other college and university campuses adopt a higher threshold in their guidelines by forbidding sexual contact with anyone who is "incapacitated." The latter approach is favored by the CEO of the higher education risk management firm NCHERM, Brett Sokolow. Sokolow argues that incapacitation is a "state beyond drunkenness or intoxication" marked by "an inability to make a rational, reasonable judgment or appreciate the consequences of your decisions." Using this standard, some-one is "incapacitated" if they display, for example, outrageous behavior, slurred speech, bloodshot eyes, and a shaky equilib-rium. Thus, by this definition, if a student is incapacitated, not "just" drunk, they are unable to give consent. Ultimately, affirmative consent does not apply in situations in which a student is intoxicated or incapacitated. In other words, even if a student verbally (or through the use of nonverbal cues) consented to sexual activity, and if he or she is incapacitated, his or her consent is invalid.

What standard of intoxication to use and how to best word sexual misconduct policies is controversial. Should they be broadly worded, negating the consent of anyone who is under the influence of alcohol or drugs? Or should they be more specific, in that only someone who is "incapacitated" is unable to consent? Either way, determining the level of intoxication is difficult after the fact. The reality is that plenty of college students have consensual sex while under the influence of alcohol, to no ill effects. However, alcohol use makes it more difficult to consent to sex and more difficult to determine if the other person consented. Unfortunately, there are also plenty of incidents in which alcohol is used by a perpetrator of sexual assault as a tool.

In recognition of the role alcohol can play in the failure to get affirmative and conscious consent, many universities and colleges are beginning to hold students responsible for sexual misconduct in situations in which they, and the victim, believe consent was impossible due to the use of alcohol or drugs. Many view this as a correct response and vastly more appropriate than blaming the victim for consuming alcohol (which happens at times too, unfortunately). However, some are more critical, citing concerns that women who have "drunk sex" that they later regret can accuse men of rape. Additionally, they argue sexual misconduct policies, especially as they relate to alcohol use and consent, are too vague and open for subjective interpretation. Others fear that in cases when both individuals have been drinking, men are held to a higher standard and disproportionately or wrongly punished. Conversely, it is argued that such policies protect victims from being taken advantage of when they are unable to make rational decisions. In cases where both parties have been drinking, the person who initiated the sexual contact is the one typically held responsible, male or female. In other words, the language in campus sexual misconduct policies is always gender neutral. Additionally, it is argued that drinking should not be used as a defense for criminal behavior.

So what is the best way for schools to approach issues of consent while intoxicated? There are no easy answers here as well. Ultimately, the relationship between alcohol consumption and consent is a tricky one. The reality is that alcohol reduces inhibitions and college students may not know their own alcohol tolerance, and it is unlikely they know the tolerance of others. Thus, anti–sexual assault advocates and campus administrators argue that the best practice is to always err on the side of caution. If someone seems impaired, it is advisable not to engage in sexual activity with them. Another common recommendation is to use a drunk driving analogy. If someone is too drunk to get behind the wheel of a car, they are likely too drunk to make conscious decisions about sexual activity. Additionally, advocates argue that it is important to teach students to be mindful of the reality that just because someone is drinking does not mean they are not consenting to sexual activity. And just because someone engaged in *some* sexual activity does not mean he or she consented to *all* sexual activity. Last, students need to be taught that alcohol use is not justification for bad decisions. If someone commits a theft while intoxicated, they are held responsible for that theft—alcohol use is not a defense. Similarly, intoxication is not an admissible defense for sexual assault, as was illustrated by the two ex–Vanderbilt University football players who recently argued that they should not be held responsible for the rape of an unconscious woman because they were too drunk to know what they were doing. They lost their case and were each convicted of four counts of aggravated rape.

Sexual Coercion

In all of the campus discussion and debate about consent, there is relatively little attention paid to the issue of sexual coercion.

Sexual coercion is defined as the use of tactics, like pressure or emotional intimidation, to get someone to do something sexual against their will, for example, if someone says "yes" to sexual activity because they are fearful of what may happen if they resist (e.g., there were threats of breaking up the relationship) or if someone says "yes" because they are persuaded or manipulated to do so regardless of their lack of desire. Sexual coercion exists in situations when someone has sex because they feel obligated to do so; feel threatened, guilty, or badgered, or were pressured to use alcohol or drugs in order to loosen inhibitions. In such situations, someone may say "yes" under duress.

Advocates argue that sexual coercion is a form of sexual assault. However, many people who have experienced being sexually coerced may not view it as abusive. Instead, they may chalk it up to a misunderstanding or view it as "normal" sexual relations in which men are supposed to be aggressive and women are supposed to passive. In fact, sexual coercion arguably plays a role in many sexual encounters. Sexual coercion complicates the issue of affirmative consent, as there are situations in which consent is given yet the sexual activity is unwanted. Thus, campus policies, and state crime laws, do not often reflect the dynamics of rape and sexual assault. Advocates will continue to stress the need to recognize the role coercion plays in sexual assault. From their perspective, there is promise in campus sexual assault prevention programs that include discussions of healthy relationships that are based on mutual respect.

Solutions

Faced with increased pressure from student activists, concerned parents, and the government, colleges and universities are scrambling to find solutions to the epidemic of sexual assault on their campuses. As discussed above, postsecondary schools are experimenting with different approaches to adjudication, improving responses to accusations, asking faculty to take increased roles, implementing additional resources for students, and drafting new sexual misconduct policies that take into account issues related to consent. Additionally, many campuses are trying various sexual assault prevention education courses and are crafting alcohol "risk reduction" policies. Moreover, there are various legislative and advocate-driven attempts to reduce campus sexual assault.

Sexual Assault Prevention Programs

The Campus SaVE Act amended Clery and was part of the 2013 reauthorization of the Violence against Women Act. One of the requirements of the SaVE Act was that college students and employees must be given "primary prevention and awareness programs" that cover the issues of sexual assault, rape, dating violence, and stalking. In response, some schools developed trainings for the first time, but many campuses already had prevention programs in place. Historically, sexual assault prevention education was centered on teaching women certain "skills." For example, after defining sexual assault and tackling commonly held rape myths, many campus programs armed women with whistles, advised them of the emergency phones on campus that connected directly to the police, and told them to never leave their drinks unattended or walk alone at night. These messages were not only based on the false notion that assailants were typically strangers, but they also failed to account for the possibility that men could be victimized as well. Additionally, they put the onus of responsibility for preventing rape and assault on women's shoulders. This perspective was faulty on many levels. While it worked to make women perpetually fearful of being attacked, it failed to actually reduce rates of sexual assault. According to the Centers for Disease Control, brief programs aimed at increasing knowledge about sexual assault and dispelling rape myths increased awareness but failed to have evidence of lasting effects on reducing sexual violence.

As a result, sexual assault prevention education today typically takes a different approach that recognizes the reality that assailants are typically known to the victim and that the responsibility for preventing rape should not be that of women alone. While some schools create their own programs, most adopt existing prevention programs that typically fall under one of three categories: online (e.g., Haven), performance based (e.g., Sex Signals), and/or workshops (e.g., Bringing in the Bystander). Most programs are meant for a mixed-gender audience, though there are some programs that are geared specifically toward women (e.g., The Women's Program), men (e.g., A Call to Men), athletes (e.g., Step Up!), and fraternities (e.g., One Act). Some programs teach about the importance of consent (e.g., Only with Consent) and healthy relationships (e.g., Know Your Power), and many take a bystander intervention approach (e.g., Green Dot).

The bystander intervention model has gained in popularity. It teaches participants that it is possible for anyone to recognize and help stop harassment before it becomes sexual violence. At its core, a bystander intervention approach is community centered, encouraging everyone to look out for one another. Such programs encourage students to be active bystanders and provides them with training on how to effectively and safely intervene in situations that are problematic. Research on some of these bystander intervention programs has indicated effectiveness. For example, Bringing in the Bystander has been shown by various studies to be effective in shifting attitudes and increasing the likelihood of participants to intervene. Research on the Green Dot program found a decrease of more than 50 percent in the frequency of sexual assaults among students who took the training.

Additionally, a randomized trial on a resistance program (not a bystander intervention program) for first-year college women in Canada found that it substantially lowered the risk of being sexually assaulted (Senn et al. 2015). The program emphasized assessing risk, learning self-defense, and defining personal sexual boundaries. While the findings indicate that teaching women skills like self-defense is useful, others argue that such an approach focuses on women as potential victims and fails to deal with the behavior of men as potential perpetrators.

Ultimately, there are many sexual assault prevention programs for schools to choose from with pros and cons to each. Many are promising, and some have research evidence to their effectiveness. Regardless of which program is used, what is clear is the need for a comprehensive approach. One training, likely given at the beginning of the year, when students are overwhelmed with information, is likely insufficient. In fact, the SaVE Act requires "ongoing prevention and awareness campaigns." Thus, to be most effective, and to follow the law, schools must make sexual assault awareness and prevention an ongoing campus mission.

Alcohol Risk Reduction Programs

In response to concerns about binge drinking and "party cultures," some schools are taking a *risk reduction* approach. By creating policies around alcohol use, these schools hope to limit alcohol consumption and the problems that are often affiliated with intoxication, such as sexual assault. For example (to name just a few), Stanford University and Bates, Bowdoin, Colby, Dartmouth, and Swarthmore colleges have all banned hard alcohol (typically defined anywhere from 10% to 20% of alcohol by volume) on campus or at public events on campus. Parties in residence halls with alcohol and over 15 guests at Denison University must be registered with the university and hosted by someone at least 21 years of age. Some schools' policies are directly aimed at the Greek system; for example, at the University of Virginia, three fraternity brothers must stay sober at parties to monitor behavior, hard liquor must be served by a sober brother, and a security guard and licensed bartender must work large parties. At Indiana University, hard liquor is banned at fraternity parties, and students patrol for a ban on kegs at fraternity parties at the University of Michigan. Further, national sorority chapters instructed members at the University of Virginia to refrain from attending fraternity social events during the week of fraternity rush, much to the consternation of many.

In addition to tighter regulations on alcohol, many schools have mandatory alcohol education classes or trainings for all students, or for those students found in violation of drinking policies. Other campuses, like Boston University, rely on stricter law enforcement of underage drinking. Advocates of tighter regulations around alcohol use believe curbing alcohol use and abuse is essential. However, these risk reduction approaches to alcohol consumption are mostly too new to know if they are effective in curbing anything, be it alcohol consumption or sexual assault. Critics fear such policies may drive alcohol consumption underground and may keep victims of sexual assault from seeking help if they are ashamed or fearful of getting into trouble for drinking. While universities and colleges may be able to reduce alcohol use on campus, curbing alcohol consumption off campus may be difficult. Additionally, critics argue that focusing on alcohol misses the mark. As sexual assault occurs on dry campuses as well, it stands to reason that a focus on campus culture, including safety issues and rape-supportive attitudes, may be a better approach.

Legislation

The ability to combat campus sexual assault is made possible with several key pieces of legislation, including Title IX, the Clery Act, the Federal Campus Sexual Assault Victims Bill of Rights, the Violence against Women Act, and the SaVE Act.

Campus sexual assault has gained the attention of many legislators. For example, the 114th Congress was scheduled to hear several controversial federal bills addressing campus sexual assault. Some bills had the goal of counteracting Title IX "overreach"; others were written with the intent to improve campus response to reports of sexual assault. The proposed legislation included the Safe Campus Act, which would prevent colleges and universities from investigating sexual assault unless the victim also reported the incident to law enforcement. The Fair Campus Act would allow schools to use the standard of proof it considers appropriate for adjudication hearings for sexual assault as opposed to always using the "preponderance of the evidence" standard. The Campus Accountability and Safety Act was aimed at boosting accountability and transparency, including allowing the Department of Education to fine schools up to 1 percent of its operating budget for violations of Title IX and providing students who report sexual assault with a trained confidential adviser. The Hold Accountable and Lend Transparency Campus Sexual Violence Act (HALT) also aimed at boosting accountability and included provisions to allow additional funding for officials to enforce Title IX and the Clery Act. The Survivor Outreach and Support Campus Act (SOS Act) would require institutions of higher education to have an independent advocate for campus sexual assault prevention and response. The Campus Sexual Assault Whistleblower Protection Act would provide student survivors and witnesses with protections so that they can report sex crimes without fear of retaliation.

Not all proposed legislation becomes a matter of law, but there have been some recent achievements. For example, the affirmative consent laws in California and New York exemplify successful legislative attempts to combat campus sexual assault. Additionally, as discussed previously, addressing campus sexual assault was a primary mission for the Obama administration. With new leadership, it remains to be seen whether there will be changes to existing policy or legislation and/or changes in federal funding for campus sexual assault programming and research.

Activism

Arguably, it is because of a wave of student activism that campus sexual assault is receiving the attention it is today. Students have not only brought the issue to the forefront of our national consciousness, but they have successfully created change. Due to the concerns and demands of students, many schools have altered their approaches to campus sexual assault—including providing increased resources for survivors, being more transparent in their handlings of campus sexual assault, altering their sexual misconduct procedures and policies, and offering more sexual assault awareness and education. Thanks to survivor-activists, college students have places to turn to learn their rights under Title IX and the Clery Act, they are provided with resources, and there is a network of legal and emotional support.

Survivor activism can come in many forms. Some survivors get involved in student groups that work to raise awareness and combat sexual assault, like peer-mentoring programs or feminist organizations. Many students who have felt as if their university or college mishandled their sexual assault allegation have filed a Title IX and/or Clery Act complaint; others have filed civil lawsuits against their schools. In an attempt to hold perpetrators responsible for their crimes, many survivors have reported sexual assault to law enforcement or to school officials. Activism occurs in more personal ways as well—for example, when survivors cease to blame themselves or when they seek support from family, friends, or therapists if they feel like they need it. Be it editorials written by survivors, performance pieces, marches/rallies/vigils, federal complaints, court cases, or a survivor who faces the day with determination—student activism, in whatever form, is a guiding force for change.

Not all campus anti–sexual assault activism is student run. For example, the gender-equality group UltraViolet created an ad campaign to draw attention to sexual assault and to put pressure on campuses. Additionally, the group circulated a petition asking the Princeton Review, an organization that publishes college rankings, to include information on campuses' sexual assault track records. They reasoned this approach would likely impact admissions which, in turn, would encourage colleges and universities to take sexual assault seriously. The Princeton Review declined.

There are many anti–sexual violence and feminist organizations, like UltraViolet, that work to combat campus sexual assault and/or provide support for campus organizations that do. Another very different tactic comes from gun advocates who support *campus-carry* legislation. Campus carry laws, like those of Colorado and Utah, allow students to carry firearms with them on campus. Advocates of campus carry argue that arming students would decrease the rate of sexual assault (in addition to reducing other criminal behavior, like mass shootings). The former president of the National Rifle Association stated that banning guns on campus provides "a sanctuary where criminals can rape and commit mass murder without fear of resistance" and that opponents to campus carry legislation are "engaging in a war against women." This is a controversial perspective on reducing campus sexual assault, and opponents argue that not only does research indicate rates of forcible rape increased in Colorado and Utah since the passage of campus carry laws, but that there is little evidence to show that women with firearms successfully fend off rapists. Additionally, opponents of campus carry legislation argue that perpetrators may use guns against their victims, and that victims are especially unlikely to use a firearm in situations in which they know their perpetrators. Political analyst and rape survivor Zerlina Maxwell spoke against arming women with firearms as a method to prevent rape in a news segment on gun control. She argued that the responsibility for preventing rape should lie with men instead. In response, Maxwell received a good deal of vitriolic backlash, including death threats. Her experience illustrates how in U.S. culture both the issues of gun control and sexual assault are incredibly divisive.

While many survivors and anti–sexual assault activists are fighting for increased accountability from their perpetrators and their schools, there are other activists who argue that colleges and universities are now overreaching and failing to provide due process for the accused. For example, the civil liberty group FIRE believes that investigation and adjudication of sexual assault cases should be done by law enforcement, as opposed to by colleges and universities. FIRE believes the lower standard of proof "preponderance of the evidence" leads to schools rushing to judgment and undermining the due process of the accused. Families Advocating for Campus Equality is an organization founded by three mothers whose sons were falsely accused of sexual misconduct at their schools. Their mission includes providing information for the wrongly accused and their families and to fight for change in policies regarding the handling of campus sexual assault. Similar to FIRE, they argue that the lower standard of proof is unfavorable to the accused.

In the end, there has been significant change and signs of progress on many college campuses. Many schools have strengthened and clarified their campus sexual assault policies. Some top administrators have publically recognized the need for change on their campus, like President "Biddy" Martin of Amherst College. The motivation for change is likely multi-layered; some colleges and universities have responded to the requests of advocates. Some schools needed the extra motivation of having a Title IX or Clery Act complaint or lawsuit filed against them in order to spur change. And many have likely been motivated by the negative publicity they have received or the pressure of fulfilling federal guidelines and mandates. Of course, there is still much to do. Many anti–sexual assault advocates argue that these changes on campuses are important first steps but that greater attempts need to be made in dismantling a rape-supportive culture that allows, if not encourages, sexual assault to occur in the first place. Such an approach requires confronting sexist or violent imagery and victim blaming and stresses the importance of involving men. From this perspective, the goal is to teach why sexual assault is wrong and why consent is necessary, as opposed to placing the onus for change on women's shoulders.

Conclusion

This chapter reviewed some of the primary debates and controversies surrounding campus sexual assault. What is evident is that regardless of how colleges and universities move forward, there are a lot of complex factors to consider.

References

Anderson, N., and P. M. Craighill. (2015, June 14). College Students Remain Deeply Divided Over What Consent Actually Means. Retrieved December 1, 2016, from: https://www.washingtonpost.com/local/education/americas-students-are-deeply-divided-on-the-meaning-of-consent-during-sex/2015/06/11/bbd303e0–04ba-11e5-a428-c984eb077d4e_story.html?hpid=z2&utm_term=.44314d90e0b8

American Association of University Professors. (2012, October). Campus Sexual Assault: Suggested Policies and Procedures. Retrieved November 22, 2016, from: https://www.aaup.org/report/campus-sexual-assault-suggested-policies-and-procedures

Association of Title IX Administrators. (2015). Mandatory Reporters: A Policy for Faculty and Professional Staff. Retrieved February 16, 2017, from: https://atixa.org/wordpress/wp-content/uploads/2012/01/Mandatory-Reporters-Policy-Template_1215.pdf

Bolger, D. (n.d.) Resisting State-Level Mandatory Police Referral Efforts. *Know Your IX*. Retrieved November 25, 2016, from: http://knowyourix.org/mandatory-referral/

Brodsky, A. (2016, April 14). Can Restorative Justice Change the Way Schools Handle Sexual Assault? *The Nation*. Retrieved December 5, 2016, from: https://www.thenation.com/article/what-if-punishment-wasnt-the-only-way-to-handle-campus-sexual-assault/

Carter, S.D. (2016, October 4). "Long Overdue": Colleges Needed Lower Standard of Evidence in Sexual Assault Cases, An Advocate Says. *The Washington Post*. Retrieved December 7, 2016, from: https://www.washingtonpost.com/news/grade-point/wp/2016/10/04/long-overdue-colleges-needed-lower-standard-of-evidence-in-sexual-assault-cases-an-advocate-says/?utm_term=.5386a1bda243

Culture of Respect. (2016). Sexual Assault Prevention Programs. Retrieved November 27, 2016, from: http://cultureofrespect.org/colleges-universities/programs/

Deamicis, C. (2013, May 20). Which Matters More: Reporting Assault or Respecting a Victim's Wishes? *The Atlantic*. Retrieved November 23, 2016, from: http://www.theatlantic.com/national/archive/2013/05/which-matters-more-reporting-assault-or-respecting-a-victims-wishes/276042/

Defilippis, E., and D. Hughes. (2015, November 9). The Numbers on Arming College Students Show Risks Outweigh Benefits. *The Trace*. Retrieved November 3, 2016, from: https://www.thetrace.org/2015/11/campus-carry-self-defense-accidental-shootings-research/

DeGue, S., L. A. Vale, M. K. Holt, G. M. Massetti, J. L. Matjasko, and A. T. Tharp. (2014). A Systematic Review of Primary Prevention Strategies for Sexual Violence Perpetration. *Aggression and Violent Behavior 19*, 4: 346–362.

Faculty against Rape. (FAR). (n.d.). Retrieved February 16, 2017, from: http://www.facultyagainstrape.net/

Families Advocating for Campus Equality (FACE). (n.d.). Retrieved February 16, 2017, from: https://www.facecampusequality.org/

Foundation for Individual Rights in Education (FIRE). (n.d.). Retrieved February 16, 2017, from: https://www.thefire.org/

Friedersdorf, C. (2016, June 17). What Should the Standard of Proof Be in Campus Rape Cases? *The Atlantic*. Retrieved December 7, 2016, from: http://www.theatlantic.com/politics/archive/2016/06/campuses-sexual-misconduct/487505/

Friedman, A. (2014, October 2). *Oh Yes* Means Yes: The Joy of Affirmative Consent. *NYMag*, *The Cut*. Retrieved November 26, 2106, from: http://nymag.com/thecut/2014/10/oh-yes-means-yes-the-joy-of-affirmative-consent.html

Friedman, J., and J. Valenti (eds.). (2008). *Yes Means Yes! Visions of Female Sexual Power & a World without Rape*. Berkeley, CA: Seal.

Friedrichs, E. (2016, May 22). 5 Questions about Alcohol and Consent You Are Too Afraid to Ask, Answered. *Everyday Feminism*. Retrieved November 26, 2016, from: http://everydayfeminism.com/2016/05/alcohol-and-consent-questions/

Gable, M. (2015, February 10). The Trouble with Oxy. *Los Angeles Magazine*. Retrieved November 22, 2016, from: http://www.lamag.com/longform/trouble-oxy/

Goldberg, M. (2014, June 23–30). Why the Campus Rape Crisis Confounds Colleges. *The Nation*. Retrieved December 8, 2016, from: https://www.thenation.com/article/why-campus-rape-crisis-confounds-colleges/

Hayes-Smith, R., T. Richards, and K. Branch. (2010). "But I'm Not a Counsellor": The Nature of Role Strain Experienced by Female Professors When a Student Discloses Sexual Assault and Intimate Partner Violence. *Enhancing Learning in the Social Sciences 2*, 3: 1–24.

Heller, Zoë. (2015, February 5). Rape on the Campus. *The New York Review of Books*. Retrieved December 8, 2016, from: http://www.nybooks.com/articles/2015/02/05/rape-campus/

Hess, A. (2015, February 11). How Drunk Is Too Drunk to Have Sex? *Slate*. Retrieved November 26, 2016, from: http://www.slate.com/articles/double_x/doublex/2015/02/drunk_sex_on_campus_universities_are_struggling_to_determine_when_intoxicated.html

Hoffman, J. (2015, June 10). College Rape Prevention Program Proves a Rare Success. *The New York Times*. Retrieved December 3, 2016, from: http://www.nytimes.com/2015/06/12/health/college-rape-prevention-program-proves-a-rare-success.html

Holmes, L. (2016, August 26). A Quick Lesson on What Trigger Warnings Actually Do. *The Huffington Post*. Retrieved November 22, 2016, from: http://www.huffingtonpost.com/entry/university-of-chicago-trigger-warning_us_57bf16d9e4b085c1ff28176d

Howard, B. (2015, August 28). How Colleges Are Battling Sexual Violence. *US News & World Report*. Retrieved November 27, 2016, from: http://www.usnews.com/news/articles/2015/08/28/how-colleges-are-battling-sexual-violence

Jozkowski, K.N. (2015, March-April). "Yes Means Yes"? Sexual Consent Policy and College Students. *Change: The Magazine of Higher Learning*. Retrieved November 26, 2016, from: http://www.changemag.org/Archives/Back%20Issues/2015/March-April%202015/yes_full.html

Kamenetz, A. (2016, September 7). Half of Professors in NPR Ed Survey Have Used "Trigger Warnings." *National Public Radio*. Retrieved November 22, 2016, from: http://www.npr.org/sections/ed/2016/09/07/492979242/half-of-professors-in-npr-ed-survey-have-used-trigger-warnings

Karasek, S. (2016, September 13). Trust Me, Trigger Warnings Are Helpful. *The New York Times*. Retrieved November 23, 2016, from http://www.nytimes.com/roomfordebate/2016/09/13/do-trigger-warnings-work/trust-me-trigger-warnings-are-helpful

Katel, P. (2011, February 4). Crime on Campus. *CQ Researcher 21*, 5: 97–120.

Kingkade, T. (2014, April 17). Harvard Accused of Retaliating against Professor Who Defended Sexual Assault Survivors. *The Huffington Post*. Retrieved November 22, 2016, from: http://www.huffingtonpost.com/2014/04/17/harvard-retaliation-professor-tenure_n_5159995.html

Kingkade, T. (2014, June 17). Oregon Professor Says She Is Facing Retaliation for Sexual Assault Criticism. *The Huffington Post*. Retrieved November 22, 2016, from: http://www.huffingtonpost.com/2014/06/17/university-of-oregon-retaliation_n_5499877.html

Kingkade, T. (2014, August 8). Colleges Are Rewriting What Consent Means to Address Sexual Assault. *The Huffington Post*. Retrieved November 26, 2016, from: http://www.huffingtonpost.com/2014/09/08/college-consent-sexual-assault_n_5748218.html

Kingkade, T. (2014, September 29). Fewer Than One-Third of Campus Sexual Assault Cases Result in Expulsion. *The Huffington Post*. Retrieved December 7, 2016, from: http://www.huffingtonpost.com/2014/09/29/campus-sexual-assault_n_5888742.html

Kingkade, T. (2016, March 8). He'd Admitted to Sexual Assault, But She's the One They Tried to Silence. *The Huffington Post*. Retrieved December 6, 2016, from: http://www.huffingtonpost.com/entry/college-sexual-assault-gag-orders_us_56ddd17ae4b0ffe6f8ea278c

Kingkade, T. (2016, August 7). Law Professors Defend Use of Preponderance Standard in Campus Rape Cases. *The Huffington Post*. Retrieved December 6, 2016, from: http://www.huffingtonpost.com/entry/preponderance-of-evidence-college-sexual-assault_us_57a4a6a4e4b056bad215390a

Koss, M. P., J. Wilgus, and K. M. Williamsen. (2014). Campus Sexual Misconduct: Restorative Justice

Approaches to Enhance Compliance with Title IX Guidance. *Trauma, Violence, & Abuse 15*, 3: 242–257.

Lam, M. (2014, April 14). Six Ways Faculty and Staff Can Fight Sexual Violence on Campus. AAUW. Retrieved November 22, 2016, from: http://www.aauw .org/2014/04/14/fight-campus-sexual-violence/

Lebioda, K. (2015, December). State Policy Proposals to Combat Sexual Assault. *American Association of State Colleges and Universities*. Retrieved December 6, 2016, from: https://www.aascu.org/policy/publications/ policy-matters/campussexualassault.pdf

Lee, P. (2011). The Curious Life of In Loco Parentis at American Universities. *Higher Education in Review 8*: 65–90.

Little, N. (2005, May). From No Means No to Only Yes Means Yes: The Rational Results of an Affirmative Consent Standard in Rape Law. *Vanderbilt Law Review 58*, 4:1321–1364.

Lombardi, K. (2010, February 24). A Lack of Consequences for Sexual Assault. *The Center for Public Integrity*. Retrieved November 21, 2016, from: https://www.publicintegrity .org/2010/02/24/4360/lack-consequences-sexual-assault

Lukianoff, G., and J. Haidt. (2015, September). The Coddling of the American Mind. *The Atlantic*. Retrieved November 22, 2016, from: http://www.theatlantic.com/ magazine/archive/2015/09/the-coddling-of-the-american- mind/399356/

Mancini, C., J. T. Pickett, C. Call, and S. P. Roche. (2016). Mandatory Reporting (MR) in Higher Education: College Students' Perceptions of Laws Designed to Reduce Campus Sexual Assault. *Criminal Justice Review 41*, 2: 219–235.

Mantel, B. (2014, October 31). Campus Sexual Assault. *CQ Researcher 24*, 39: 913–936.

Nelson, C. (2010, December 21). Defining Academic Freedom. *Inside Higher Ed*. Retrieved November 23, 2016,

from: https://www.insidehighered.com/views/2010/12/21/
defining-academic-freedom

New, J. (2015, February 19). First, Do No Harm. *Inside
Higher Ed*. Retrieved November 25, 2016, from: https://
www.insidehighered.com/news/2015/02/19/open-letter-
calls-legislators-reconsider-campus-sexual-assault-bills

New, J. (2015, July 10). States Requiring Colleges to Note
Sexual Assault Responsibility on Student Transcripts. *Inside
Higher Ed*. Retrieved December 4, 2016, from: https://
www.insidehighered.com/news/2015/07/10/states-requirin
g-colleges-note-sexual-assault-responsibility-student-
transcripts

New, J. (2014, June 27). Expulsion Presumed. *Inside Higher
Ed*. Retrieved December 6, 2016, from: https://www
.insidehighered.com/news/2014/06/27/should-expulsion-
be-default-discipline-policy-students-accused-sexual-
assault

New, J. (2014, October 17). The "Yes Means Yes" *World.
Inside Higher Ed*. Retrieved November 26, 2016, from:
https://www.insidehighered.com/news/2014/10/17/
colleges-across-country-adopting-affirmative-
consent-sexual-assault-policies

The New York Times. (2016, October 29). No Kegs, No
Liquor: College Crackdown Targets Drinking and Sexual
Assault. Retrieved December 3, 2016, from: http://
www.nytimes.com/2016/10/30/us/college-crackdown-
drinking-sexual-assault.html

Nunez, V. (2015, February 25). What Role Do College
Faculty Members Play in the Discussion around
Campus Sexual Assault? *Generation Progress*. Retrieved
November 22, 2016, from: http://genprogress.org/
voices/2015/02/25/35022/what-role-do-college-faculty-
members-play-in-the-discussion-around-campus-sexual-
assault/

RAIIN. (n.d.). 97 of Every 100 Rapists Receive No Punishment, RAINN Analysis Shows. Retrieved December 6, 2016, from: https://www.rainn.org/news/97-every-100-rapists-receive-no-punishment-rainn-analysis-shows

Reilly, K. (2016, August 24). Why Banning Hard Alcohol on College Campuses May Not Be the Answer. *Time* magazine. Retrieved November 27, 2016, from: http://time.com/4463227/stanford-hard-liquor-ban/

Senn, C., M. Eliasziw, P. Barata, W. Thurston, I. Newby-Clark, L. Radtke, and K. Hobden. (2015). Efficacy of a Sexual Assault Resistance Program for University Women. *The New England Journal of Medicine 372*: 2326–2335.

Smith, T. (2014, June 13). A Campus Dilemma: Sure, "No" Means "No," but Exactly What Means "Yes"? *National Public Radio*. Retrieved November 26, 2016, from: http://www.npr.org/2014/06/13/321677110/a-campus-dilemma-sure-no-means-no-but-exactly-what-means-yes

Smith, T. (2016, May 11). Push Grows for a "Scarlet Letter" on Transcripts of Campus Sexual Offenders. *National Public Radio*. Retrieved December 4, 2016, from: http://www.npr.org/2016/05/11/477656378/push-grows-for-a-scarlet-letter-on-transcripts-of-campus-sexual-offenders

Strong, E. (2015, April 16). Is It Rape If You Say Yes? Five Types of Sexual Coercion, Explained. *Bustle*. Retrieved December 3, 2016, from: https://www.bustle.com/articles/67926-is-it-rape-if-you-say-yes-5-types-of-sexual-coercion-explained

Thomas, J. R. (2013, November 13). UConn Prof Says Her Support of Outspoken Student May Cost Her Job. *The CT Mirror*. Retrieved November 22, 2016, from: http://ctmirror.org/2013/11/13/uconn-prof-says-her-support-outspoken-student-may-cost-her-her-job/

Wheeling, K. (2015, May 28). One Woman's Quest to Fix the Process of Reporting Sexual Assault. *Pacific Standard*. Retrieved November 27, 2016, from: https://psmag.com/one-woman-s-quest-to-fix-the-process-of-reporting-sexual-assault-61c12d0b8647#.qflkxhhx7

Zimmerman, E. (2016, June 22). Campuses Struggle with Approaches for Preventing Sexual Assault. *The New York Times*. Retrieved December 3, 2016, from: http://www.nytimes.com/2016/06/23/education/campuses-struggle-with-approaches-for-preventing-sexual-assault.html

3   Perspectives

Introduction

This chapter is comprised of essays written by people who, by virtue of their professions or experiences, have a range of perspectives on campus sexual assault. Contributors include a college psychologist (Dr. Jodi Caldwell), a campus advocate (Kathryn Woods), a community educator and advocate (Ron Roberts), a Title IX investigator (Erika Krouse), a sexual assault nurse examiner (Rosemary Schuster), and survivors of sexual assault perpetrated in high school (Kaili Miller) and on college campuses (Caroline Asher and Sarah Gilchriese). Together, these voices illustrate the various ways people work not only to assist survivors of sexual assault but actively strive toward eradicating campus rape culture altogether. Their courage, strength, determination, vision, and hope serve to inspire us all.

How Far We Have Come and How Far We Have Yet to Go: The Perspective of a College Psychologist
Jodi Caldwell

I felt privileged, and not just a bit intimidated, to be asked to write about my perspective of working with issues related to

---

Columbia art student and sexual assault survivor Emma Sulkowicz began carrying around a 50-pound dorm mattress in the fall of 2014 as part of her senior art thesis entitled "Carry That Weight." Sulkowicz vowed to carry the mattress until her alleged perpetrator was expelled or left the university (neither occurred and she carried the mattress across the stage during her graduation). Her performance piece inspired similar protests against campus sexual assault across the nation and the globe. (Andrew Burton/Getty Images) sexual violence on a college campus. After considering many different angles from which I could write, it occurred to me that to be authentic, I had a responsibility to share where my perspective on sexual violence first began. From the time I was about 14 years old to about 15, I was sexually assaulted by someone I knew well, someone that my family knew well. And, yet, almost 30 years later, reading this essay will be the first time most people in my life will become aware of my experience.

My experience is relative to this piece because of the irony life often provides. I clearly remember starting my first professional job and thinking, "The one area of counseling I don't want to work in is sexual violence!" Life had other plans for me. Within a year of beginning my new job and establishing my professional identity, the chair of the Georgia Southern University Sexual Assault Response Team (SART) approached me, explained that she was moving to a new position, and outlined all of the reasons why she and my boss believed that I should be the next person to chair the team. I was stunned. I could not think of a reason that I was willing to share for saying, "no, thanks." Seemingly before I knew what was happening, it was a fait accompli. Life knew what it was doing—the work I have done in this area has been a tremendous inspiration for me and has allowed me to make my own transition to being a survivor.

In the almost 15 years that I have worked on sexual violence education, reduction, and response, there have been a great deal of cultural shifts that I have witnessed, especially living in a rural southern town. In 2001, on this campus, there were no coordinated response services for victims of sexual violence, no large-scale educational efforts in place. Nationally, extremely few campus SARTs even existed. And, advocates had to play a tense balancing game of exposing the epidemic of campus sexual violence while not promoting the image that their own campus was especially dangerous! As conferences emerged to address this issue, programming tended to focus on debunking myths related to sexual violence and making the issue relevant to students by putting a personal face on sexual assault—educating students that statistically, they already knew victims of sexual assault—those victims were their relatives, friends, classmates, educators, and so on. Campus men were enlisted as educational allies since sexual assault had the reputation of being "a woman's issue." These efforts were difficult, especially in conservative areas, where educators were discouraged from talking about healthy sexual education, let alone sexual education that focused on the potentially violent and/or traumatizing impact of sexual interactions! It took courage on the part of our administrators to acknowledge that sexual assault did happen on their campuses, while advocates were trying to educate that sexual violence happened on all campuses. It took courage for our first peer educators and staff educators to go into the campus communities and discuss a topic to which most audiences had never been exposed. It took a courage that continues to humble me to be one of those first victims to utilize response protocols and be willing to come forward, report their experience, and access services that became available.

Educational efforts have continued to expand, and the perspective from which sexual violence is approached has evolved over the years. What has remained is the idea that sexual violence impacts every person on the college campus: It impacts the victims themselves, it impacts every relationship the victim has (whether romantic, platonic, professional, familial), and it impacts those in whom the victim confides as they are secondarily traumatized. Long before the Dear Colleague letter, and the updates to the Violence against Women Act, there were well-researched educational efforts on university campuses regarding risk factors associated with sexual violence, risk reduction strategies, and responding to victims. The pendulum had been swinging from pervasive stereotypes about sexual violence and its victims, to open communication, trained adjudication, and comprehensive services for those who had been victimized. However, as often happens in history, my perception is that the pendulum may be swinging back.

Sexual assault has moved from a social issue to a politicized issue. There are now federal mandates on what universities *must* provide by way of education, response to, and reporting of sexual assault cases. What is not clearly outlined in the mandates is who should be responsible for the programming, how will the responses be funded, and how will the programming be instituted? As a result, universities are scrambling to figure out where to house their sexual assault response teams, how to adapt their judicial code policies, and more. A whole new field of online education has popped up, many of which have little evidence to support their efficacy, but make big promises in terms of allowing universities to be "compliant" with federal regulations. And, in the worst cases, issues of sexual violence education and response have been taken out of the hands of those core groups of people who did the work because it was their passion and put onto the plates of offices that do not have the history and experience of addressing these issues and people who may feel coerced into taking on this new role. As campus folks become frustrated with the new ambiguity surrounding universities' obligations related to sexual violence, what seems to be getting lost is the victim.

Like many political decisions, the intent was likely a heartfelt and ambitious one: to ensure that there was education and response on every campus; to highlight the epidemic that is sexual violence in college communities; to attempt to reduce the incidence rates of sexual violence. And, on many campuses, the new regulations have created a sense of urgency for the development of such resources. However, on other campuses, confusion has been created. Being in contact with many universities, I have seen conduct definitions of sexual misconduct change, in a way that is not more sensitive to victims. I have heard campus frustrations about new procedures for reporting and adjudicating cases and Title IX offices being overwhelmed, and in that frustration, there is a current of irritation that seems inappropriately directed toward victims, who bring all of these issues to light. I can't help but wonder about the impact these changes are having on today's victims—do they feel more or less safe coming forward when education is more prevalent, but procedures are less clear? Do they know how and where to go, as policies are shifting?

What has changed in my 14 years? I am energized by students' responses to this issue. In my experience, today's students are more open to discussing healthy communication, consent, bystander intervention, and sexual intimacy than ever before. I have listened to 14 years of audiences respond to *Sex Signals*, one of the primary educational programs we bring to our campus each year and have been rocked by the evolution of audience reactions to a scenario that addresses acquaintance rape. *Sex Signals*, written and performed by Catharsis Productions, has always been based on empirical evidence regarding social norms, sexual violence education, and bystander intervention. Over the last 14 years, as research has suggested that norms have changed, the *Sex Signals* script has changed in response. Each year, it seems that more students vocally support the victim in these scenarios and speak out against their peers who make sexist or stereotypical comments. Recently, our university newspaper did a series of comprehensively researched and well-written articles on sexual violence in college and university campuses—because the students wanted the issues addressed! Nationally, the most recent college sexual assault cases to be picked up by media focused on how investigations were handled, as opposed to headlines in the past that focused on victim blaming. This shift tells me that all of the advocates and educators out there *have* made a difference in our culture—young adults have been hearing our messages. But we have more work to do.

What has not changed is how difficult it is for victims to come forward. During educational programs, I continue to cringe as some students make those stereotypical crude or victim-blaming comments, because I know that every audience contains unseen victims who are hearing their worst fears confirmed. What has not changed is how invasive the judicial and legal processes are, for victims. Now, with the increased pressure for all *responsible campus agents* to file Title IX reports, victims have less confidential resources and are more likely to be questioned regarding their assaults—even if they do not want any report filed. What has not changed is the tendency for victims to feel blamed or shamed for a crime that is perpetrated against them, in a way that we do not culturally shame the victims of any other crimes. We have come a long way, and we have a long way to go.

Almost 30 years after I was raped, less than a dozen people in my life know what happened to me. I do this work for a living, I promote victims' empowerment and healing, I talk about these issues to crowds of every size. I no longer feel the shame I initially associated with my rape. Yet, I would do a disservice to all survivors if I did not admit that there is a part of me that is reluctant to have folks read this essay. And, the fact that *I* feel that reluctance tells me that as a culture—as campus communities—we still have a long way to go.

Jodi Caldwell received her PhD in Counseling Psychology from Texas Tech University. Dr. Caldwell has worked at Georgia Southern University since 2000 as a Staff Psychologist, Assistant Director for Training, and now Director of the Counseling Center. Since 2001, Dr. Caldwell has chaired the university's Sexual Assault Response Team. In addition, she was involved in the conception and development of the Statesboro Regional Sexual Assault Center. This grant-funded, full-service rape crisis center serves the three counties within its judicial circuit, as well as three additional underserved counties and a correctional facility, with which it has MOUs. Dr. Caldwell has served as the elected president of the Board of Directors for Statesboro Regional Sexual Assault Center since inception in 2009. Dr. Caldwell has also consulted with universities nationwide on the establishment of their own campus sexual assault response teams.

Campus Victim Advocacy and Its Role in Supporting Survivors of Interpersonal Violence
Kathryn Woods

It was a Friday morning. I was at my desk, enjoying my morning caffeine and appreciating the quiet since most students were still sleeping or in class. And then my phone rang: "Come quick. We need you." I rushed out of my office into our lobby area and was greeted by a very unusual scene. There were two women at the front desk. One was on the floor sobbing, and the other was swinging a plastic bag over her head screaming, "We have the DNA. We have the DNA." A little stunned, the only thing I could think was that plastic destroys DNA, so she should have it in a paper bag. With an inexplicable urge to laugh at my thought, I quickly pulled myself together. I called for another advocate and asked her to talk with the woman with the bag. I then sat down on the floor next to the crying student: "Would you like to come to my office where we can talk in private?" Still sobbing, she got up and accompanied me to my office. While this was an unusual start to my interaction with this particular student, it was not at all unusual to have students walk in and speak with a victim advocate. We got referrals from other sources as well—police, campus Title IX investigators, conduct officers, residence life staff, and many other staff and faculty on campus. But most survivors either walked in to our office or called our 24-hour, 365-day-a-year campus-specific hotline.

College campus victim advocacy is a unique niche within the larger field of victim services. College campuses are bound by federal laws and mandates that govern how reports of sexual assault, domestic violence, dating violence, and stalking are handled by the school. There are requirements for responding to reporting, investigating, providing support, and adjudicating. Many campuses now have dedicated victim advocates whose role is to respond to and support survivors. On some campuses, victim advocates are considered confidential. On other campuses, they have to report what they are told to the Title IX investigator and/or the police. Whether an advocate is confidential on a given campus is largely determined by a combination of federal laws and policies, state laws, and campus policies. My campus and state law considers campus-based advocates to be confidential, which I believe best facilitates my ability to fulfill my role.

I see the role of campus advocates as threefold: providing emotional support, providing resource education and accompaniment, and helping the victim develop trauma-specific coping skills. However, when I begin a relationship with a survivor, I first determine what *they* need. Their primary focus is my primary focus. If they are most worried about making up a missed class, I don't start with explaining how to report to the police. I see us as beginning a partnership, to which the survivors bring their experiences, trauma symptoms, existing coping skills, and support systems and to which I bring knowledge about options and resources, knowledge about trauma, and concrete coping skill strategies. They are the expert on their own experience and what will work best for them.

Emotional Support

Emotional support is the primary goal for an advocate, and is the first order of business when working with a survivor. Advocates should listen much more than they talk, and active listening is a crucial skill. Skills combined with active listening are validation and normalizing the survivor's experience. Many survivors experience similar symptoms, and it can be helpful for survivors to know they are not alone in their reactions. Another component of emotional support is educating the survivors about trauma and what they may have experienced during and after their assault.

Resource Education and Accompaniment

Resource education and accompaniment involves explaining options to survivors neutrally and then supporting the decision they make. The resources may be in the areas of legal options (such as reporting to the police), medical options (including medical forensic exams), campus disciplinary options (such as reporting to the university and explaining which employees are required to report sexual assault, dating violence, domestic violence, and stalking), academic options (including academic accommodations for missing classes and needing extensions on exams or assignments), and emotional support options (including counseling, safety in living situation, safety in classes, continued advocacy and support groups). Depending on the campus, advocates often accompany survivors to access restraining orders, report to police, report to the university, have medical forensic exams, or talk to professors or residence life staff. Many campus advocates have the unique potential to provide advocacy for survivors from the time they first access advocacy until the end of their university careers, if needed.

Developing Trauma-Specific Coping Skills

All people learn coping skills as they grow. Some are effective, some ineffective. However, most people do not develop trauma-specific coping skills until they encounter a traumatic event. These coping skills include techniques such as sensory grounding, managing triggers, and breaking down overwhelming tasks into smaller steps.

Conclusion

At the end of the day that started in such a surprising way, I had accompanied the survivor and her friend, both much calmer, to report a sexual assault to the police, have a medical forensic exam, and talk to residence life staff. We had made an appointment for the next morning to talk about academic accommodations and to work on trauma-specific coping skills. It was a long day, and the survivor ultimately wanted to sleep. I made it home around 10 p.m. and was reminded that long days like this often turned into many months of relationship building and system navigation. But, for that moment, sleep was first on my agenda as well.

Campus advocacy has a critical role in providing support for survivors of interpersonal violence. Consider this: without campus advocacy, the woman whose story I told here would have had to navigate those systems alone. I have valued my time as a campus advocate because of being able to witness survivors' stories. I remain honored that they allowed me to walk part of their journeys with them.

Kathryn Woods, MSW, MPA, LCSW, is an Assistant Professor of Social Work at Ferris State University in Big Rapids, Michigan. Most recently, she worked as a campus-based victim advocate at Colorado State University for nine years. Prior to moving to Colorado, she worked as an advocate and crisis therapist at a nonprofit agency in Tempe, Arizona, and worked as a victim advocate and prevention specialist at Arizona State University. She enjoys reading and watching the Food Network while snuggling with her two dachshunds.

The Importance of Being Proactive
Ron Roberts

It was 5:30 a.m. and the phone was ringing. I had no idea that phone call would change my life. It was my sergeant with the police department. I wasn't due at work that particular morning until 6:45 a.m. Why was he calling? In a very matter-of-fact tone, he told me I needed to get to the hospital because one of my family members was there. I asked him what was wrong and he told me he would talk to me when I got to the hospital. I quickly dressed and was on the way to the hospital—I don't remember a lot of that 20-minute drive. When I arrived at the hospital, I saw several police cars in the emergency room parking lot. As I approached the emergency room, I was met by a lieutenant with the police department. He told me that a male had broken into my female relative's home around 2:30 a.m. and had beaten, raped, and robbed her. The perpetrator was caught a few days later and was eventually sentenced to 14 years in prison. He served ten years and is currently out of prison. I saw how this assault altered my relative's life forever. I thought I knew everything, but I realized I knew nothing. I realized then how the world is so different for women. As a male, I never realized how safety issues are a part of a women's reality every day. I decided I needed to try and make a difference.

For 15 years, I served as a violence prevention coordinator and educator at a rape crisis center. I supervised a staff of several prevention specialists and also presented programming and information on issues that included child sexual abuse, bullying, sexual harassment, dating violence, domestic violence, sexual assault awareness, masculinity, and drug-facilitated sexual assault. In general, sexual violence prevention can be divided into the following three categories:

- Primary Prevention: Approaches that take place before sexual violence has occurred to prevent initial perpetration or victimization
- Secondary Prevention: Immediate responses after sexual violence has occurred to deal with the short-term consequences of violence
- Tertiary Prevention: Long-term responses after sexual violence has occurred to deal with the lasting consequences of violence and sex offender treatment interventions

Much of prevention activities and responses tend to be secondary and tertiary in nature: that is to say, reactive and not proactive. If we are to reduce sexual violence, we must move prevention efforts upstream. That is not to say that we should abandon secondary and tertiary prevention, but instead, greater effort and resources need to be expended on primary prevention of sexual violence if we are to have meaningful positive change. The National Sexual Violence Resource Center (2008), in the document Sexual Violence and the Spectrum of Prevention: Towards a Community Solution, says it best:

> It is critical that a prevention strategy addresses norms because of their power in influencing behavior. If violence is typical and this expectation is reinforced by the media, school, and community, it is far more likely to occur with greater frequency. If norms discourage safe behavior or do not support healthy, equitable and safe relationships, then programs focused on individual change will not prevent sexual violence unless related norms are changed as well. Thus, norm change is essential; it is best accomplished through a community approach. The community has a stake in preventing sexual violence and all members have a valuable role to play.

Some of the best proactive work that can be done is working with males and changing negative social norms. Helping males understand what a healthy relationship is and normalizing the healthy behavior is essential. Training on issues like social skills building, character education, healthy relationships, healthy dating, and healthy masculinity should start in elementary school and be reinforced through middle school, high school, and college.

Years after that tragic assault on my family member, I was presenting a program to a group of junior and senior males at a high school. I had been speaking about 20 minutes on sexual assault awareness issues and started speaking specifically about drug-facilitated sexual assault and how this behavior becomes normalized, especially among certain groups of males (sports teams, fraternities, military, etc.). I noticed a male about three rows up with a big grin on his face. He turned and looked around like he was looking for someone behind him. I saw him make eye contact with another male and both of them had a big smile on their face and nodded to each other. When the male closest to me turned around, I looked directly at him and let him know, by my stern facial expression, that I knew what he and his friend had been doing. I looked directly at him and his friend the rest of the hour-long presentation, especially when I was talking about consequences. As I spoke, both of their faces turned red and they had trouble making eye contact with me. They likely had engaged in troubling, if not abusive and illegal, behavior in the past. However, because they experienced that anti–sexual assault and healthy relationship program I was leading that day, I felt that they learned how they could, and how they needed to, make better decisions in their future.

My years of experience leading both healthy relationship and anti–sexual assault education have led me to believe that proactive education is a key ingredient in creating change. Such programming should occur throughout the school year for students so that they are engaged in ongoing conversations about healthy relationships. If not already offered, I strongly urge readers to demand your local schools to implement ongoing proactive prevention programs.

Reference

National Sexual Violence Resource Center. (2008). Sexual Violence and the Spectrum of Prevention: Towards a Community Solution. National Sexual Violence Resource Center. Enola, Pennsylvania.

Ron Roberts served as the senior prevention coordinator for the Rape Crisis Center of the Coastal Empire located in Savannah, Georgia, for 15 years. In this position, he operated the most successful violence prevention program in the state, reaching well over 50,000 children, adults, teachers, administrators, and organizations with prevention programming. Recently retired from the crisis center, Roberts currently owns and operates a prevention educational center for adults and youth on the topics of alcohol, drugs, and safety issues. Roberts has presented at numerous local, state, and national conferences on the issue of gender violence.

A Private Investigator's Perspective on College Rape
Erika Krouse

For the past 13 years, I've worked as a private investigator (PI) for Title IX sexual assault cases. Title IX prohibits sex-based discrimination in education, and those protections extend to college rape—a student has the right to pursue her (or his) education free from sexual harassment or sexual violence.

As a PI, I get to choose my cases, so I work for the survivor. In most of my cases, a college athlete raped my client, on or off campus. Working closely with the survivor's attorney, I locate and interview potential witnesses to the attack. I also try to find other survivors who were raped by the same perpetrator or by members of the same football or basketball team. The work is difficult and emotionally tricky. Sometimes, I talk to a survivor who has never talked about her rape before. Sometimes, I even talk to potential rapists.

Through these experiences, I learned that rape cases work very differently from what I had previously assumed. I am not an attorney (nor is this legal advice), but below are some facts and trends in college rape that have surprised me over the years and ways to address them.

- If sexually assaulted, you may have to demand that physical evidence be collected. Some hospital staff may refuse to give you a rape kit and/or collect a DNA sample. Don't leave without these vital tests. If necessary, insist on a victim advocate. DNA comes from your attacker's semen, blood, saliva, sweat, urine, and skin tissue (including from under your fingernails, if you scratched your perpetrator). Rape kits are used to determine whether rape occurred, not mere sexual contact. Medical or police photographs of bruises are important evidence in court.

- If your blood alcohol or drug level was high enough for you to be unconscious or incapacitated, it automatically proves sexual assault, since you would have been unable to defend yourself, or consent to sex. Insist on blood and urine tests.

- People may risk their jobs if they ignore a rape case. Most professionals are wonderful; some are not. Even with indisputable physical evidence, some police officers refuse to investigate a rape case. Administrators disobey college policies to avoid scandal. For political reasons, some DAs refuse to prosecute even open-and-shut cases. In a Title IX case, the judge may be a graduate and/or donor of the college you're suing and refuse to recuse himself or herself. I've worked on cases where all these events occurred. If you can't prosecute criminally, you can prosecute civilly. If a judge is biased, you can appeal.

- It's in the college's best interests to ignore your assault and for your case to fail. Rape is bad PR for them. They're legally bound to begin an investigation within 60 days of the assault, and many colleges fail to do so, or "find" that your assault never took place. Don't rely on the college to protect your interests—rather, assume it will hinder them.

- Social media has an important role in rape cases. Right after calling 911, it's a good idea to email your friends or write a Twitter or Facebook post something like "Help me." You may want to avoid details to protect your anonymity (see below), but a nonspecific public plea for help can establish a timeline and act as proof in a later case. If you know the identity of your attacker, take daily screenshots of his or her Facebook and Twitter page after the attack. Often, an attacker will post something incriminating, such as misogynistic posts or pictures or even an admission of guilt. However, it may hurt you if you post on Facebook or Twitter, take or post smiling pictures or selfies, or Friend your attacker in the weeks afterward.

- Technology is your friend. Security tapes can establish your timeline and prove your attacker was with you. Even if the tape shows the two of you willingly leaving a bar together, that evidence can work to your advantage, especially if your attacker denies knowing you. Bars and restaurants often reuse the same tape, so time is of the essence in requesting them for the tapes. Also, there's a strange trend in sexual assault where an attacker enlists a friend to record the assault with his phone. A lawyer can subpoena the accomplice's phone and computer.

- It's all about the timeline. The more concrete your timeline, the more solid your case. Write down the names and contact information for everyone you interacted with. Collect pictures from the day of the event, and see if they have a time and date stamp on them.

- You have Title IX rights. The college is legally bound to help you change your housing, classes, sports schedule, campus job, and extra-curriculars so you don't experience any further sexual violence, harassment, or discrimination. You have other protections, too—investigate your Title IX sexual harassment rights. The college may not enforce them, but they are liable for them in court.

- Even in a court case, you can protect your anonymity. If your attacker is an athlete or public figure and you go public, your fellow students may harass you. I've seen witnesses and survivors receive death threats, get fired from their jobs, and even have fountain drinks thrown at them in public. However, I've also worked on cases where the survivor's attorney was able to successfully protect the identity of the survivor and other witnesses, leaving them free to live their lives.

- The rumor mill is usually reliable. Many rapists rape more than once before they're caught. If you hear of other people who were possibly assaulted by your attacker, write those names down and consider discreetly talking to those people, or enlisting an investigator or attorney to do so.

- For court cases, time is your enemy. For certain crimes, some states have a statute of limitation, which is the time limit in which the prosecutor can file charges. Statutes of limitations vary by state (often between 3 and 20 years), and some states don't have any, or have exceptions. Also, witnesses morph over time. A sympathetic witness at the time of the assault will turn into a blaming, shaming witness in a year or perhaps an apathetic witness who doesn't want to get involved once she or he graduates. For this reason, it's a good idea to have your attorney collect depositions from witnesses as quickly after the attack as possible.

- Your diary can hurt you. Many survivors naturally begin to question their sanity, or wonder if such a thing really happened, and it feels therapeutic to write it down. However, the defendant's attorney can subpoena diaries, journals, blogs, letters, emails, and social media posts and use them against the survivor in court. If you write anything that could discredit your experience, you may want to destroy it.

- Your attorney is busy; you'll need outside help. Your attorney often doesn't have time to call a witness or track down difficult-to-obtain contact information. You can ask your attorney to obtain outside help. PIs tend to be more approachable for witnesses, have fewer investigative restrictions, and charge about 70 percent less than an attorney by the hour. You can also enlist free help from discreet friends and/or family members to do any legwork that may help you later.

In all the rape cases I've worked, the most damaging force is not sexism, but apathy. I've heard "All that was so long ago, does it even matter anymore?" or even, when the perpetrator was a winning football or basketball player, "It was for a greater cause." In the face of such apathy, often the last thing a rape survivor wants to do is immediately think about collecting evidence, documenting his or her trauma, or pursuing justice.

However, time changes the experience. Many survivors eventually want accountability and closure. And some find that their experience can create a positive change, so their college can be a safer place in the future.

Erika Krouse is a writer, creative-writing teacher, and private investigator living in Boulder, Colorado. She is the author of two books, most recently a novel entitled Contenders.

Treating Survivors: The Experience of a Sexual Assault Nurse Examiner
Rosemary Schuster

About seven years ago, I found myself at crossroads in my career. I had worked as a registered nurse for much of my adult life, taking a 13-year hiatus to raise children and travel abroad for my husband's work. I was working as a retired nurse in a health clinic for a small private school when I came across a newspaper article describing the need for sexual assault nurse examiners (SANEs) in our community. I had always been curious about sexual assault and violence in our society, convinced on a visceral level that it had something to do with gender inequality, the violent movies and videos so prevalent in our society, and childhood neglect and abuse. Additionally, I always feared being out alone and after dark.

My first professional job involved working with criminally committed sex offenders. For better or worse, this job catapulted me into adulthood and the realities of the limits of psychiatric care for sex offenders in the late 1970s and early 1980s. It also solidified my fear of sexual predators and my desire to do everything in my power to never become a victim.

The article about the need for SANEs spoke to me on several levels: my desire to impact victims of sexual assault, my need to decrease fears by doing something proactive to counter them, and my fascination with forensic science. I wish I could say the decision to become a SANE was a noble one; instead it was a pragmatic one.

My work as a SANE covered a five-year period in which I performed approximately 25 to 30 exams. During this time, I had one male victim. Several of my patients were college students attending one of the local universities. Most of the victims knew the person who assaulted them, usually an acquaintance, not a close friend, and most remembered the assault with certain events very vivid in their memory and others less clear. The majority of the victims who requested the sexual assault exam also wished to file charges against their assailant(s).

So how does a victim of sexual assault become a SANE patient? How do they tap into their local resources? What does the sexual assault exam consist of, and, most importantly, what does this process ask of the victim who becomes a SANE patient? It is important to note at this time that the SANE exam varies, and the process plays out differently in different locations.

Victims of sexual assault seek help in many ways. Calling the police directly, coming to the hospital emergency room for care, and calling the rape crisis center are just some of the ways to report an assault and ask for help. No matter how the victims access the system, several things will happen almost simultaneously for them. A special victims detective is assigned to the case, a rape crisis center advocate is assigned to the victim and stays with the victim throughout the interview and exam, and a SANE is called in to perform the SANE exam. If there is no SANE available, emergency room personnel are often called upon to complete the sexual assault kit.

The exam begins with an interview by the special victims detective. The SANE then takes over and obtains a medical and assault history, rules out medical injury requiring immediate attention, takes photographs for identification and injury, collects specimens for DNA and toxicology, administers prophylactic medications for STDs and pregnancy prevention, and provides follow-up education and instructions. The advocate remains with the victim throughout this process, providing support and counseling as needed along with facilitating safe return to home or significant others.

It is important to understand that photographs and specimens are taken of all areas that have been touched or injured in the assault. This includes the oral, vaginal, penile, and anal areas of victims along with any other areas on the body that are painful or visibly injured.

The SANE exam takes upwards of two hours for a victim. Certainly, it can be much longer if there are extensive injuries. For me, the SANE exam took approximately eight hours from start to finish: completing the sexual assault kit, transferring the kit to the detective, and documentation of the exam for the SANE chart after the victim has been discharged. My thoughts during the exam are hyper-focused on collecting the evidence in as gentle and efficient way as possible while ensuring that no detail is missed. The intrusive nature of this exam is obvious. I can only guess at what my patients are feeling and thinking undergoing this so close after the assault. If I am exhausted, what must they be feeling?

This exam is in no way the end of the process for the patient; it really is just the beginning of a long journey toward obtaining justice and healing. My hope is that they can recognize the power and control they have taken back by choosing to complete the SANE exam. I take every opportunity during the exam to reinforce their choice to do so. It is in no way the end of the process for the SANE either; subpoenas and court appearances await both the victim of the assault and the SANE. I can be called upon to testify as the SANE in a specific case or as an expert witness, depending on the needs of the court.

Here, I would like to speak to the "needs of the court." I found, through my SANE training and practice, that performing these exams really is serving the court and the community as well as the victim who has become my patient. My job as a SANE is to be the best evidence collector possible so that all people involved in the case are served well. Interestingly enough, I came to understand that this also serves the alleged assailant; it could very well prove that particular suspect's innocence and point to the need for further investigation.

During my exams, I made every effort to connect on a human level with my patients. By respecting their person, listening to their story, acknowledging their pain, and reinforcing their decision to undergo this exam, it is my hope that

I assisted them in beginning the healing process and road to recovery. Their courage and strength certainly empowered me.

Rosemary Schuster, BSN, RN, graduated from the University of Wisconsin Madison in 1978 with a Bachelors of Science in Nursing. Her work experience is varied with the majority of time spent working in inpatient psychiatry and school health. The Gwinnett Sexual Assault Center provided her SANE training (40 hours). Her SANE clinical training was supervised by a local, experienced SANE (40 hours). Rosemary thanks her son, Robert Schuster, for assistance with this essay.

It Still Counts: Reflection on a High School Assault
Kaili Miller*

It was Saint Patrick's Day of my sophomore year in high school. I was 15 years old. The varsity baseball team was having a party, and my girlfriends and I were invited. We started off by playing shot pong at April's house. We headed to the baseball party after.

I remember being poured shots by John.* I thought he, another guy on the team, and I were all drinking together. (I learned later they were pouring me shots of vodka, and themselves shots of water.) There were a lot of people there, and the house was huge. I remember socializing and having fun.

John and I had a bit of history. He was good looking and a varsity baseball and football player. Before, I thought he was cute. I remember chatting with him online and telling him I wasn't ready to have sex yet. He didn't show much interest in me after that. But a few weeks later at the party, we were flirting throughout the night. The drunker I got, the heavier became the flirting. At the end of the night, he went into a room, and I followed him.

Rather quickly, I found myself in bed with him. This is the part of my story that made me question for years whether or not it was my fault. *Did it still count as sexual assault if you walked into the room by yourself?*

---

* Name has been changed.

I was borderline incoherent from the alcohol. We started kissing. This is something I knew I wanted to do. However, then he started pressuring me to go further. It wasn't long before my pants and underwear came off. I had only ever been that naked around one guy one time before, sober, and I didn't even like it then. This is something I knew I did not like and did not want to do. He left the room briefly at some point to grab his jacket, which had condoms in the pocket.

He was at the bottom of the bed and I felt extreme discomfort in my body. I remember being in pain. When I asked him to stop, he told me he just had to put on lotion or something so it wouldn't hurt. I was not enjoying myself, but to him that wasn't relevant. He decided that meant I wasn't lubricated enough to enjoy it. He left the room again and came back. I assume he got lotion. When his continual attempts did not produce the results he wanted, he stopped and went to sleep.

Did it count as sex? I lay up all night with that confliction, and by morning I was still significantly drunk, but I was functional. I woke up my friends early, and we left to go home. I got home and put the underwear I was wearing into the trash. I never slept at a party again.

That Monday, I missed school. There was a perpetual sense of heaviness in my stomach that was not letting up. I went to my gynecologist to get tested and get clarity. I couldn't figure it out so I thought she could. *Was I no longer a virgin?* She told me that technically it did count as intercourse. It began to feel like the world was shifting against me. Upon hearing the truth that I did not want to accept, I decided I didn't want to see that doctor anymore.

I just remember lying in my bed wondering how I could escape this. It all felt so wrong—and in such a permanent way. I was confused because John was not violent. He didn't use physical force. *So how was it really assault?* I hated him. But I didn't want to because I knew what I was up against. I decided to confront him about it anyway.

I let him know I didn't want to have sex. Looking back, I'm not sure why because he knew. But he kept telling me that I wanted to and that's why it happened. He used me going into that room with him against me, like me feeling violated didn't matter because I had pardoned it with my actions. My expressions of discomfort and unwillingness did not matter because I kissed him in the first place.

No matter what happened—in his mind it was okay because I walked into the room where he was. All of my previous actions should have been negated once I said "no"—not used against me as a reason why I actually meant "yes."

The biggest confusion of everything was internal. I knew I didn't want it. I knew I wanted to be a virgin. I knew I wanted a shot with John (before I knew what kind of guy he was). I knew I drank because I wanted to. But I also knew that I told him to stop. I also knew that I was too intoxicated to consent. I knew all of these things—but I was being told a different story. He kept telling me it's what I was seeking that night, but I knew that I didn't. *Or did I?* I knew I would be even more of an outcast if I claimed rape. I wasn't even comfortable saying that because I felt an undue burden of responsibility. Word spreads quickly in the walls of any high school. His friends hastily assured me it was not rape. At the time, I took their word over mine.

On Tuesday, his ex-girlfriend saw me at school. She mentioned she had heard about my weekend and the fun I had had. She said it with such a confidence as if she knew what had happened and was judging me for it. *Did what she thought she knew count?* Because I still didn't even know. These sorts of things are what perpetuate the nightmare in the aftermath of a sexual assault.

I felt like I could only be identified by that event after it happened. I would go out, meet new people, or see old friends and wonder if they knew. *Had anyone told them? Did they think of me as a slut?* I didn't want to be a girl who wondered whom she technically lost her virginity to. So much of my worth came into question from this one drunken night. This night had more value to me than any other in my life for such a long period of time. I was no longer a high school student who worked three jobs, an animal lover, an athlete, a daughter, or a good friend. None of your accomplishments seems to matter when you don't even understand who you are anymore.

I moved away to go to Georgia for college, in hopes of escaping my past. But I developed serious trust issues that wouldn't allow that to happen. I couldn't maintain a healthy relationship, so I decided relationships didn't matter. It felt easier to pretend that sex didn't have any meaning. I carried this belief for years. It did not provide me with the comfort I was seeking. Nothing did.

Time has passed, but nine years later, I recognize the effects my assault has had on my life and my relationships. What I came to understand in time was that it didn't just matter what he told me, what his friends told me, or that I was drunk and began the night with flirtation.

It still counted that I said "no."

Kaili Miller is a pseudonym for a legal professional who works at an intellectual property firm in Washington, D.C. She is infatuated with her two Yorkshire terriers and enjoys reading and writing in her spare time.

Survivor Reflection
Caroline Asher*

Friday night, band party, can't wait to get there
I put on my best clothes that I have to wear.
Only to be pinned against a wall
Mouth covered by a sweaty hand
Who happened to be my best friend after all.

---

* Name has been changed.

Being dragged away
I giggled, thinking it was all a joke.
Come on Billy, let me go
Reeking of alcohol and smelling of cigarette smoke.

Behind the door, his three friends stood,
Smiles on their faces, a brew in hand,
Billy let me go, I wish you would.
What are you doing to me?
What is happening? What did I do to deserve this?

Screaming, fighting to stop this torture.
Only to have them continue this horror.
Alcohol and sweat are all I smell,
When will someone save me from this hell?

Using me for their only satisfaction,
Not caring at all about my negative reaction.
He was someone I thought I could trust,
But in his dorm room
He and his friends take my innocence with every thrust.

I dare not to utter a word,
For I know I will be blamed for this
They will say, "you could have done"
"You should have done"
"What did you do to ask for this?"

I see you at school,
You say hey,
I can't believe you lack the decency
To even look my way.
Do you know what you have done?
Do you know what it's like
To be pinned down, and unable to run?

Unable to flee from this pain
From the torture you put me through
Absolutely humiliated, my innocence exposed.
Your pleasure, not mine, it happened because of you.
I look in the mirror today
Stained, scarred, completely violated.
Scarred by the pain that will forever stay.

When will society accept me as a victim?
For I will never know,
I guess hiding in the shadows
Is where I will forever stay.

My voice will stay silent,
I might as well run along,
I hope the world will someday see
That a victim should never be the one in the wrong.

Carolyn Asher is a pseudonym for a college student who was sexually assaulted by someone she thought was a friend. She remains silent about her assault for fear of being blamed.

I Think about It Every Day: Pursuing Justice on My College Campus
Sarah Gilchriese

February 2013

The moments or minutes following all I can think is, run. Run far away from the toxic, poisonous environment. Run away from the man who held you down and violated you. Run from the apartment he led you to after he fed you vodka, coating your body in a fuzzy haze. *Run* from this street, *run* to campus, *run* to your bike, *run away*.

Early March 2013

Let me tell you about this night, three weeks ago. Let me sit here in this room on campus, so close to where it happened, and tell my university that I need help. I need help, I need you to get him in trouble, find him guilty of violating your code of conduct. I need you to contact him, tell him not to contact me, tell him he raped me, tell him he can't do that. I need my university to protect me.

March 2013

Over spring break, I lead a volunteer trip outside Yosemite National Park to build trails with the Bureau of Land Management. I had been planning this trip since the beginning of the fall semester and was one of two leaders going. For multiple days I battled over whether or not to go—to subject myself to leadership and surroundings of 12 people I barely knew for six days straight. Crippled with PTSD and anxiety, I had barely left my bed the past month. Driving and travelling to California seemed like it may stretch me too thin beyond my boundaries.

The day before we were supposed to leave, I received a call from the investigator on my case at the university. The report was finished, and my assailant had been found guilty of "non-consensual sexual intercourse" along with three other violations of the student code of conduct. The allocation of his guilt replenished my comfort and confidence in facilitating the trip.

This trip was a turning point in my healing. This was the first time that I shared with a large group of people that I was a rape survivor and that it had only happened a little more than a month before the trip. When I was hugged by these participants, and received with only support, I knew that going on the trip was the right decision.

April 2013

I get the email from the interim director of student code of conduct and silently scream. After almost five torturous weeks of emails, phone calls, and meetings, I finally get the sanctions for my rapist. After five weeks of waiting by the phone and by my email to see how they would punish him, I finally received the news. He was sentenced with only eight months of suspension, a $75 fee, and a five- to seven-page paper on emerging adulthood. Anger, fear, and the drive to seek appropriate justice filled me that day.

Early May 2013

I walk into my meeting with the dean of students with my friend. I came prepared for conflict, to fight and demand justice with my case or I'll go straight to the government and file a Title IX complaint with the Office for Civil Rights under the Department of Education. While my statement was well heard, the dean of students told me that I could simply appeal the sanctions that were imposed on my rapist but that she couldn't do anything to change the initial sanctions. His eight-month suspension stood, although I would still be a student when he returned to campus. His agreement to write a five- to seven-page paper remained intact as well, as did his $75 fine. I left the meeting with only one thought: *file a Title IX complaint with the government against the University of Colorado Boulder.*

May 2013

After speaking with a friendly lawyer from Take Back the Night, I contacted the Department of Education and filed a Title IX complaint. I filled out a form, wrote a generic paragraph about my experience, and waited to hear back from the government. I did not think the university would change anything based on my conversation with the dean and knew that if I did not ask someone above them to change, other survivors would go through the same thing as I did. I also dreaded every day seeing my rapist, ever again.

June 2013

Time to go to the police station, file a report, sit through the entire process. Time to start this grueling conversation with the officer and detective so I can achieve what I want: a permanent protection order. After three court dates, the city of Boulder granted me a permanent protection order. Part of this order, which will last me my entire life, stated that my rapist could not come within 100 yards of my dog, University of Colorado, or myself. Because of the order, he is not allowed back on campus again.

July 2013

Going public in *The Huffington Post* about my Title IX complaint was like coming out from under a rock. Until then, I was carrying around the burden that I had filed a complaint against this beloved university. When that article hit, the local and national community was in uproar. I felt like I had support from the general public for the first time, and this national attention finally began to impact the way the university conducted themselves in regards to sexual assault cases, as well as their treatment of me.

January 2014

Sitting in my living room in Boulder, my lawyer calls me with joy in his tone. He lets me know that the University of Colorado decided to settle with me and were going to write a check for two semesters' worth of tuition to me. He told me "congratulations" and that I should feel "empowered" for what I had done. We talked logistics: when to meet to sign the paperwork and the check itself and got off the phone. All I noticed was elation pulsing through my body. I had successfully settled with the university that did me wrong. While this settlement did not negate my assault, or how the university handled it, I was refunded the tuition I lost in the process. The university denied liability over Title IX, but settled regardless. Therefore, I had won: though a small feat, yet a big one for all the money I lost over tuition and for the roller-coaster year I had been yanked through.

January 2015

I walk into my class of 80 people the Tuesday after filming *CBS Sunday Morning* with my sunglasses still on. *Does anybody recognize me? Does anyone in college even watch* CBS Sunday Morning? A few heads turn as I walk to my usual seat in the front of the room. I pull out my notebook and look over my calendar, all standard for the beginning of the week. Someone taps me on the shoulder. *Oh, no, here we go.* "Hey, I saw you on TV two days ago. I didn't know you were raped. I didn't know that CU could even get away without expelling a rapist. Man, I'm sorry," my classmate tells me. *Whew, at least that was a positive response.* I thanked my classmate and went back to attempting to hide in the small confinement of my desk, burying my eyes from the class.

February 2016

Three years ago, I was raped. Three years ago on Valentine's Day, someone who I thought was my friend pushed me to intoxication and held me down as he forced something upon me, something that will follow me for the rest of my life. Three years ago, I was bleeding, drunk, and crying hysterically. Today, I am happy, healthy, and focused on myself and my future. I have graduated from the university that did me wrong, landed a job in the communication field, and physically distanced myself from the city I was raped in. My new life in California has opened up the door for many opportunities and a bright future. I am not the girl who was raped anymore, but the woman who turned into a survivor.

Sarah Gilchriese is a recent Magna Cum Laude graduate in communication from the University of Colorado Boulder. She now resides in Northern California with her dog, Koa.

Introduction

Divided into two sections, this chapter provides profiles on select campus sexual assault cases and campus sexual assault activists. Listed alphabetically by school, the profiles begin with the following case summaries: the Jameis Winston scandal at Florida State University, the rape and murder of Jeanne Clery at Lehigh University, the sexual assault of children by assistant football coach Jerry Sandusky at Pennsylvania State University, the sexual assault by Brock Turner at Stanford, the gang rape by Steubenville High School football players, the sexual assault that led to a historic Title IX case at the University of Colorado, multiple incidents at the University of Montana, and the false report chronicled by *Rolling Stone* magazine about an alleged gang rape at the University of Virginia. The second section of this chapter includes profiles of prominent activists, activist organizations, and a critically acclaimed documentary credited with raising awareness. Listed alphabetically, they include Joseph Biden and the Obama Administration, Laura Dunn, End Rape on Campus, Angie Epifano, *The Hunting Ground*, Know Your IX, Katie Koestner, Mary P. Koss, Emma Sulkowicz, and the "Womyn and Antioch College."

Vice President Joe Biden speaks at Syracuse University during an "It's on Us" event to raise awareness of sexual assault on college campuses in November 2015. The Obama administration made combating campus sexual assault a primary policy initiative, largely due to Biden's legislative experience and interest in reducing violence against women. (AP Photo/Mike Groll)

Taken all together, this chapter provides an overview of cases and activists that have gained public recognition and helped to bring the topic of campus sexual assault to the forefront of our contemporary national consciousness.

Selected School and/or Campus Sexual Assaults

With roughly 200 colleges and universities under investigation by the Department of Education for possible Title IX violations for their handling of sexual assault, it is difficult to narrow down just a few schools and cases to highlight. The following schools are included here because they were home to sexual assault cases that are particularly notable. However, the failure to make the nightly news does not mean a sexual assault case is not worthy of concern. In reality, for better or worse, most campus sexual assaults do not become the center of media attention and public scrutiny. High-profile cases are likely high profile because they are especially "scandalous" or have details that make the case especially intriguing. Cases that involve student athletes and beloved football teams generate a good deal of public attention. Additionally, it is only relatively recently that the news industry has shown interest in covering stories of campus sexual assault and only relatively recently that the public has shown interest in hearing about them. While the public debates these prominent scandals, the reality is that the majority of sexual assaults that occur every day on college and university campuses do not make it into our public consciousness. We cannot forget that the epidemic of sexual assault spans far beyond what we read in our newsfeeds.

Florida State University

In a community that rallies behind the local football team, a sexual assault allegation against the star quarterback is scandalous. The sexual assault allegation against Florida State University's (FSU's) star quarterback, Jameis Winston, created an uproar that called into question the priorities of both the school and the local police force. Many believe the eventual bungled investigations were an attempt to protect the FSU football team and the football career of the accused.

On the evening of December 6, 2012, Florida State University freshman Erica Kinsman was at the Tallahassee nightclub Potbelly's with friends. While there, Kinsman was followed around and harassed by a man in the bar, and Jameis Winston pretended to pose as her boyfriend to drive the man away. Winston and Kinsman were not previous acquaintances, and Kinsman stated she did not recognize him as the star quarterback of the college football team or know who he was. After successfully driving away the harassing man, Winston offered Kinsman a shot of alcohol. Kinsman accepted the shot, which she believed to be tainted because her memory became hazy and fragmented afterward, despite having not consumed much alcohol that evening. Kinsman stated she remembered being in a cab with Winston and two other men unknown to her, which she said was personally uncharacteristic behavior. The cab dropped them off at Winston's apartment. In the apartment, Kinsman alleged that after partially blacking out, she awoke to find Winston raping her despite her verbal protests and physical attempts to get him off. She recounts that at some point one of the other men came into the bedroom because the door did not lock and told Winston to stop because she was saying "no." He did not stop and instead, she stated, he took her to the bathroom, locked the door, and continued to rape her while pushing her face against the tile floor.

After the alleged assault, Winston dressed Kinsman and dropped her off near her apartment on his scooter. Kinsman immediately posted a plea on Twitter asking for help. Kinsman told a friend who responded that she thought she was just raped, and the friend convinced Kinsman to allow her to call the police. A campus police officer responded to the 911 call reporting a sexual assault by an unknown assailant, and the officer drove Kinsman to the hospital in order to have evidence collected. Semen was found in her underwear, and bruises were forming on her body while she was at the hospital, indicating recent trauma.

Because the campus officer believed it to be an off-campus incident, the case was referred to the Tallahassee Police Department. A city police officer began the interview and was later joined by an officer from the Special Victims Unit, Scott Angulo. Angulo was an FSU alum who did private security work for the Seminole Boosters, a nonprofit that provides finances for Florida State athletics. Angulo's subsequent investigation was limited. He failed to review video footage from the bar, failed to locate the cab driver, and failed to locate the three men Kinsman left the bar with.

About a month after the alleged assault, Kinsman identified her assailant when his name was read out loud during roll call in a class they were both enrolled. Kinsman immediately provided the name to Detective Angulo, who, according to Kinsman, cautioned that "this is a huge football town. You really should think long and hard if you want to press charges." While the investigation was slow and spotty at first, it all but ground to a halt after the alleged assailant was identified. Angulo did not attempt to interview Winston for two weeks after hearing his identity, at which point Winston declined an interview through his attorney. Winston maintained, throughout it all, that any sex that occurred was consensual. The two other men in the cab and at the apartment, later identified as football players Chris Casher and Ronald Darby, backed Winston's account. Casher admitted to having taken video footage of some of the sexual encounter when he was finally interviewed months later but that he had deleted it a few days after the incident. Arguably, the police could have reviewed the video had there not been such a delay in locating the witnesses.

Meanwhile, a victim advocate at FSU informed Kinsman that another student had sought counseling after a problematic sexual encounter with Winston. While the advocate did not identify the incident as rape, she believed the account to be troubling enough to alert Kinsman, because she felt it shed "some light on the way Mr. Winston operates."

Angulo closed the case 66 days after meeting with Kinsman in the hospital, citing "lack of cooperation" from the victim, an assertion denied by Kinsman. Not only did he not inform Kinsman that he was closing the case but he did so after failing to interview witnesses, failing to obtain communication records, and failing to acquire Winston's DNA. In November 2013, spurred by a public records request by the *Tampa Bay Times*, the police department released documents about the sexual assault case. The state attorney, Willie Meggs, directed his staff to reinvestigate. After Megg's office took over the case, the authorities obtained Winston's DNA sample, which was a match for what was found on Kinsman's clothing. Ultimately, the state attorney's office decided that there was not sufficient evidence to prove that Winston sexually assaulted Kinsman against her will. In closing the investigation, Meggs argued that law enforcement "missed all the basic fundamental stuff that you are supposed to do" but cautioned he was unsure what the result would have been had the case been properly investigated. In an interview, however, Meggs conceded that he thought what happened that evening "was not good."

The university, for its part, failed to investigate until after the football season was over, despite having known early on that Winston was charged with a serious crime. Winston won the Heisman Trophy in 2013. In December 2014, nearly two years after the alleged assault, Winston attended a two-day hearing to determine whether he should be found in violation of the student conduct code for sexual misconduct. Of the four people present in the apartment the night in question, only Kinsman was questioned and cross-examined. Winston read from a prepared statement and indicated he was not going to answer questions, citing FSU's student conduct rules that permitted him to not answer questions. According to the transcript, the hearing was marred by confusion. The judge in the case, a retired Florida Supreme Court justice, was often unsure what the procedures of the hearing were. The judge ultimately cleared Winston of wrongdoing due to a lack of sufficient evidence, which cleared the way for Winston to play in the upcoming championship game.

Kinsman publicly identified herself. Once her identity was known, people were quick to defend Winston and condemn Kinsman. Prominent sportscasters defended Winston, calling into question the timing of the investigation. Kinsman, on the other hand, was harassed, threatened, and called a liar, among many other things, by students who believed she made the rape allegations up. Kinsman ultimately dropped out of FSU. Kinsman's story is predominately featured in the documentary *The Hunting Ground*. The film was also aired on CNN, despite Winston threatening to sue the network if they showed it. After the film's release, FSU president John Thrasher came to the defense of the school, saying the film "contains major distortions and glaring omissions."

Kinsman filed a Title IX complaint, and the Office of Civil Rights has agreed to examine whether FSU responded appropriately to sexual violence complaints. Kinsman sued FSU, claiming it violated Title IX by not taking seriously her sexual assault allegation. The lawsuit against FSU was settled out of court in January 2016 for $950,000 and a five-year agreement to take steps to prevent sexual abuse on campus. Kinsman also filed a civil suit of forcible rape against Winston in April 2015, requesting a jury trial and monetary damages for sexual battery, assault, false imprisonment, and intentional infliction of emotional distress. Winston countersued for defamation and tortuous interference a month later. A federal judge dismissed Winston's tortuous interference claim but did not dismiss the defamation claim. The two suits were combined and are scheduled to begin in the summer of 2017.

An investigation by *The New York Times* found that the police in this case conducted a "flawed investigation." Additionally, investigations by *The New York Times* and *Fox Sports* accused FSU of taking steps to "hide, and then hinder" the criminal investigation into the rape allegations against Winston. Ultimately, Winston was never charged with a crime and was the first overall draft pick in 2015. He is currently the starting quarterback for the Tampa Bay Bucanneers.

Lehigh University

On April 5, 1986, Jeanne Ann Clery, a student at Lehigh University in Bethlehem, Pennsylvania, awoke in her dorm room to someone robbing her. The man proceeded to attack, rape, sodomize, bite, and strangle Clery. Clery had never previously encountered her assailant, Josoph Henry, who had been drinking all night and was also a student at Lehigh. In order for Henry to reach Clery's room, he had gone through three doors with automatic locks that had been propped open with pizza boxes by students.

Henry was subsequently convicted of first-degree murder, rape, involuntary deviate sexual intercourse, indecent assault, burglary, theft, robbery, and aggravated assault and sentenced to death for his crimes. His death sentence was overturned in 2002, and he traded appeal rights for life in prison.

After the death of their daughter, Connie and Howard Clery learned that there had been 38 violent crimes (including rape, robbery, and assault) reported on Lehigh's campus in the three years preceding Jeanne's murder. The Clerys were convinced that Lehigh not only provided insufficient security but was misleading about their campus crime rates. They sued Lehigh University for negligence and settled out of court for an undisclosed amount and a promise from the university to strengthen campus security.

The Clerys recognized that what happened to their daughter was not an isolated incident, and they were vocal about the need for better security across all college campuses. Additionally, they argued that schools should make their crime statistics public information. Using the settlement from their lawsuit against Lehigh, the Clerys created the advocacy and education clearinghouse Clery Center for Security on Campus (http://clerycenter.org). Additionally, they lobbied state legislatures and Congress for legislation requiring colleges to publicize their crime statistics. Successful in passing legislation in a few states, including Pennsylvania, their greatest success was the federal Campus Security Act passed in 1990, which was later renamed the Jeanne Clery Act.

The Clery Act requires schools that participate in federal financial aid programs to publish an annual report that details their campus security policies and crime statistics over the past three years. The statistics must include forcible and non-forcible sex offenses, and other crimes like arson, burglary, motor vehicle theft, aggravated assault, and robbery. Additionally, the act requires schools to give timely warnings of crimes that represent an ongoing threat to the campus community and imposes certain basic requirements on handling cases of sexual assault, stalking, and domestic and dating violence. Schools found in violation can, and have been, fined by the U.S. Department of Education.

The Clery family was successful in raising awareness and spurring important legislative changes in the wake of a terrible tragedy. Due to their hard work, college campuses are more accountable for the safety of their students.

Pennsylvania State University

We most often hear of campus sexual assaults that involve crimes perpetrated by college students against their peers; however, one of the most egregious cases involves a college football coach found guilty of sexually assaulting young boys over the course of decades and an athletic staff and campus administrators who seemingly turned a blind eye to the abuse.

Jerry Sandusky joined renowned football coach Joe Paterno's staff at Pennsylvania State University as a defensive line coach in 1969. In 1977, Sandusky created The Second Mile, a group foster home for troubled boys. The Second Mile eventually grew into a nonprofit charity for at-risk and underprivileged youth.

It was through his work with the charity that Sandusky met, and lured, his numerous victims. In 2011, a grand jury report outlined Sandusky's sexual abuse of eight victims. For example, between 1994 and 1997, Sandusky engaged in improper sexual conduct with three different boys he met through The Second Mile. The children, who were aged 7 or 8, 10, and 12 or 13 at the time of the assaults, were subjected to abusive conduct ranging from sexual touching to sexual encounters.

In 1998, Sandusky showered with an 11-year-old boy in the locker room. The boy's mother reported the incident, which was then investigated by Penn State Police and the Pennsylvania Department of Public Welfare. Sandusky admitted to showering with the child, stating to the boy's mother, "I understand. I was wrong. I wish I could get forgiveness. I know I won't get it from you. I wish I were dead." The district attorney chose not to file charges, and the university police chief closed the case. Both the athletic director Tim Curley and the university's vice president for business and finance Gary Schultz were informed of the incident.

In 1999, Sandusky retired with full access to campus and sports facilities. He remained an active volunteer with The Second Mile. In 2000, janitor James Calhoun witnessed Sandusky performing oral sex on a young boy pinned against the wall in the showers. Calhoun told a colleague, but neither reported the incident, fearing their job security. His supervisor was also informed, and he also failed to report the incident. In March 2002, graduate assistant Mike McQueary, who later became the assistant coach, witnessed Sandusky raping a 10-year-old boy in the showers. McQueary reported the assault to Paterno, who in turn reported the assault to the athletic director Tim Curley. McQueary met with Curley and Schultz and informed them of the assault. McQueary later testified that he told all of them that he witnessed Sandusky raping the boy; however, Curley, Schultz, and Paterno all alleged that they were merely told of sexual misconduct and did not know the extent of the assault. Sandusky's keys to the locker room were taken away, and the incident was reported to The Second Mile. However, no one filed formal charges, and no law enforcement investigation occurred.

In 2006 or 2007, Sandusky began to spend a good deal of time with an 11- or 12-year-old boy he met through The Second Mile. He took the boy to sporting events, bought him gifts, and performed oral sex on him numerous times. The boy broke off contact with Sandusky in 2008. His mother reported the sexual assaults to her son's principal, who in turn informed the police. By November 2008, Sandusky was under investigation and removed from all Second Mile activities involving children. In 2010, Sandusky retired from The Second Mile permanently.

On November 4, 2011, the grand jury report was released containing testimony that Sandusky abused eight young boys over a period of at least 15 years and that officials at Penn State knew of some of the incidents but failed to notify the police. Sandusky was arrested and released on bail. Curley and Schultz were also charged with numerous counts, including perjury and failure to report sexual abuse allegations. The two stepped down from their positions at Penn State. On November 9, 2011, Paterno released a statement saying he was going to retire at the end of the season. By the end of the same day, the school board fired Paterno and the university's president, Graham Spanier. Spanier was also charged with numerous counts, including perjury and endangering the welfare of children.

By December 7, 2011, the number of Sandusky's victims had risen to ten. In 2012, Sandusky was ultimately convicted of sexually abusing 10 boys, and found guilty of 45 of the 48 counts against him. He was sentenced to 30 to 60 years, which he is currently serving in a maximum security prison in Pennsylvania. Other victims continued to come forward, including one of Sandusky's adopted sons. Penn State has reached settlements with 30 of Sandusky's victims, resulting in almost $90 million paid by the university. The earliest year of alleged abuse covered in one of Penn State's settlements was 1971.

Paterno died in January 2012 from lung cancer. He maintained until his death that he did not know of Sandusky's predatory sexual behavior. In July 2012, a former federal judge and director of the FBI released a report of his independent investigation into the case, and accused Paterno, Spanier, and others of deliberately hiding facts about Sandusky's behavior. Ultimately, the NCAA fined Penn State $60 million, banned the football team from postseason play for four seasons, reduced scholarships for four years, and vacated the university's football victories from 1998 to 2011. Paterno's wins were later restored as a result of a 2015 lawsuit. In 2016, new allegations arose asserting Paterno knew Sandusky was sexually abusing children as early as 1976. While many defend Paterno and believe he had little or no knowledge of Sandusky's behavior, many others are critical of what they believe to be Paterno's inaction. After the release of the independent investigation, university president Rodney Erickson had a bronze sculpture of Paterno removed from campus because it became a "source of division and obstacle to healing in our university." Paterno's name, however, remains on the campus library.

Most recently, in 2016, McQueary, the former assistant coach who, as a graduate assistant had reported witnessing Sandusky sexually assault a boy, filed a lawsuit against Penn State, claiming it retaliated against him, defamed him, and led him to believe they would take appropriate actions with his report. McQueary was put on administrative leave when Sandusky was charged and his contract was not renewed, actions McQueary believe were in retaliation for assisting with the investigation against Sandusky. Additionally, millions of dollars have been spent in legal fees challenging the charges the three administrators face as a result of the scandal. The efforts have begun to pay off, as the charges of perjury, conspiracy, and obstruction of justice have been thrown out for Spanier, Schultz, and Curley. The men who had supervised Sandusky, but claim not to have known the extent of his predatory behavior, are currently only facing counts of failure to report suspected abuse and endangering the welfare of children, which are second- and first-degree misdemeanors.

Throughout it all, Sandusky claimed he was innocent of the charges against him, that he only "horsed around" with them, and stated that "in retrospect, I shouldn't have showered with those kids." His wife of 37 years, Dottie, believes in his innocence and feels that the accusers are motivated by financial gain. Meanwhile, many believe that the evidence points to campus officials who swept abuse allegations under the rug and allowed a pedophile to walk free in order to protect a college football team and university from negative publicity. In 2016, the Department of Education levied the largest fine for Clery Act violations against Penn State. The nearly $2.4-million fine was based on the finding of 11 acts of "serious" noncompliance tied to Sandusky and other compliance failures on campus. The Department of Education's scathing report said the university's "football culture" was partially to blame for some of the violations.

Stanford

The rape of an unconscious woman by a Stanford swimmer became the focal point of a national conversation about campus sexual assault and specifically spurred a debate about the sentencing of perpetrators. On January 18, 2015, around 1 a.m., two Swedish graduate students, Carl-Fredrik Arndt and Peter Jonsson, were biking near the Kappa Alpha fraternity house on Stanford's campus. They saw a man on top of a woman behind a dumpster and noticed the woman did not seem to be moving. The man attempted to flee when Arndt and Jonsson pulled him off of the unconscious and partially naked woman. They caught him and held him down until the police arrived. The assailant was identified as Stanford University freshman Brock Turner. Turner was an Olympic hopeful athlete, attending Stanford on a swimming scholarship.

The victim, who has remained anonymous, was a 22-year-old recent college graduate from the University of California–Santa Barbara who had moved back home with her parents. On the night of January 17, after dinner at home with her family, her younger sister persuaded her to attend a fraternity party on Stanford's campus. At the Kappa Alpha fraternity house, Turner, who was unknown to the sisters beforehand, made advances on the younger sister but was rebuffed. According to Turner's account a year later, he and the very intoxicated older sister kissed on the dance floor and agreed to leave together. In the early hours of that morning, after being apprehended by the passing graduate students behind the fraternity house, the police arrested him on suspicion of attempted rape, and he was released on bond later in the day. Turner stated to police that he had been drinking alcohol, did not know the woman's name, and would not be able to identify her, but that the sexual contact was consensual.

The victim had a blood-alcohol level more than triple the legal driving limit, and she didn't wake up for at least three hours after the assault. When she did gain consciousness, she was in the hospital with no recollection of what had occurred. She later learned the details of her assault by reading about it in the newspaper. Turner was formally charged with two counts of rape, two counts of penetration, and one count of assault with attempt to rape on January 28, 2015. During his arraignment in February, he pleaded not guilty to five felony charges. The victim believed he would admit guilt, formally apologize, and choose to settle; however, he hired a defense attorney and pursued a trial. In October, the judge threw out the two rape charges and ordered him to stand trial on the remaining counts. In March 2016, a jury found Turner guilty of three felonies: assault with intent to rape an intoxicated woman, sexually penetrating an intoxicated person with a foreign object, and sexually penetrating an unconscious person with a foreign object. As a result, USA Swimming later barred Turner from renewing his membership, meaning he would be unable to participate in competitive swimming.

Turner faced a possible sentence of ten years in prison. Prosecutors recommended that Turner be given a six-year prison sentence, arguing a severe sentence was needed because of

Turner's predatory behavior in isolating the victim and taking advantage of her extreme intoxication. However, on June 2, 2016, Santa Clara Superior Court Judge Aaron Persky handed Turner a six-month jail sentence (with possibility of early release for good behavior) followed by three years of formal probation and lifelong registration as a sex offender. Persky stated that a longer sentence would have a "severe impact" on Turner. The sentence drew national outrage for its leniency. There was a push to recall Persky from the bench, and there were protests, threats against him, and online petitions opposing him with over a million signatures. Jurors refused to sit in juries in which he presided. A juror who served in the Turner case wrote a letter published in the *Palo Alto Weekly* to Persky that said he was "absolutely shocked and appalled" by the sentence. Lacking in confidence that Persky could preside over another sexual assault case, the Santa Clara district attorney removed him from a different case later in the year. Persky later removed himself from all criminal cases. The sentence also inspired a proposed law that would give mandatory prison sentences for anyone convicted of sexually assaulting an unconscious and intoxicated person.

For multiple reasons, this case spurred a national conversation about the prosecution and sentencing of known sexual offenders. First, it took over a year for Turner's mug shot to be released, which meant images used in the media were often of him as a smiling athlete. The failure to use a mug shot is largely inconsistent with how the media typically portrays images of others arrested for crimes, especially minorities. This prompted the Twitter hashtag #NoMugShot and calls for the mug shot to be released. Second, the case became a symbol of unequal protection under the law, specifically for minorities convicted of similar crimes. Pointing to the data on racial disparities in sentencing, many argued that Turner's lenient sentence was influenced by his status as a white, blonde-haired, blue-eyed athlete at a prestigious university. Additionally, anti–sexual assault advocates argued that Turner's light sentence not only strengthened the perception that perpetrators of sexual assault are not likely to be punished but also illustrated why so few victims of sexual assault choose not to report their experiences in the first place.

The case also drew a fair amount of media attention because of various statements made by the people involved. For example, in a statement to the court, Turner's father argued for leniency. His comment that a prison sentence would be "a steep price to pay for 20 minutes of action" was met with widespread indignation. A childhood friend of Turner's wrote in support of him in a pre-sentencing letter, saying alcohol was to blame. The release of this letter prompted the cancellation of many shows for her band. In Turner's letter to the judge, he blamed his own actions on the college atmosphere of drinking, peer pressure, and sexual promiscuity. His statement is criticized for his failure to understand the difference between sexual promiscuity and sexual assault. Ultimately, the most significant statement came from the victim herself. She wrote a powerful 12-page impact letter that she read in court, directly addressing Turner. In this letter, the victim articulated the profound impact of the assault, how she felt revictimized by the trial proceedings, and her astonishment at the lenient sentence. The letter was published on Buzzfeed and quickly went viral. It was picked up by many major news outlets, read on air by a CNN anchor, and read out loud by bipartisan senators on the floor of Congress. The victim's statement was read by New York City's first lady, celebrities, and other New York officials in a live stream on New York City's Mayor de Blasio's Facebook page. The cast of HBO's show *Girls* dedicated their public service announcement to the victim. The public service announcement (PSA) urged people to take action against sexual assault and to support survivors. Additionally, in response to the victim's statement, Vice President Joe Biden wrote a long open letter published in Buzzfeed to the victim, indicating his anger over the incident and lauding her courage.

Stanford, like many universities and colleges, is accused of having a history of mishandling sexual assault and is one of the many schools currently under investigation for Title IX violations. In this particular case, Stanford banned Turner from campus two days after his arrest, and Turner withdrew before he had to face any disciplinary proceedings. Graduating students protested against Turner's sentence and in support of the victim during their graduation ceremony with signs and cap decorations. Additionally, a petition on Change.org called for the school to apologize to the victim, offer her counseling, and bolster efforts to prevent campus sexual assault and assist victims. Stanford has maintained they have acted appropriately in handling the case.

Turner was ultimately released after serving three months in jail. He will serve three years of probation and has registered as a sex offender. After his release, armed protestors gathered outside of his home with signs that read, for example, "castrate rapists." While justice was not served to the victim in this case, her letter raised awareness, prompted others to speak out about their experiences, and reminded women that they are not alone: *"And finally, to girls everywhere, I am with you. On nights when you feel alone, I am with you. When people doubt you or dismiss you, I am with you. I fought everyday for you. So never stop fighting, I believe you."*

Steubenville High School

What happened in Steubenville, Ohio, caused national outrage. While this is a case that occurred at a high school and not a college campus, it illustrates how in this new era of social media, bad behavior can be documented and widely disseminated in a short period of time.

On August 11, 2012, there were a number of end-of-summer parties for students of Steubenville High School. A 16-year-old girl who attended a different school near her home across the river in West Virginia told her parents she was spending the night at a friend's and went to a party at the house of a volunteer football coach at Steubenville High. While she was there, she drank alcohol and became so intoxicated that she slurred her words and had difficulty walking. She left the party with star football players Trent Mays and Ma'lik Richmond, both 16 years of age.

Mays and Richmond took the girl to a few more locations. Over the course of several hours, while the girl was unconscious, Mays and Richmond sexually assaulted her and images were captured by the party attendees and shared via social media. There were photos of her naked. Various tweets included the words *rape*, *drunk girl*, and *whore* and one tweet that said "the song of the night is definitely Rape Me by Nirvana." In one video, another football player taped Mays flashing her breasts and digitally penetrating the girl in the backseat of a car. There was a photo of Mays and Richmond carrying the girl, clearly passed out, by her ankles. There was a video of Mays attempting to get the girl to give him oral sex, but the girl was unresponsive. Witnesses recall Richmond digitally penetrating her and there was a photo of her naked body with Richmond's semen on her stomach. One witness made a video laughing while saying things like "she is so raped right now" and "she's deader than a door knob."

The girl awoke the next morning in a basement living room, naked and surrounded by Mays, Richmond, and another boy. She had no recollection of what had happened except for a short period of vomiting. She had no idea where she was, and she could not find her underwear, earrings, shoes, or phone. Meanwhile, the images of what had happened had been widely disseminated via Twitter, text, Instagram, and Facebook. After the girl's parents had been shown some of the images, they notified the police on August 14, 2012.

Steubenville, Ohio, is a steel town, once booming, that has suffered economically for decades. As is true of many small towns, the community rallies around their high school football team, packing the stadium for the games. The love for the Steubenville Big Red football team fueled a great deal of divisiveness in the community as the news of the events of that night unfolded. Many people blamed the victim saying she put herself in that position, while others argued high school football players in that town have gotten away with bad behavior for too long.

The assault made the local news on August 22, when it was announced that Mays and Richmond were arrested and charged. Despite the abundance of images on social media, the police did not have an air-tight case. Witnesses were not coming forward. And while 15 phones and 2 iPads were confiscated, cybercrime experts found that most images had been deleted and were not retrievable. Ultimately, investigators were able to retrieve two photos, and they analyzed hundreds of text messages. The involvement of two Steubenville outsiders also played a critical role.

A crime blogger, Alexandria Goddard, who had once lived in Steubenville, heard about the case early on and immediately started investigating. She was able to take screen shots of many images and messages taken by the partygoers before they were erased and specifically named athletes she believed were implicated in the crimes. While she was able to help the case unfold, her involvement upset many in the community, and one family of a football player, who had not been charged, sued for defamation. Additionally, Deric Lostutter, a member of the hacker collective Anonymous, leaked evidence, including text messages and photos. It is possible Lostutter may face a more severe punishment for hacking then what the assailants themselves received. Lostutter's role is reportedly being turned into a movie produced by Brad Pitt.

Ultimately, the Juvenile Court handed Mays a two-year sentence in juvenile detention for rape and distribution of a nude image of a minor, and Richmond received a one-year sentence for rape. None of the party goers who witnessed her assault, but failed to intervene, was charged. Three other boys, two of whom were on the Big Red team, recorded parts of the assault and were granted immunity to testify. A grand jury investigating into a possible cover-up by school officials later charged the school superintendent, Mike McVey, with a felony for tampering with evidence and obstruction of justice. Additionally, a former football coach, elementary school principal, and director of information technology were indicted on several misdemeanor counts ranging from allowing underage drinking to perjury and tampering.

The case drew national attention largely for the role social media played and for the implication of high school football stars in a town united for their love of football. But this is not an isolated incident, and high school sexual assaults occur all too often. It is worth noting that in this case, like many others, partygoers failed to intervene when they saw what was happening, and they failed to come forward as witnesses' afterward. This speaks volumes about rape culture and the need for bystander training.

University of Colorado–Boulder

On December 7, 2001, University of Colorado–Boulder (CU) students Lisa Simpson and Anne Gilmore were having a small get-together playing drinking games with friends in Simpson's off-campus apartment. Later in the evening, a friend of theirs invited football players, and the high school recruits they were hosting, to the party. The party grew to include almost 20 football players and recruits. At some point in the evening, Simpson passed out on her bed and stated she awoke to two football players undressing and orally and vaginally raping her. Meanwhile, Gilmore alleged she was sexually assaulted by one man and asked to fondle another. Additionally, a third woman, Monique Gillaspie, stated she was assaulted after she left the same party by two football players in her dorm room. The events of that evening set off a scandal that exposed the university's problematic recruiting techniques, resulted in sweeping reforms and an historic Title IX case, and contributed to the resignations of high-level campus officials.

After the alleged assault, Simpson went to the hospital and also filed a police report. The police subsequently interviewed many of the players and recruits who had been at the party, and the players maintained the sex was consensual. Prosecutors decided not to press criminal charges against the accused assailants; however, they charged four football players with providing alcohol to minors. The players received deferred sentences and lost their scholarships for one semester.

Simpson filed a civil suit against the University of Colorado in 2002 under Title IX, and Gilmore filed a similar complaint in 2003. The cases were consolidated in 2004. The complaints claimed that CU knew of the risk of sexual harassment for female CU students in connection to the football recruiting program and that the university failed to take any action to prevent further harassment. Gillaspie also filed suit but later chose to drop it because she felt the school used "guerilla warfare" tactics to challenge her character and credibility in their litigation strategy.

The accusations against the football players and the recruits spurred controversy over CU's recruiting techniques. In a deposition filed in conjunction with the civil suit, Boulder District Attorney Mary Keenan accused the university of using sex and alcohol to entice recruits. Head football coach Gary Barnett and the athletic department denied the allegations. Keenan stated that part of the reason they had decided not to charge the young men with sexual assault was because the men believed the purpose of the party was to have sex. Additionally, Keenan argued that the athletic department was well aware of the inherent danger for women, pointing to a case in 1997 when a 17-year-old high school student accused a CU football player of rape after a recruiting party. After that accusation, Keenan had put the football department "on notice" because she believed sex and alcohol were used as bargaining tools.

Meanwhile, additional facts were surfacing that painted the football team, and the university, in poor light. For example, according to a deposition by a CU police detective, the night before, Simpson's party recruits were taken to a party in a hotel and shown films of players and women engaging in sexual activity. The detective reported that one of the recruits said a player stated "this is what you get when you come to Colorado." Also, an escort service said that CU football players hired strippers for recruiting parties. A cell phone assigned to a former recruiting assistant showed a call to the escort service. That assistant was later indicted by a grand jury for improperly using a university-issued cell phone and for soliciting a prostitute.

In the midst of this scandal, at least nine additional women came forward to say they had been sexually assaulted by CU football players or recruits since 1997. Katie Hnida, the University of Colorado's first female kicker, told *Sports Illustrated* she was raped by a teammate in 1999 and was the victim to consistent sexual harassment from fellow players before she transferred. In response, Barnett made disparaging comments about her playing skills, including, "Katie was not only a girl, she was terrible. . . . There's no other way to say it." As a result, CU president Betsy Hoffman suspended Barnett, placed him on paid leave, and reinstated him a little over a month later. Additionally, in 2004, an investigative panel convened by the university's Board of Regents found that university officials failed to monitor the recruiting process, exercise sufficient oversight, or explain appropriate standards of behavior to the players hosting the recruits.

While the university vigorously defended itself against the lawsuits, the allegations did lead to sweeping athletic department reforms and changes to their recruiting efforts. Additionally, the scandal likely contributed to the resignations of Chancellor Richard Byyny in 2004, Athletic Director Dick Tharpe in 2004, President Betsy Hoffman in 2005, and, after a $3 million financial settlement with the school, Head Coach Gary Barnett in 2005.

In 2005, a federal judge dismissed Simpson and Gilmore's lawsuit, saying the women did not have a claim under Title IX because they failed to prove that the university knew about previous similar incidents and showed "deliberate indifference." Gilmore and Simpson appealed, and the U.S. Court of Appeals for the 10th Circuit ruled in their favor in 2007, concluding that the university "had an official policy of showing high-school recruits a 'good time' on their visits to the CU campus." Additionally, the appeals court found that the assaults occurred because of a lack of supervision over the players, and the lack of supervision was the result of "deliberate indifference." Thus, the lower court's decision was reversed and a trial date was set for January 2009.

In 2007, six years after the party in Simpson's apartment, the University of Colorado settled with Simpson and Gilmore, awarding one of the largest settlements in a Title IX civil suit against a college or university to date. In exchange for settling all claims against it, the university paid $2.5 million to Simpson and $350,000 to Anne Gilmore, hired a Title IX advisor, and added an additional part-time counselor to the Office of Victim's Assistance. The university also spent about $3 million in outside legal fees to defend itself against the lawsuit, in addition to the money it spent on a public relations consultant to handle the university's image during the scandal and the loss of tuition money due to a significant drop in out-of-state enrollment.

The University of Colorado made headlines again in 2013 when Sarah Gilchriese filed a Title IX complaint against the school, alleging they were slow to punish her rapist and levied sanctions that were too light. Her assailant was found responsible for non-consensual sexual intercourse by the school's student discipline office. He was suspended for eight months, but it took four weeks to remove him from campus, during which time he repeatedly violated an order to have no contact with her. His punishment also included a $75 fine and an assigned five- to seven-page paper reflecting upon his experience. Gilchriese settled with CU in 2014. Additionally, the *Simpson v. University of Colorado* case resurfaced recently in light of the sexual assault scandal at the University of Tennessee–Knoxville. In February 2016, eight women filed a federal lawsuit under Title IX against the University of Tennessee, claiming the school created a culture that enables sexual assault and other bad behavior by student-athletes, especially football players, and uses a disciplinary system that favors the players. The suit mirrors complaints made by Simpson and Gilmore, and the plaintiffs' attorneys stated that the precedent for the case lies with the federal appeals court decision in the Simpson case, specifically that officials at the University of Tennessee knew of prior sexual assaults and showed "deliberate indifference" to the reports. In July 2016, the university settled with the women, agreeing to pay $2.8 million to the plaintiffs, hire six positions in its Title IX office, and appoint a special independent commission to review the response to sexual assaults at all universities within the University of Tennessee system.

University of Montana

Missoula, Montana, has been dubbed by critics as the "Rape Capital of America" due to the high number of reported rapes within the last several years, many of which have occurred at the University of Montana (UM). In fact, the numbers of rapes reported in Missoula align with national averages; however, the city police, city prosecutors, and the university came under intense criticism and scrutiny for how they handled sexual assault cases.

The Grizzlies, University of Montana's beloved football team, made headlines in 2011 for reported sexual assaults by players. In response, UM's president, Royce Engstrom, appointed a former Assistant U.S. Attorney and Montana Supreme Court member, Diane Barz, to investigate. Barz's final report, released on January 31, 2012, stated that sexual assaults on the UM campus "require immediate action and swift compliance with Title IX mandates" and that "a rape-tolerant campus with ineffective programming, inadequate support service for victim survivors, and inequitable grievance procedures threatens every student."

On May 1, 2012, the federal Department of Justice (DOJ) launched an investigation of the University of Montana, the Missoula Police Department, and the Missoula County

Attorney's Office over the handling of reported sexual assaults, specifically because so few rape cases brought to authorities resulted in actual charges. The DOJ found that prosecutors pursued charges in only 14 of 85 rape cases sent to them by the police between 2008 and 2012 and that the Missoula county attorney failed to prosecute in nearly every case that involved drugs or alcohol—even if the rapist had confessed. The report went as far as to say the county prosecutor's office had disregarded sexual assaults to such a degree that it was placing "women in Missoula at increased risk of harm." In response, the county attorney argued that this was a case of overreach and that the DOJ overstepped its bounds and had no legal authority to investigate his office. However, in the wake of the investigation, the Missoula police and county attorney's office made significant changes.

Additionally, two separate probes, one by the Justice Department's Civil Rights Division and another by the Department of Education's Office of Civil Rights, investigated the University of Montana in 2012. They found that the campus police force discriminated against female students and botched rape reports. Additionally, they found that officers discouraged women from reporting sexual assault and relied upon "unwarranted gender-based assumptions and stereotypes." Additionally, they discovered that the delayed and inadequate responses to the students who reported sexual assault led to a variety of problems for the survivors, including not feeling safe on campus, mental health problems, suicidal feelings, and dropping out or withdrawing from classes. In the wake of these investigations, the University of Montana signed an agreement with the DOJ agreeing to policy changes. In the letter to the university, the DOJ said the agreement will "serve as a blueprint" to protect students from sexual harassment and assault at universities and colleges across the nation. The "blueprint" designation has put the University of Montana under increased national scrutiny.

The headlines from Missoula got the attention of investigative reporter Jon Krakauer. Krakauer looked into the rash of sexual assaults at the University of Montana between 2010 and 2012. His best-selling book, *Missoula: Rape and the Justice System in a College Town* (2015), documents the experiences of five women who reported surviving rape or attempted rape during those years. He examines how they were treated by the community, the university, and the criminal justice system. His book presents a police department that failed to believe and support victims, allegations of cover-ups, and a town that was divided by the accusation of football players from an adored team. Krakauer's stated intent was to spur a national conversation about the epidemic of rape that occurs everywhere, not just in the bucolic town of Missoula.

One of the women Krakauer profiled in his book was Kelsey Belknap. Belknap attended an off-campus party at the end of the fall semester in December 2010. In the course of playing drinking games, she consumed anywhere from 8 to 11 shots of 99-proof alcohol within an hour and was slipping in and out of consciousness. Belknap told the police that a Grizzly football player tried to have sex with her, that she pushed him away and said "I don't want to," but that he grabbed her by the jaw and forced himself on her. She stated that three of his teammates then proceeded to rape her as well. She passed out during the alleged attacks, and after she awoke she went to the hospital, had a rape kit performed, and reported the assaults to the police. Belknap maintains the police were not sympathetic, blaming the assaults on her decision to consume alcohol and wanting her to keep the incident "hush-hush." Prosecutors never charged the four football players for gang raping Belknap, citing a lack of probable cause. Montana law states a victim is incapable of giving consent if he or she is "mentally defective or incapacitated." The definition of *incapacitated* is murky, and while she was clearly drunk, the Missoula county attorney said she was not legally incapacitated because she was in and out of consciousness. After that process failed her, Belknap turned to university officials. One of her attackers was expelled from school, another agreed to leave voluntarily, and the other two had already dropped out.

Another woman profiled by Krakauer is Allison Huguet. Huguet attended a college out of state, but she returned to her hometown of Missoula in December 2010. She attended a party at the home of her childhood friend and Grizzly football star Beau Donaldson. After drinking at the party, she crashed on Donaldson's couch for the night. She awoke to a lot of pain, and realized Donaldson was raping her. She kept her eyes closed and waited for him to finish and leave the room. Huguet then fled barefoot and called her mother for help. As she was running, she realized Donaldson was chasing her and begging her not to tell anyone what happened. She got away and had a rape kit performed at the hospital, but she chose not to file a police report at the time.

Later, Huguet and her mother invited Donaldson to their home and secretly taped his confession. Huguet asked him to get counseling and promised that in exchange she would not report the incident to the police. A year later, she was still plagued with nightmares and anxiety. Huguet found Donaldson had not sought the help he had promised, and she reported him to the authorities. In an interview with the police, Donaldson confessed. In the process of getting the case moved through the criminal justice system, Huguet discovered a woman named Hillary McLaughlin, who came forward to say Donaldson had sexually assaulted her in 2008 but that she never reported it to the police. McLaughlin told her story in court on Huguet's behalf. In September 2012, Donaldson pleaded guilty to rape and was sentenced to 30 years with 20 years suspended in federal prison. In 2015, Donaldson's first request for parole was denied, but he was allowed to attend boot camp. In 2016, Donaldson's second request for parole was granted, contingent upon successful completion of a prerelease program and the stipulation of regular sex offending and chemical dependency counseling upon release.

In another incident with a Grizzly football player, Krakauer describes a woman, who has chosen to remain anonymous, who alleged she was raped by the quarterback Jordan Johnson. On a late evening in February 2012, the woman said that she and Johnson were watching a movie on her bed, had taken their shirts off, and were kissing. She stated that when Johnson attempted to go further, she said "no." Johnson then allegedly became aggressive, pinned her down, turned her over, and raped her. The woman did not file a police report in hopes that the incident would not become public; however, she did report the alleged assault to the university. She later filed a temporary restraining order against him, prompted by seeing him on campus. News of the restraining order made it to the press, and the woman decided to report the alleged assault to the police. When the allegations first surfaced, Johnson was briefly suspended from the football team. He was later kicked off of the team under the school's student-athlete code of conduct when the felony charge of sexual intercourse without consent was filed against him. Eventually, multiple university proceedings found Johnson responsible for rape and the University Court voted to expel him.

Johnson subsequently petitioned the state commissioner of higher education, Clayton Christian, to overturn the ruling and ultimately Johnson was not expelled but it is unclear as to why. Assuming Christian had overturned the expulsion, Krakauer wished to see the records about the disciplinary proceeding concerning Johnson in order to see why it was decided to overturn the decision made by the University Court. Christian refused to release the records, citing the Family Educational Rights and Privacy Act, which restricts releasing anything from a student's "educational records" without permission from the student. In an interesting twist, Krakauer hired an attorney to file a petition to ask the commissioner to unseal the documents to see what action the commissioner took, arguing the public's right to know outweighs privacy concerns. The court originally sided with Krakauer, Christian appealed, and now Krakauer is awaiting a ruling from the Montana Supreme Court.

Johnson took his felony charge of sexual intercourse without consent to trial, and the jury acquitted Johnson of the charges in March 2013, having failed to find Johnson guilty beyond a reasonable doubt. Johnson promptly sued the university for mishandling the rape allegation against him, arguing that his due process and civil rights were violated and that he was the victim of sexual discrimination. The University of Montana chose to settle, paying Johnson $245,000.

These examples are some of several that illustrate why Missoula spent a good deal of time under the spotlight for the way the university, the police, and the county attorney's office responded to sexual assault. In many ways, Missoula served as an example of what not to do when survivors come forward after being sexually assaulted. In the end, all of this resulted in significant and much needed changes, and now universities and colleges are looking to UM's policy on sexual assault for guidance.

University of Virginia

On November 19, 2014, *Rolling Stone* magazine published an article online (and in the print edition of the magazine on December 4) entitled "A Rape on Campus." The article, written by Sabrina Rubin Erdely, chronicled the story of an alleged gang rape in a Phi Kappa Psi fraternity house at the University of Virginia. The article was later retracted, as it was discovered that Erdely failed to properly fact-check the alleged victim's claims. The article, and the resulting controversy surrounding it, roiled the college campus, created widespread debate, and fueled a media frenzy.

Erdely was originally interested in investigating how college campuses handle sexual assault cases. She contacted a staff member who worked on sexual assault issues at the University of Virginia for a recommendation of a student rape survivor who could provide an emblematic illustration of a campus sexual assault case. Erdely was put in touch with Jackie, a pseudonym for an alleged victim of a gang rape that occurred when she was a freshman in 2012. Erdely's original 9,000-word article in *Rolling Stone* described the brutal gang rape of Jackie by seven men at the Phi Kappa Psi house. According to Jackie's account to Erdely, Jackie went on a date a few weeks after she arrived on campus with a junior Phi Kappa Psi brother, referred to in the article by the pseudonym Drew. Jackie said she met Drew at the university aquatic center where they both worked as lifeguards. After dinner, she alleged Drew brought her to a party at the Phi Kappa Psi house and led her upstairs. In the dark room, Jackie said seven men took turns raping her in what she understood to be a hazing ritual over the course of three hours, while Drew and one other man gave directions and encouragement. She indicated she passed out and later awoke alone, injured and bleeding, in the early morning hours. She said she fled the fraternity and called a friend to come and get her. Her three best friends, two men and one woman, came to pick her up. Jackie said that one friend suggested going to the hospital but that the other friends disagreed and discouraged her from reporting for fear of harming her reputation.

After the assault, Jackie recounted that she failed classes and suffered from depression and suicidal thoughts. Jackie reported the assault at the end of her freshman year to Dean Nicole Eramo, who was in charge of University of Virginia's Sexual Misconduct Board. However, she said, after the dean provided her with her options, she ultimately chose not to file any criminal reports or formal complaints with the university. Urged by Eramo, Jackie became involved in a campus sexual assault peer advocacy group, where she said she heard from other students who experienced assault on UVA's campus. Jackie said she met with Dean Eramo again after being hit with a bottle on campus in retaliation for being a public advocate against sexual assault and after hearing of other women who had similar experiences with the same fraternity. Throughout the article, Erdely reported that UVA neglected to warn the university community of the alleged assaults and portrayed the administration as consistently failing to take action against sexual assault assailants. After the release of the *Rolling Stone* article and in response to mounting campus pressure, UVA placed all Greek system activities under temporary suspension and asked the Charlottesville police to investigate Jackie's rape. Phi Kappa Psi also put the UVA chapter under suspension.

By all accounts, the investigation portrayed UVA's response to Jackie, and other alleged victims of campus sexual assault, as problematic. After the release of Erdely's article, the campus community responded with outrage and protests against UVA's mishandling of Jackie's case. The *Rolling Stone* article went viral, and it received praise for shining a light on a university seemingly willing to sweep sexual assault cases under the rug. However, shortly thereafter, the story began to unravel as *The Washington Post* and other news outlets found discrepancies and inconsistencies in the report. An investigation by *The Washington Post* found that Jackie's account varied on key details. For example, the three friends who came to her aid the night in question said Jackie reported being forced to perform oral sex on five fraternity brothers but that she did not identify a specific fraternity. They did not recall seeing any injuries and they recalled that she said her date was not a lifeguard but someone from her chemistry class.

Erdely interviewed Jackie a total of eight times and believed her to be a reliable source. However, Jackie refused to provide the last name of the individual who orchestrated the attack, stating that she was scared of him. Editors at the magazine acquiesced to proceeding not only with an alias for the ringleader but also without verifying his existence. After the story was released, Erdely finally convinced Jackie to provide the last name of the perpetrator. With his full name in hand, Erdely was unable to confirm that he worked at the pool or that he was a member of the fraternity. As a result, Erdely told her editor that she had doubts about the article's accuracy.

Ultimately, many of Jackie's claims were repudiated not only by *The Washington Post* investigation, but by school officials, the fraternity, her peers, and the police. After a four-month investigation, the Charlottesville, Virginia, police department found there was no corroborating evidence to support the claims in Jackie's account. Dean Eramo said that Jackie provided different details to her when the two had met. The fraternity found no record of a social event on the date in question, nor did they have any fraternity members who worked at the campus aquatic center as a lifeguard. Not only was Jackie's alleged date never located or interviewed, but the three friends who came to her aid said they were never contacted by Erdely for an interview. Erdely's story, it turns out, relied upon a single and unidentified source.

In light of the controversy surrounding the article, *Rolling Stone* asked the Columbia University School of Journalism to review the editorial process of the article. Columbia's nearly 13,000-word report found the article failed "basic, even routine journalistic practice" in both reporting and fact-checking and that the "journalistic failure" was "avoidable." Pointing to gaps in reporting and the failure to state where important information came from, the report recommended several changes. For example, the report recommended that the editorial management at *Rolling Stone* review their policies on pseudonym use and their process for checking "derogatory" information. Throughout the course of the controversy, *Rolling Stone* issued multiple apologies, and the article was officially retracted. Ultimately, three lawsuits were leveled at the magazine. Dean Eramo filed a complaint for defamation against *Rolling Stone*, and a jury subsequently awarded her $3 million to be paid by the magazine and Erdely. Additionally, the UVA fraternity chapter of Phi Kappa Psi is seeking $25 million in damages in a libel trial set to go to court in October 2017.

This is not the first time that UVA, and specifically UVA's Phi Kappa Psi fraternity chapter, has found itself in the news for campus sexual assault. In 1984, Liz Seccuro, a student at UVA, was gang raped in the Phi Kappa Psi house in what was an apparent hazing ritual. One of Seccuro's assailants, William Beebe, contacted her decades later to apologize and ultimately admitted to raping her. Seccuro was successful in pressing charges and Beebe served five years in prison. Seccuro's memoir *Crash into Me* (2011) chronicles her experience pursuing justice. Given the similar nature of Jackie's alleged case, Erdely contacted Seccuro. Seccuro granted multiple interviews with Erdely. At the beginning, Seccuro was an ardent supporter of the story and was quick to defend Jackie's account because something so similar happened to her. She later spotted red flags in Jackie's narrative and noted the many uncanny similarities. Whether Jackie's account was influenced by that of Seccuro's is unknown. It is worth noting that Jackie's friends, along with Seccuro and other experts who have followed this case, believe that Jackie likely did experience a traumatic event. However, the nature of that traumatic event is unknown.

One of the greatest tragedies of this story is the possibility that it spread the notion that many women invent rape allegations. In fact, statistics indicate false reporting of rape is rare. However, when false reporting does occur, it is damaging not only to the wrongly accused but also to actual survivors of sexual assault whose credibility is questioned. In 2006, similar concerns were raised after members of the Duke Lacrosse team were found to be wrongly accused of sexual assault by an exotic dancer they had hired to perform at a party. The Duke Lacrosse scandal was racially charged, but much like the UVA case, it ignited public debate and fears that the false accusation would lead the public to wrongly believe "crying rape" was a common occurrence.

In this case, there were plenty of other sexual assault survivors on UVA's campus (or on any campus) that Erdely could have profiled instead. Her decision to primarily focus on one unverified account did more harm than good. This scandal calls into question basic journalistic practice in reporting sexual assault. On one hand, experts caution that journalists should believe sexual assault victims and respect their autonomy so as not to re-traumatize them. However, as this case illustrates, journalists need to weigh these concerns with the need to verify their facts. The fallout from this article has fueled a continuing debate among journalists regarding the best practices in reporting sexual assault.

Selected Activists

The following is a list of brave individuals who, by virtue of their hard work and activism, helped to bring the issue of campus sexual assault to the forefront of our national consciousness. This list is limited in its scope to select individuals who have received public accolades over the last few decades for their activism. However, this is not to forget the hundreds of activists who are unnamed here. Students who confront their institutions of higher learning for mishandling cases of sexual assault, survivors who speak publically, and anyone who challenges the very existence of rape culture all deserve recognition for their courage and dedication.

Joseph Biden and the Obama Administration

President Barack Obama's administration made sexual assault awareness and prevention a priority. Obama and his Vice President Joseph "Joe" Biden were vocal advocates in fighting the epidemic of sexual assaults on college and university campuses. As a result of their efforts, they are credited with "re-writing the rulebook" on campus sexual assault and moving the issue to the top of the national agenda.

Biden was a U.S. senator from Delaware before serving as vice president to the United States for two terms with President Obama (2008–2016). In 1990, with wide support from advocacy groups, Biden introduced the Violence against Women Act (VAWA) in Congress. VAWA passed in 1994 and was the first federal legislative package designed to end violence against women with the goal of improving criminal justice and community-based responses to intimate partner violence, sexual assault, and stalking. To name a few of the accomplishments, the act included a criminal law against battering, provided funds for victim services and for the investigation and prosecution of violent crimes against women, and fostered federal prosecution of interstate domestic violence and sexual assault crimes. VAWA was reauthorized in 2000, 2005, and 2013 and has expanded the rights and protections to women, Native Americans, immigrants, college students and youth, and LBGT victims. Biden refers to the act as his "proudest legislative accomplishment."

As vice president, Biden oversaw the Office of Violence against Women. He appointed the first White House Advisor on Violence against Women, Lynn Rosenthal. Rosenthal advised Biden on issues of domestic violence and sexual assault and promoted collaboration across federal agencies. In 2011, Biden launched the 1 is 2 Many initiative to reduce dating violence and sexual assault among teens and young adults. The same year, the Department of Education's Office of Civil Rights released a Dear Colleague letter. The letter, written by Assistant Secretary for Civil Rights Russlynn Ali, an Obama appointee, informed schools that sexual violence is a form of sexual harassment and that schools that failed to adequately address sexual assault risked losing federal funds for violation of Title IX.

In January 2014, the Office of the Vice President and the White House Council on Women and Girls published a report on sexual violence entitled Rape and Sexual Assault: A Renewed Call to Action. The report analyzed data on sexual assault and noted that it was a particular problem on college campuses. In an effort to "redouble the work" to combat sexual assault, Obama established the White House Task Force to Protect Students from Sexual Assault. Cochaired by the White House Council on Women and Girls and the Office of the Vice President, the task force was charged with providing resources, improving transparency, and raising awareness. Three months later, based on conversations with thousands of people related to the issue, the task force released a report entitled Not Alone, which addressed the problem of sexual assault on college and university campuses. Not Alone provided recommendations and action steps for best practices. A resulting public awareness campaign and pledge, called It's on Us, encouraged people to be active bystanders and to intervene in problematic scenarios before a sexual assault occurred. Since its inception, hundreds of thousands of people have taken the White House pledge, and hundreds of schools have active It's on Us chapters. Additionally, a corresponding website (www.changingourcampus .org) provides data and resources for students and schools.

Biden often met privately with survivors of sexual assault and regularly gave speeches on the topic, asking men to step up and be active bystanders. Biden received a standing ovation at the 88th Academy Awards after advocating for survivors of sexual assault. He introduced singer Lady Gaga who performed her Oscar nominated song "'Til It Happens to You." The powerful song was featured in the documentary *The Hunting Ground* about campus sexual assault (see *The Hunting Ground* later in this chapter). Biden also wrote an open letter published in Buzzfeed in response to the heart-wrenching victim impact statement read by the survivor of sexual assault committed by Brock Turner from Stanford. Biden's letter, which went viral, applauded the survivor's strength in coming forward, praised the bystanders who intervened, and criticized a national campus culture marred by high rates of sexual assault and victim blaming. In his letter, Biden stated, "I join your global chorus of supporters, because we can never say enough to survivors: I believe you. It is not your fault. What you endured is never, never, never, NEVER a woman's fault."

While Obama and Biden's accomplishments in raising awareness about violence against women are laudable, their actions were not without criticism. Some disapproved of the Obama administration's role in combating campus sexual assault because they viewed it as heavy-handed government overreach. Others have pointed to Biden's questionable performance when he presided over the 1991 Supreme Court confirmation hearings of Clarence Thomas as chairman of the Senate Judiciary Committee. Specifically, Biden is criticized for doing little to stop the verbal attacks on Anita Hill, who maintained she was sexually harassed by Thomas. Despite these critiques, Obama and Biden's joint interest in eliminating violence against women paid off. Their efforts transformed the way colleges and universities respond to allegations of sexual misconduct, and they left a legacy of combating campus rape culture.

Laura Dunn

In 2004, at the end of her freshman year at the University of Wisconsin–Madison, two men from Laura Dunn's crew team brought her home after she consumed a lot of alcohol at a party. Dunn says the men raped her as she passed in and out of consciousness. Immediately afterward, she kept quiet about the assault and struggled with weight loss and an inability to sleep. Over a year later, prompted by a professor who told them students could report sexual assault to the dean, Dunn told the university what had happened. By that time, one of the accused had graduated; the other said the sex was consensual. The university took nine months to investigate and chose not to punish the alleged assailant, citing a lack of eyewitnesses and the role of alcohol. Frustrated with the time it took the school to investigate, Dunn filed a Title IX complaint against the University of Wisconsin–Madison. However, after an additional two years, the Department of Education ruled against her, stating the University of Wisconsin–Madison's nine-month inquiry was justified. A criminal investigation also ended without charges against the accused.

The alleged assault on Dunn occurred before the release of the 2011 Dear Colleague letter that provided Title IX guidance and in an era of less-than-aggressive enforcement of Title IX in sexual assault cases. Dunn had ultimately quit the crew team and her grades suffered. However, she graduated and entered the Teach for America program and later went to law school at the University of Maryland and graduated with her JD in 2014. Dunn gained media attention when her story was profiled by a 2010 investigative report on campus sexual violence by the Center for Public Integrity. She remained committed to working on the issue of campus sexual violence and attended the release of the 2011 Dear Colleague letter as a VIP guest of Vice President Joe Biden, successfully lobbied for the 2013 Violence against Women Act Reauthorization, and advised the White House Task Force to Protect Students from Sexual Assault. Additionally, Dunn founded the national nonprofit organization ServJustice, where she currently serves as the executive director. ServJustice provides legal assistance for survivors of sexual assault, in addition to policy advocacy and institutional training.

End Rape on Campus

Annie E. Clark and Andrea L. Pino first met as undergraduate students at the University of North Carolina–Chapel Hill. Clark graduated and moved to Oregon, and Pino remained on campus to finish her undergraduate degree. The two bonded over their experiences of sexual assault by strangers at campus parties and their shared outrage at University of North Carolina–Chapel Hill's mishandling of sexual assault complaints and failure to provide support for survivors. Both women felt unsupported by the university; Clark recounts an administrator responded to her by saying, "Rape is like football, if you look back on the game, and you're the quarterback . . . is there anything you would have done differently?" The pair found that there were other sexual assault survivors on campus who felt that the institution failed them, and so in 2013, along with three other women, they filed two federal complaints against their school, for violations of both Title IX and the Clery Act. In order to write their complaints, they spent all of their free time researching and came across a strategy proposed by Catharine MacKinnon in the 1970s, who argued sexual harassment was a form of sex discrimination. Ultimately, they wrote, without legal assistance, a 32-page complaint that combined personal narratives with legal arguments.

In the months after they filed and after an article in the *New York Times* featured their work, Pino and Clark heard from survivors across the nation who also wanted to hold their campuses accountable for mishandling their reports of sexual assault. The pair became increasingly aware that sexual assault, and institutional callousness, was not just an issue on their campus. With the desire to change how all campuses handle sexual assault, they worked diligently to launch a nationwide campaign to advise students on how to file a Title IX complaint against their college or university. In the summer of 2013, along with other students, survivors, and professors, they cofounded the organization End Rape on Campus (EROC). EROC provides free and direct assistance to survivors who seek to file Title IX and/or Clery complaints and provides mentorship in campus organizing, survivor support, and policy reform.

The two dedicated activists, who weathered threatening phone calls and death threats, are notable for their outspoken advocacy and their desire to "give Jane Doe a face." President Barack Obama credited Pino and Clark, in part, for launching the 2014 White House Task Force on college sexual assault. Pino and Clark have visited colleges and universities across the nation to talk about sexual assault and have provided countless media interviews. Their advocacy was predominately featured in the 2015 documentary *The Hunting Ground*; the film also profiled another EROC cofounder, Sofie Karasek, who survived sexual assault at the University of California–Berkeley.

Notably, the pair also walked into Senator Kristen Gillibrand's office, without an appointment, and shared their experiences and concerns with her. In 2014, Pino and Clark joined a bipartisan group of senators, including Gillibrand and Claire McCaskill, to introduce the Campus Accountability and Safety Act to Congress. The act would hold universities accountable for how they handle sexual assaults. The bill was reintroduced in 2015 and is, as of this writing, currently being debated by Congress. Additionally, Clark and Pino cowrote the book *We Believe You: Survivors of Campus Sexual Assault Speak Out* (2016), a collection of

36 stories written by survivors of campus sexual assault. Without a doubt, with their outspoken leadership, they have made significant strides in empowering students to hold their campuses accountable for how they handle sexual assault. Pino and Clark currently run EROC in Washington, D.C.

Angie Epifano

In October 2012, the student newspaper at Amherst College published Angie Epifano's first person account of being raped in a dorm room by an acquaintance in 2011. Her wrenching essay describes the insensitivity she faced by school administrators when she reported the assault. According to Epifano, the sexual assault counselor told her she couldn't change dorms, questioned if it was really rape, and told her to "forgive and forget." She was steered away from officially reporting the assault and was forcibly admitted by the college to a psychiatric ward for depression and suicidal thoughts. She alleges Amherst tried to deny her re-admittance after she was released from the ward and after the school changed course and agreed to allow her back, her dean prevented her from studying abroad in Africa. Frustrated, she withdrew from the college to work on a ranch in Wyoming and later wrote the essay in an attempt to improve the atmosphere at Amherst for sexual assault survivors. Her alleged rapist graduated with honors and was never sanctioned by Amherst.

Epifano's account went viral and crashed the newspaper's server. It prompted other Amherst students, past and present, to disclose their experiences with assault on campus and how they too were treated poorly. Her story also gained widespread national and media attention. After Epifano's story was published, the president of Amherst College, Dr. Carolyn "Biddy" Martin, released a statement that was uncharacteristic of most institutional responses. Instead of taking a defensive tone, Martin argued that things "must change, and change immediately." Martin then made a series of administrative modifications: she overhauled the judicial review process, improved reporting

procedures, hired more counselors trained in sexual misconduct, and implemented intervention and prevention programs.
Additionally, the sexual assault counselor who was portrayed
negatively by Epifano resigned.

Epifano maintains that Amherst College hurt her more than
her rapist, and she has remained publicly critical of the institution's handling of sexual assault. Epifano was not alone in her
criticism of Amherst's mishandling of sexual assault. Survivor
Dana Bolger was urged to take time off by an Amherst dean
after her assault. Additionally, on June 17, 2012, Amherst student Trey Malone, unable to cope with the sexual assault he suffered as a student, committed suicide. The letter he left behind
described Amherst's response as "emotionless hand washing."
He said he failed to find support and indicated Dr. Martin
responded with callousness. Malone's letter was published,
with approval of his family, on The Good Men Project website.
Already under scrutiny for the mishandling of Epifano's assault,
Dr. Martin released an open letter in response to Malone's suicide note, stating that the college responded immediately to
Malone's report of assault and provided him with ongoing support. Malone's story has a tragic ending, but his heartbreaking
letter educates readers about sexual assault and urges us all to
remember that "there are millions more just like me that need
help and no, someone who is drunk cannot give consent."

Ultimately, in 2013, Epifano and an anonymous former student with a similar experience filed a Title IX complaint against
the school. Epifano's story was profiled in the 2015 documentary *It Happened Here*. Her essay also inspired the creation of
the organization Know Your IX. After taking some time off to
travel, Epifano transferred to Lewis and Clark. Her advocacy is
responsible for significant changes at Amherst College, and she
can be credited for raising awareness and inspiring the action
of many across the nation.

The Hunting Ground

In 2012, director Kirby Dick and producer Amy Ziering
released *The Invisible War*, a documentary that revealed the

prevalence of sexual assault in the military. The award-winning film sparked a national outcry and spurred the secretary of defense to make significant policy changes. While screening *The Invisible War* at colleges and universities, students approached Dick and Ziering to recount analogous situations occurring on their campuses. These stories inspired the pair to research and craft a new documentary on the topic of campus sexual assault. Written and directed by Dick and produced by Ziering, *The Hunting Ground* premiered at the 2015 Sundance Film Festival and was released in February of the same year. In November 2015, CNN aired an edited version.

The Hunting Ground is an exposé of sexual assaults on college and university campuses in the United States. The film follows the stories of sexual assault survivors who attempt to get justice from their universities but are faced with institutional cover-ups, unsympathetic administrators, and a campus climate that both blames and silences the victim. The documentary predominately features the activism of Andrea Pino and Annie Clark as they navigate the process of using Title IX to hold schools accountable for mishandling sexual assault cases.

Singer Lady Gaga produced and performed the original song "'Til It Happens to You" for the soundtrack of the documentary. Lady Gaga, who cowrote the song with Diane Warren, is a survivor of sexual violence. At the 88th Academy Awards, Vice President Joe Biden introduced Lady Gaga after urging people to take the "It's on Us" pledge to intervene in potentially dangerous situations. Lady Gaga followed with a performance of the Oscar-nominated song and was joined on stage by 50 sexual assault survivors.

Critically acclaimed, *The Hunting Ground* is the recipient of multiple awards, including two Emmy nominations. It was screened at the White House in addition to nearly a thousand college and university campuses. Additionally, the documentary spurred important campus policy changes at various colleges and universities across the nation. However, the film is not without its critics. Some question the specific statistics utilized and the accounts of some of the survivors. For example, faculty at Harvard Law School published an open letter in attempts to discredit the account of Kamilah Willingham, who was profiled in the documentary, and the Florida State University president said the film had "major distortions" in its coverage of the Jameis Winston case. Kirby and Dirk released a companion book *The Hunting Ground: The Inside Story of Sexual Assault on American College Campuses* with their response to critics in addition to various essays written by experts.

By all accounts, *The Hunting Ground* is a powerful documentary that has had a significant impact on raising national awareness about campus sexual assault. The documentary has spurred policy changes, prompted government response, and inspired campus activism. While smaller in scope, another important documentary on the issue of campus sexual assault was released around the same time. *It Happened Here* (2014) focuses on the experiences of five survivors of campus sexual assault and illustrates the problem of college and university administrators mishandling sexual assault cases. Together, both films provide an opportunity for survivors of campus sexual assault to have their voices heard.

Know Your IX

During her freshman year at Yale University, Alexandra Brodsky reported her experience of attempted rape and subsequent harassment by an assailant to the school's Sexual Harassment Grievance Board. The board allegedly informed Brodsky that they would tell the harasser to leave her alone and advised her to keep quiet to protect her reputation. In 2011, Brodsky joined 15 other students in filing a Title IX complaint against Yale for mishandling cases of sexual harassment and sexual assault. After the Office of Civil Rights (OCR) conducted their investigation, Yale agreed to a settlement that included strengthening their antiviolence programming, taking additional steps against sexual violence, and continued monitoring. The OCR investigation did not find the school to be in compliance with Title IX; however, it did not determine that Yale was in noncompliance of Title IX either. Brodsky felt as though the school was let off too easily.

In 2011, Amherst College sophomore Dana Bolger was raped by a fellow student. After she reported the assault and the continuous harassment and stalking by her assailant, a dean allegedly urged her to take time off and "get a job at Starbucks or Barnes and Noble, and come back after he's graduated." She took a semester off, and when she returned she joined a survivor's group on campus. In that group she heard from other students who had similar experiences receiving unsympathetic and inept responses from administration. In response, Bolger created a website about sexual violence at Amherst called It Happens Here. The website featured photos of Amherst campus sexual assault survivors holding signs with the insensitive comments they received from peers and administrators.

At the time of their complaints, Brodsky and Bolder both knew that they were not being treated well by their schools. However, they did not know they had the legal right to demand better. The two eventually met through a mutual friend and decided that students needed to be better informed of their rights. What started as a social media campaign, motivated by the accounts of many survivors, including Angie Epifano's, they cofounded the national nonprofit Know Your IX in 2013. Know Your IX is a survivor-led organization that informs students of their rights under Title IX, provides guidance on campus activism, and advocates for policy change at the campus, state, and federal levels to end gender violence.

Know Your IX organized the ED Act Now campaign with the purpose of demanding the Department of Education to be tougher on schools found noncompliant of Title IX and to conduct more timely and transparent investigations. In July 2013 student activists delivered a petition that outlined their demands and had over 100,000 signatures to the Department of Education's office in Washington, D.C. After their protest, they were granted the first of many meetings with top officials. Following the early meetings, the Department of

Education made notable changes, including increasing transparency by releasing a list of colleges and universities under Title IX investigations. The Department of Education also agreed to swifter investigations and found six schools in violation of Title IX in 2014.

Know Your IX continues to thrive as an important resource for students. Brodsky is a recent graduate of Yale Law School, is an editor at feministing.com, and serves as board chair for the Know Your IX organization. Bolger is a student at Yale Law School, is a senior editor at feministing.com, and serves as the policy and advocacy coordinator for Know Your IX. Both women have written extensively on the topic of campus sexual assault, granted numerous interviews for major news outlets, and have testified in front of Congress on the issue of campus sexual assault.

Katie Koestner

On June 3, 1991, Katie Koestner was on the cover of *Time* magazine. At that moment in history, rape was understood to be something that strangers forcibly did to victims, and there was little awareness of, or discussion about, rape perpetrated by acquaintances. Koestner changed this, and made the reality of "date rape" take root.

During her first week of her freshman year at the College of William and Mary, Koestner was raped in her dorm room after going out to dinner with a man she had recently met. She went to the health center the next day and was sent home with sleeping pills. She attempted to report the incident to her dean, and he asked her to reconsider what she was saying. Koestner failed to get support from her father as well, who said it would not have happened had she not let the perpetrator into her room. She reported the incident to the campus police, where she was peppered with questions about sex and what she was wearing. The district attorney ultimately felt there was very little chance of winning a case, as at the time for a forcible rape conviction she would have had to prove she had fought him off. Instead, Koestner chose to go through the university disciplinary system, and her case was the first sexual misconduct hearing at a university or college.

In the hearing, Koestner's rapist admitted that she had said "no" more than a dozen times. The school found him responsible and banned him from going into any dorm room other than his own for the remainder of the semester. The dean also made a recommendation to Koestner that she "get back together in the spring semester . . . because he really likes you a lot and you make a nice couple." The insubstantial punishment and administrative callousness angered Koestner, and she sent a letter to her local newspaper, which was quickly picked up by media outlets across the nation. As a result, Koestner was asked to do many interviews, HBO made a movie based on her experience, and she made the infamous cover of *Time* magazine.

The media firestorm gave Koestner the platform to explain that rape can be perpetrated by an acquaintance. Her bravery paved the path for public recognition of the existence and seriousness of date rape. Still an activist to this day, Koestner is a public speaker and the executive director of the Take Back the Night Foundation.

Mary P. Koss

In the early 1980s, rape was still largely understood to be a crime perpetrated by strangers, and very little was known about sexual assault on college campuses. The groundbreaking research of clinical psychologist Mary P. Koss altered the conventional wisdom of the time and brought the issue of date rape to light.

The Ms. Foundation for Research and Education partnered with Koss to conduct a three-year study on sexual assault on college campuses. The study was federally funded through a competitive grant and surveyed more than 7,000 students at 35 schools. At the time, existing research on sexual assault was often based on incidences reported to law enforcement (e.g., the FBI's Uniform Crime Statistics). Additionally, existing research often asked respondents whether they had experienced "rape" or "sexual assault." Koss recognized that these methods were problematic, that existing research failed to account for victims of sexual assault who chose not to report and for victims who did not recognize or acknowledge they had been raped. To address these shortcomings, the survey Koss and her colleagues developed used graphic language to describe rape and other forms of sexual assault without using the actual word *rape*.

In 1985, *Ms.* magazine published an article "Date Rape: The Story of an Epidemic and Those Who Deny It," highlighting some of the early findings of Koss's study. Shortly thereafter in 1987, Koss and her colleagues from Kent State, Christine Gidycz and Nadine Wisniewsk, published their research findings in *The Journal of Consulting and Clinical Psychology*. The research was groundbreaking for numerous reasons. It was the first national study of rape and the first to look extensively at sexual assault on college campuses. Additionally, the measure they developed, the Sexual Experiences Survey, has since become a frequently used tool to study unwanted sexual encounters. Most importantly, their findings were eye opening, introducing readers to both the existence and prevalence of date rape. Koss found that one in four women in college have experienced rape or attempted rape since the age of 14 and that most sexual assaults are perpetrated by acquaintances. This research continues to be widely cited, and the findings have been replicated.

Currently a professor in the Mel and Enid Zuckerman College of Public Health at the University of Arizona, specializing in sexual violence, Koss has authored 2 books and over 175 articles on sexual assault. She is credited with coining the term *hidden rape* to refer to those who have been assaulted but do not report the crime to authorities and *unacknowledged rape* to refer to those who have experienced the legal definition of rape but fail to recognize it as such. She has testified before the U.S. Senate, participated in congressional briefings, and served on expert panels, including a think tank to create a comprehensive approach to sexual violence prevention as part of the White House's Not Alone initiative. At the University of Arizona, Koss has implemented a restorative justice program for those found responsible for campus sexual misconduct. Restorative justice includes therapeutic approaches and allows victims to confront their assailants. Those found responsible for misconduct are often assigned counseling and/or community service as punishment. In sum, Koss's groundbreaking research is invaluable to our understanding of campus sexual assault.

Emma Sulkowicz

On the first day of her sophomore year at Columbia University, Emma Sulkowicz says, she was raped by a classmate in her dorm room. The alleged perpetrator, who maintained that the sex was consensual and later came forward as Paul Nungesser, was brought to a university hearing seven months after the incident occurred. Sulkowicz maintains the university mishandled the case, citing, for example, that she had to draw a diagram because the administrators were unclear as to how anal rape could occur. Nungesser was found not responsible by the panel and remained on campus. Two other women also came forward alleging they were sexually assaulted by Nungesser and believe Columbia mishandled their cases.

In anger and frustration, Sulkowicz, who was a visual arts major, based her senior thesis on her assault in a protest piece titled "Carry That Weight." Starting in September 2014, Sulkowicz carried an extra-long twin-sized dorm mattress around with her on campus as a symbol of her burden as a victim and vowed to put the mattress down only if the alleged perpetrator was expelled, left the university, or graduated. One of the rules of her performance was that she could not ask for help carrying the mattress, but that if others offered to help she could accept. Her protest gained national and international attention, spurring a national day of action on October 29, 2014, in which students at 130 universities and colleges carried mattresses in solidarity with survivors and in order to raise awareness about the need to reform campus sexual assault policies. On that day, a group of Columbia students, armed with a list of demands, put 28 mattresses outside the university president's home. The mattresses symbolized the 28 students, Sulkowicz included, who filed a Title IX complaint against the school for mishandling sexual assault cases.

Sulkowicz's haunting protest piece brought the private into the public and drew attention to the reality that most sexual assaults are committed by acquaintances. She has won awards for her activism and was invited to attend the State of the Union address as a guest of Senator Kristin Gillibrand. Sulkowicz has become a symbol of bravery and an inspiration to activists and sexual assault survivors. She ultimately carried that mattress with her on stage to receive her diploma upon graduation, and the university president turned away as she walked by.

Womyn of Antioch College

In 1990, students at Antioch College met to discuss two reported rapes on campus. In one incident, the perpetrator was removed from campus but remained enrolled; in the other, the perpetrator was not removed from campus. Angry that the administration failed, in their view, to adequately punish the perpetrators, the students formulated a list of demands. The group called themselves the Womyn of Antioch and requested a host of changes, including the formation of a permanent support group for survivors, an orientation program that included rape education, and immediate campus-wide notification if a sexual assault occurred.

Numerous additional meetings were held to discuss the inadequate campus administrative response to rape and to strategize how to get a sexual offense policy on the college's official agenda. A group of over 30 women, dressed in black with symbolic rape whistles around their necks, stood in the back of the room during a meeting of the Advisory Committee to the President. This action was successful, and the issue of campus sexual assault was put on the official agenda. The group also staged an awareness protest at a weekly campus community meeting—every six minutes a woman was slapped on the back with a sign that said "Raped" to symbolize the common occurrence of rape in the United States.

Ultimately, a group of 15 students crafted the Antioch Sexual Offense Policy, many sacrificing their grades and even timely graduation to develop the document. The policy outlined forms of sexual offense, used non-gender-specific language, included the need for antirape education and counseling services, and provided guidance on disciplinary measures. The policy also required that all sexual contact be consensual and stated that verbal consent was needed at each progressive level of sexual contact. It read, in part:

> The person(s) who initiate(s) the sexual activity is responsible for asking for consent.
>
> The person(s) who are asked are responsible for verbally responding.
>
> Each new level of sexual activity requires consent.

After some revisions from the original list of demands, the final version of the Antioch Sexual Offense Policy was passed by the Advisory Committee to the President and approved by the University Board of Directors in June 1992. In 1993, the media picked up on the policy, specifically the affirmative consent clause, and the small community of Antioch College received a great deal of national and international attention. Many universities contacted Antioch for a copy, but in general the policy was mocked for being an example of political correctness run amok. A policy that was easy to parody, it was even the premise of a *Saturday Night Live* skit called "Is It Date Rape?"

While Antioch's policy was widely ridiculed at the time, it turned out to be prophetic. Over 20 years later, affirmative consent policies, different only in that they allow nonverbal consent cues as well, have been adopted by California and New

York, in addition to many colleges and universities across the nation. The Womyn of Antioch, now in their forties, are finally able to see their ideas prevail on a larger scale.

References

Bogdanich, W. (2014, April 16). A Star Player Accused and a Flawed Rape Investigation. *The New York Times*. Retrieved October 16, 2016, from: http://www.nytimes.com/interactive/2014/04/16/sports/errors-in-inquiry-on-rape-allegations-against-fsu-jameis-winston.html?_r=0

Burleigh, N. (2014, June 4). Confronting Campus Rape. *Rolling Stone Magazine*. Retrieved October 16, 2016, from: http://www.rollingstone.com/politics/news/confronting-campus-rape-20140604.

CampusClarity. (2013, October 18). One in Five Women in College Sexually Assaulted: Source of Statistic. *CampusClarity*. Retrieved October 16, 2016, from: https://home.campusclarity.com/one-in-five-women-in-college-sexually-assaulted/.

Center for Changing Campus Culture. (n.d.). Online Resource Center Supported by the Office of Violence against Women. Retrieved October 16, 2016, from: http://www.changingourcampus.org/

Chang, J., N. Capote, A. Louszko, and L. Effron. (2015, April 22). "Missoula" Shines Spotlight on Campus Rape, Women Share How Their Allegations Changed Them Forever. *ABC News*. Retrieved October 16, 2016, from: http://abcnews.go.com/US/missoula-shines-spotlight-campus-rape-women-share-allegations/story?id=30505851

Chappell, B. (2012, June 21). Penn State Abuse Scandal: A Guide and Timeline. *National Public Radio*. Retrieved October 16, 2016, from: http://www.npr.org/2011/11/08/142111804/penn-state-abuse-scandal-a-guide-and-timeline

Clark, A., and A. Pino (eds.). (2016). *We Believe You: Survivors of Campus Sexual Assault Speak Out*. New York: Henry Holt.

Clery Center For Security On Campus. (n.d.). Retrieved October 16, 2016, from: http://clerycenter.org/

Coronel, S., S. Coll, and D. Kravitz. (2015, April 5). Rolling Stone and UVA: The Columbia University Graduate School of Journalism Report. *Rolling Stone Magazine*. Retrieved October 16, 2016, from: http://www.rollingstone.com/culture/features/a-rape-on-campus-what-went-wrong-20150405

Dick, K., and A. Ziering. (2016). *The Hunting Ground: The Inside Story of Sexual Assault on American College Campuses*. New York: Hot Books.

Eilperin, J. (2016, July 3). Biden and Obama Rewrite the Rulebook on College Sexual Assaults. *States News Service*. Retrieved October 16, 2016, from: http://www.highbeam.com/doc/1G1–457641148.html?refid=easy_hf

Eisenstadter, D. (2015, February 12). Former Amherst College Student Angie Epifano Speaks Out in Documentary about College Rape. *Daily Hampshire Gazette*. Retrieved October 16, 2016, from: http://www.gazettenet.com/Archives/2015/02/Epifanodoc-hg-021215

End Rape On Campus. (n.d). Retrieved October 16, 2016, from: http://endrapeoncampus.org/

Epifano, A. (2012, October 17). An Account of Sexual Assault at Amherst College. *The Amherst Student*. Retrieved October 16, 2016, from: http://amherststudent.amherst.edu/?q=article/2012/10/17/account-sexual-assault-amherst-college

Gold, J., and S. Villari (eds.). (2000). *Just Sex: Students Rewrite the Rules on Sex, Violence, Activism, and Equality*. Lanham, MD: Rowman & Littlefield.

The Good Men Project. (2012, November 5). Lead a Good Life Everyone: Trey Malone's Suicide Note. The Good

Men Project. Retrieved October 16, 2016, from: https://
goodmenproject.com/ethics-values/lead-a-good-life-
everyone-trey-malones-suicide-note/

Grasgreen, A. (2013, October 18). "Blueprint" Balancing
Act. *Inside Higher Education*. Retrieved October 16, 2016,
from: https://www.insidehighered.com/news/2013/10/18/
montana-adjusts-life-blueprint-sexual-assault-response

Herman, K. (2000)."Demands from the Women of Antioch,"
in Gold, J., and S. Villari (eds.), *Just Sex: Students Rewrite
the Rules on Sex, Violence, Activism, and Equality*. Lanham,
MD: Rowman & Littlefield.

The Hunting Ground. (2015). [Motion Picture, Chain Camera
Pictures]. Retrieved October 16, 2016, from: http://
thehuntinggroundfilm.com/

It Happened Here. (2014). [Motion Picture, Neponsit
Pictures]. Retrieved October 16, 2016, from: http://www.
ithappenedhere.org/

Johnson, R. (2014, October 9). Campus Sexual Assault:
Annie E. Clark and Andrea Pino Are Fighting Back—And
Shaping the National Debate. *Vogue Magazine*. Retrieved
October 16, 2016, from: http://www.vogue.com/2210627/
college-sexual-assault-harassment-annie-e-clark-andrea-pino/

Jones, K. (2010, February 25). Sexual Assault on Campus:
Laura Dunn Interview, Part One. The Center for Public
Integrity. Retrieved October 16, 2016, from: https://www
.publicintegrity.org/2010/02/25/4375/sexual-assault-
campus-laura-dunn-interview-part-one-0

Jones, K. (2010, February 25). Sexual Assault on Campus:
Laura Dunn Interview, Part Two. The Center for Public
Integrity. Retrieved October 16, 2016, from: https://www
.publicintegrity.org/2010/02/25/4376/sexual-assault-
campus-laura-dunn-interview-part-two-0

Kingkade, T. (2015, May 6). Ending Campus Rape Won't
Be Easy, But These Activists Aren't Going Anywhere. *The*

Huffington Post. Retrieved October 16, 2016, from: http://
www.huffingtonpost.com/2015/05/06/campus-rape-
activists_n_7165478.html

Know Your IX: Empowering Students to Stop Sexual
Violence. (n.d.). Retrieved October 16, 2016, from: http://
knowyourix.org/

Koestner K. (2016, June 2). How I Convinced the World
You Can Be Raped by Your Date. BBC News. Retrieved
October 16, 2016, from: http://www.bbc.com/news/
magazine-36434191

Koss, M.P., C.A. Gidycz, and N. Wisniewski. (1987).
The Scope of Rape: Incidence and Prevalence of Sexual
Aggression and Victimization in a National Sample
of Higher Education Students. *Journal of Consulting
and Clinical Psychology 55*, 2: 162–170. doi:10.103
7/0022–006x.55.2.162.

Krakauer J. (2015). *Missoula: Rape and the Justice System in a
College Town.* New York: Doubleday.

Krakauer, J. (2016, January 21). How Much Should a
University Have to Reveal about a Sexual-Assault Case? *The
New York Times.* Retrieved October 16, 2016, from: http://
www.nytimes.com/2016/01/20/magazine/how-much-
should-a-university-have-to-reveal-about-a-sexual-assault-
case.html?_r=0

Kushner, D. (2013, November 13). Anonymous vs. Steubenville.
Rolling Stone Magazine. Retrieved October 16, 2016, from:
http://www.rollingstone.com/culture/news/anonymous-vs-
steubenville-20131127?page=4

Lederman, D. (2007, December 6). Settlement in Sexual
Assault Case. *Inside Higher Ed.* Retrieved October 16,
2016, from: https://www.insidehighered.com/news/2007/
12/06/settle

Lisak, D., L. Gardinier, S.C. Nicksa, and A.M. Cote. (2010).
False Allegations of Sexual Assault: An Analysis of Ten

Years of Reported Cases. *Violence against Women 16*, 12: 1318–1334. doi:10.1177/1077801210387747.

Macur, J. (2013, November 26). In Steubenville Rape Case, a Lesson for Adults. *The New York Times*. Retrieved October 16, 2016, from: http://www.nytimes.com/2013/11/27/sports/ in-steubenville-rape-case-a-lesson-for-adults.html

Macur, J., and N. Schweber. (2012, December 16). Rape Case Unfolds on Web and Splits City. *The New York Times*. Retrieved October 16, 2016, from: http://www.nytimes .com/2012/12/17/sports/high-school-football-rape- case-unfolds-online-and-divides-steubenville-ohio .html?_r=0

Namako, T. (2016, June 9). Joe Biden Writes an Open Letter to Stanford Survivor. *BuzzFeed*. Retrieved October 16, 2016, from: https://www.buzzfeed.com/tomnamako/ joe-biden-writes-an-open-letter-to-stanford-survivor?utm_ term=.ai1oO6Wob#.lr12WGl26

Nathanson, R. (2014, December 1). How "Carry That Weight" Is Changing the Conversation on Campus Sexual Assault. *Rolling Stone Magazine*. Retrieved October 16, 2016, from: http://www.rollingstone.com/politics/news/ how-carry-that-weight-is-changing-the-conversation-on- campus-sexual-assault-20141201

Payne, M. (2015, February 19). Erica Kinsman, Who Accused Jameis Winston of Rape, Tells Her Story in New Documentary "The Hunting Ground." *The Washington Post*. Retrieved October 16, 2016, from: https://www .washingtonpost.com/news/early-lead/wp/2015/02/19/ erica-kinsman-who-accused-jameis-winston-of-rape-tells- her-story-in-new-documentary-the-hunting-ground

Peterson, M. (2011, April 5). Murder at Lehigh University Shocked the Nation 25 Years Ago. *Emmaus, PA Patch*. Retrieved October 16, 2016, from: http://patch.com/ pennsylvania/emmaus/murder-at-lehigh-university-shocked- the-nation-25-years-ago

Rios, E., and M. Pauly. (2016, March 3). This Explosive Lawsuit Could Change How Colleges Deal with Athletes Accused of Sexual Assault. *Mother Jones*. Retrieved October 16, 2016, from: http://www.motherjones.com/politics/2016/03/sexual-assault-case-against-university-tennessee-explained

Saltman, B. (2014, October 22). We Started the Crusade for Affirmative Consent Way Back in the '90s. *New York Magazine*. Retrieved October 16, 2016, from: http://nymag.com/thecut/2014/10/we-fought-for-affirmative-consent-in-the-90s.html?mid=twitter_nymag

Sander, L. (2007, December 6). U. of Colorado at Boulder Settles Lawsuit over Alleged Rapes at Football Recruiting Party for $2.85 Million. *TitleIX Info*. Retrieved October 16, 2016, from: http://www.titleix.info/Resources/Legal-Cases/Colorado-Lawsuit-Alleged-Rape-Football-Recruiting-Party.aspx

Seccuro, L. (2011). *Crash into Me: A Survivor's Search for Justice*. New York: Bloomsbury.

Shapiro, J. (2010, February 24). Campus Rape Victims: A Struggle for Justice. National Public Radio. Retrieved October 16, 2016, from: http://www.npr.org/templates/story/story.php?storyId=124001493

Shapiro, T.R. (2014, December 5). Key Elements of Rolling Stone's U-Va. Gang Rape Allegations in Doubt. *The Washington Post*. Retrieved October 16, 2016, from: https://www.washingtonpost.com/local/education/u-va-fraternity-to-rebut-claims-of-gang-rape-in-rolling-stone/2014/12/05/5fa5f7d2-7c91-11e4-84d4-7c896b90abdc_story.html

Stack, L. (2016, June 6). Light Sentence for Brock Turner in Stanford Rape Case Draws Outrage. *The New York Times*. Retrieved October 16, 2016, from: http://www.nytimes.com/2016/06/07/us/outrage-in-stanford-rape-case-over-dueling-statements-of-victim-and-attackers-father.html

SurvJustice. (n.d.). Retrieved October 16, 2016, from: http://survjustice.org

Sweet, E. (2012, February 23). Date Rape Revisited. Women's Media Center. Retrieved October 16, 2016, from: http://www.womensmediacenter.com/feature/entry/date-rape-revisited

von Hoffmann, Emily. (2016, June 8). Stanford Rape Case Stands Out from Most Sexual Assaults. InsideGov. Retrieved October 16, 2016, from: http://political-issues.insidegov.com/stories/14275/sexual-assault-numbers-united-states-brock-turner-rape

The White House. (2011). About Vice President Biden's Efforts to End Violence against Women. 1 is 2 Many. Retrieved October 16, 2016, from: https://www.whitehouse.gov/1is2many/about

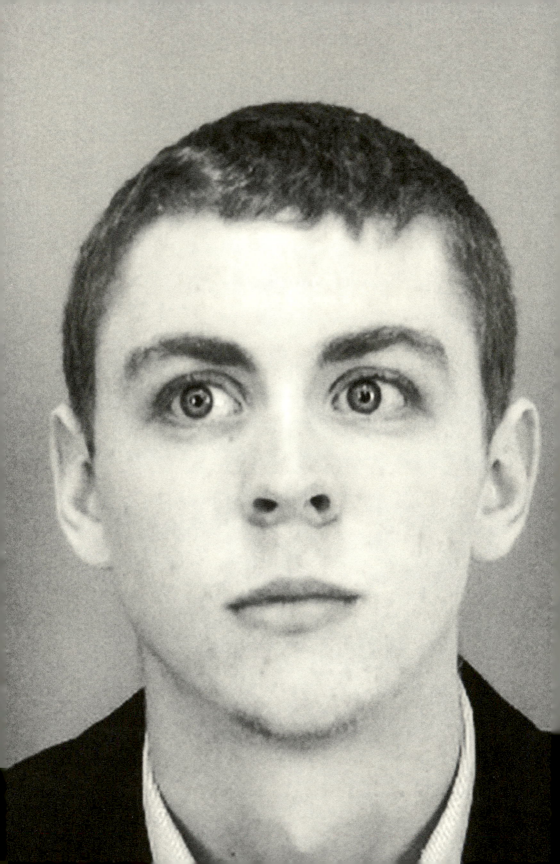

5   Data and Documents

Introduction

This chapter provides some of the key findings on prevalence, reporting, and disciplinary action from some of the most highly cited studies on campus sexual assault, including the National College Women Sexual Victimization Study (2000), Campus Sexual Assault Survey (2007), Campus Climate Survey on Sexual Assault and Sexual Misconduct administered by the American Association of Universities (2015), the Washington Post–Kaiser Family Foundation Poll (2015), the National Institute of Justice Campus Climate Survey (2016), and a recent list of colleges and universities under investigation for possible Title IX violations for their handling of sexual assault cases (2016). Additionally, this chapter includes some pertinent language from a variety of key documents and pieces of legislation. Items include Title IX (1972), the Jeanne Clery Disclosure of Campus Security Policy and Campus Crime Statistics Act (Clery Act) (1990), expansions to the Clery Act, the Dear Colleague letter sent from the Office for Civil Rights, a sub-agency of the U.S. Department of Education (2011), the executive summary of The First Report of the White House Task Force to Protect Students from Sexual Assault (2014), a list of Title IX rights for survivors of campus sexual assault, and

---

Brock Turner, a former Stanford University swimmer who received a sentence of six months in jail for sexually assaulting an unconscious woman. The sentence drew widespread outrage for its leniency, and the case became a focal point for a national conversation about campus sexual assault. (Santa Clara County Sheriff via AP Photo)

a portion of a powerful victim impact letter written by a survivor of sexual assault at Stanford (2016). Taken as a whole, these documents comprise the governmental response and legislative foundation to addressing sexual assault on college campuses.

Data

What follows is a sample of key findings from recent research on campus sexual assault. Statistics on sexual assault are not only difficult to obtain, but there are numerous variables that can impact the findings. It is noteworthy that the data on prevalence discussed in this chapter is based on research in which students are asked to disclose their experiences, as opposed to data on assault cases reported to law enforcement or campus personnel (e.g., FBI Uniform Crime Statistics, campus crime statistics) as most survivors of sexual assault do not report their attack to authorities. Additionally, the National Crime Victimization Surveys have been criticized by many, including the National Academies of Sciences, for failing to employ best practices. Thus the results of these surveys are not discussed in this chapter, but are covered earlier in the book.

One in Five Women Experience Sexual Assault while in College

The definition of sexual assault typically includes a range of behaviors, from unwanted sexual touching to rape. The *one in five* statistic is gleaned from various research reports that have similar findings. For example, the National College Women Sexual Victimization Study (2000) estimated that the percentage of completed or attempted rape victimization among women in higher educational institutions may be between 20 percent and 25 percent over the course of a college career. The results of the Campus Sexual Assault (CSA) Survey (2007) were used as the basis of the one in five statistic put forth by the Obama administration in their White House initiative to combat campus sexual assault. The CSA survey found that

19 percent of college women experienced attempted or completed sexual assault. In 2015, the Association of American Universities released the results of their study on college sexual assault and misconduct. Notable for its scope, the survey was administered at 27 universities and had over 150,000 student responses. Their report found that 23 percent of female undergraduates reported they were victims on nonconsensual sexual contact. The Washington Post-Kaiser Poll on Campus Sexual Assault (2015) found that 20 percent of women who attended college over the past four years experienced sexual assault. Additionally, based on data from 23,000 students in 9 schools, the National Institute of Justice's Campus Climate Survey (2016) found the average sexual assault prevalence rate for women since entering college was 21 percent; the prevalence rate for fourth-year female undergraduates was 25 percent (or one in four). This study also illustrated how the prevalence of sexual violence varies depending on the school, with the rate ranging from an alarming one in two at some schools to one in eight in others.

Sources

Association of American Universities. (2015). *Campus Climate Survey on Sexual Assault and Sexual Misconduct*. Retrieved May 20, 2016, from: https://www.aau.edu/Climate-Survey.aspx?id=16525

Fisher, Bonnie S., Cullen, Francis T., and Turner, Michael G. (2000). The Sexual Victimization of College Women Research Report. National Institute of Justice, Bureau of Justice Statistics. Retrieved May 20, 2016, from: https://www.ncjrs.gov/pdffiles1/nij/182369.pdf

Krebs, Christopher P., Lindquist, Christine H., Warner, Tara D., Fisher, Bonnie S., Martin, Sandra L. (2007). *The Campus Sexual Assault Study*. Justice Department's National Institute of Justice. Retrieved May 20, 2016, from: https://www.ncjrs.gov/pdffiles1/nij/grants/221153.pdf

Krebs, Christopher, Lindquist, Christine, Berzofsky, Marcus, Shook-Sa, Bonnie, Peterson, Kimberly. (2016). Campus Climate Survey Validation Study. Final Technical Report. National Institute of Justice, Bureau of Justice Statistics. Retrieved May 20, 2016, from: http://www.bjs.gov/content/pub/pdf/ccsvsftr.pdf

Washington Post–Kaiser Family Foundation Poll. (2015). *Survey on Current and Recent College Students on Sexual Assault*. Retrieved May 20, 2016, from: http://kff.org/other/poll-finding/survey-of-current-and-recent-college-students-on-sexual-assault/

One in 20 Men Experience Sexual Assault while in College

The numbers on male survivors of sexual assault are more variable than the statistics on female survivors, perhaps due to the taboo nature surrounding male victimization in our culture. The finding that 1 in 20 men (or 5%) experience sexual assault while in college is based on the Association of American Universities' Campus Climate Survey on Sexual Assault and Sexual Misconduct (2015) and the Washington Post-Kaiser Poll (2015). The Campus Sexual Assault Survey (2007) found 1 in 16 men (6.1%) experienced completed or attempted sexual assault since entering college. The Campus Climate Survey (2016) found that among undergraduate males, the average prevalence rate for sexual assault since entering college was 7 percent. It is worth noting that male survivors are not only likely to have fewer resources available to them but also face additional hurdles in reporting their assaults.

Sources

Association of American Universities. (2015). *Campus Climate Survey on Sexual Assault and Sexual Misconduct*. Retrieved May 20, 2016, from: https://www.aau.edu/Climate-Survey.aspx?id=16525

Krebs, Christopher, Lindquist, Christine, Berzofsky, Marcus, Shook-Sa, Bonnie, and Peterson, Kimberly. (2016). Campus Climate Survey Validation Study. Final Technical Report. National Institute of Justice, Bureau of Justice Statistics. Retrieved May 20, 2016, from: http://www.bjs .gov/content/pub/pdf/ccsvsftr.pdf

Krebs, Christopher P., Lindquist, Christine H., Warner, Tara D., Fisher, Bonnie S., and Martin, Sandra L. (2007). *The Campus Sexual Assault Study.* Justice Department's National Institute of Justice. Retrieved May 20, 2016, from: https:// www.ncjrs.gov/pdffiles1/nij/grants/221153.pdf

Washington Post–Kaiser Family Foundation Poll. (2015). *Survey on Current and Recent College Students on Sexual Assault.* Retrieved May 20, 2016, from: http://kff.org/ other/poll-finding/survey-of-current-and-recent-college-students-on-sexual-assault/

Most Female Victims of College Sexual Assault Knew Their Assailant

A commonly held myth about sexual assault is that the assailants are generally strangers to the victim. This is not the reality for perpetrators of rape in general or for perpetrators of campus sexual assault specifically. The Sexual Victimization of College Women Report (2000) found that nine out of ten survivors of college sexual assault knew their assailant, most often a boyfriend, an ex-boyfriend, a classmate, a friend, or an acquaintance or coworker. Similar findings attest to the fact that most perpetrators are not unknown to the victim, including the Campus Sexual Assault Study (2007), which found that 23 percent of victims of physically forced sexual assault and 12 percent of victims of incapacitated assault did not know their assailant. The Washington Post-Kaiser Poll (2015) found that 28 percent of women who experienced campus sexual assault did not know their perpetrator.

In general, the vast majority of sexual assault perpetrators are male: 98 percent of female victims and 93 percent of male victims indicate a male assailant (Black et al. 2011). Despite the common assumption that perpetrators of campus sexual assault make one-time regrettable decisions, research indicates that most campus sexual assaults are being carried out by a minority of male students. Clinical psychologist David Lisak found that serial rapists account for 90 percent of campus assaults, with the average of six rapes each (2002).

Sources

Black, M.C., Basile, K.C., Breiding, M.J., Smith, S.G., Walters, M.L., Merrick, M.T., Chen, J., and Stevens, M.R. (2011). The National Intimate Partner and Sexual Violence Survey (NISVS): 2010 Summary Report. Atlanta, GA: National Center for Injury Prevention and Control, Centers for Disease Control and Prevention.

Fisher, Bonnie S., Cullen, Francis T., and Turner, Michael G. (2000). *The Sexual Victimization of College Women Research Report*. National Institute of Justice. Bureau of Justice Statistics. Retrieved May 20, 2016, from: https://www.ncjrs.gov/pdffiles1/nij/182369.pdf

Krebs, Christopher P., Lindquist, Christine H., Warner, Tara D., Fisher, Bonnie S., and Martin, Sandra L. (2007). *The Campus Sexual Assault Study*. Justice Department's National Institute of Justice. Retrieved May 20, 2016, from: https://www.ncjrs.gov/pdffiles1/nij/grants/221153.pdf

Lisak, David, and Miller, Paul M. (2002). Repeat Rape & Multiple Offending among Undetected Rapists. *Violence & Victims, 17*(1): 73–84. http://www.davidlisak.com/wp-content/uploads/pdf/RepeatRapeinUndetectedRapists.pdf

Reporting of Campus Sexual Assault

While most survivors of campus sexual assault disclose to friends, and sometimes family, few report their experiences to campus officials or law enforcement. The Sexual Victimization of College Women Research Report indicates that less than 5 percent of completed or attempted rapes against college women were reported to law enforcement (2000). The National Institute of Justice's Campus Climate Survey (2016) found that female victims reported only 12.5 percent of rapes and 4.3 percent of sexual battery incidents to any official (university administrator, law enforcement, or crisis center). Both the Washington Post–Kaiser Poll (2015) and research by Kilpatrick et al. (2007) reported that among female campus sexual assault victims, 12 percent reported their attacks to police or university officials. As an illustration of common findings, Table 5.1 shows data from the Campus Sexual Assault survey (2007) on sexual assault reporting, organized by assault type (forced sexual assault or incapacitated sexual assault). Using the same data set, Table 5.2. shows the reasons stated for not reporting sexual assault to law enforcement.

Table 5.1 Reporting of Sexual Assault, by Assault Type

Reporting Variable	Forced Sexual Assault (n = 131) (%)	Incapacitated Sexual Assault (n = 526) (%)
Disclosed incident to family/friend	68.9	63.7
Contacted a victim's, crisis, or health care center	15.8	7.5
Reported incident to the police or campus security	12.9	2.1

This study defined *forced sexual assault* as "assaults occurring because of physical force, or threats of physical force." It defined *incapacitated sexual assault* as "any unwanted sexual contact occurring when a victim is unable to provide consent or stop what is happening because she is passed out, drugged, drunk, incapacitated, or asleep, regardless of whether the perpetrator was responsible for her substance use or whether substances were administered without her knowledge."

Percentages are weighted percentages.

Source: Krebs et al. (2007).

Table 5.2 Reasons for Not Reporting Sexual Assault to Law Enforcement

Reporting Variable	Forced Sexual Assault (n = 131) (%)	Incapacitated Sexual Assault (n = 526) (%)
Did not want anyone to know	41.7	28.6
Afraid of reprisal by the assailant	17.9	11.7
Did not think it was serious enough to report	55.6	66.5
Unclear that it was a crime or that harm was intended	38.6	35.9
Did not have proof that the incident happened	23.3	14.9
Did not know how to report it	14.1	7.4
Did not think the police would think it was serious enough	20.6	11.9
Fear of being treated poorly by police or other parts of the justice system	13.6	5.6
Did not think anything could be done to the assailant	24.0	7.5
Did not want anyone to know about alcohol or drug use	7.5	10.7
Did not remember/know what really happened	n/a	31.1
Victim thought she was partially/fully responsible	n/a	49.8
Other reason	16.9	15.2

This study defined *forced sexual assault* as "assaults occurring because of physical force, or threats of physical force." It defined *incapacitated sexual assault* as "any unwanted sexual contact occurring when a victim is unable to provide consent or stop what is happening because she is passed out, drugged, drunk, incapacitated, or asleep, regardless of whether the perpetrator was responsible for her substance use or whether substances were administered without her knowledge."

Percentages are weighted percentages.

Source: Krebs et al. (2007).

Sources

Fisher, Bonnie S., Cullen, Francis T., and Turner, Michael G. (2000). *The Sexual Victimization of College Women Research Report*. National Institute of Justice. Bureau of Justice Statistics. Retrieved May 20, 2016, from: https://www.ncjrs.gov/pdffiles1/nij/182369.pdf

Kilpatrick, Dean G., Resnick, Heidi S., Ruggiero, Kenneth J., Conoscenti, Lauren M., McCauley, Jenna. (2007). *Drug-facilitated, Incapacitated, and Forcible Rape: A National Study*. US Department of Justice. Retrieved May 20, 2016, from: https://www.ncjrs.gov/pdffiles1/nij/grants/219181.pdf

Krebs, Christopher P., Lindquist, Christine H., Warner, Tara D., Fisher, Bonnie S., Martin, Sandra L. (2007). *The Campus Sexual Assault Study*. Justice Department's National Institute of Justice. Retrieved May 20, 2016, from: https://www.ncjrs.gov/pdffiles1/nij/grants/221153.pdf

Krebs, Christopher, Lindquist, Christine, Berzofsky, Marcus, Shook-Sa, Bonnie, Peterson, Kimberly. (2016). *Campus Climate Survey Validation Study Final Technical Report*. National Institute of Justice, Bureau of Justice Statistics. Retrieved May 20, 2016, from: http://www.bjs.gov/content/pub/pdf/ccsvsftr.pdf

Washington Post–Kaiser Family Foundation Poll. (2015). *Survey on Current and Recent College Students on Sexual Assault*. Retrieved May 20, 2016, from: http://kff.org/other/poll-finding/survey-of-current-and-recent-college-students-on-sexual-assault/

School Sanctions for Sexual Assault

Many students on college campuses feel as though sexual assault is not taken seriously and that perpetrators of sexual assault are unlikely to face significant sanctions, or for that matter any punishments at all. Research indicates that most students found

Table 5.3   How Colleges Resolve Sexual Assault Cases

Punishment	Percentage
Expulsion	12
Suspension	28
Reprimands	13
Counseling orders	12
Community service, and other non-specified	4

Source: Anderson (2014).

responsible for sexual assault are allowed to stay in school. While there is no comprehensive national data on how schools punish sexual misconduct, the *Washington Post* obtained data through a Freedom of Information Act request from the U.S. Department of Justice's Office on Violence against Women, which shows the pattern of resolution in about 100 schools surveyed in 2012 and 2013. Table 5.3 illustrates how the 478 sanctions for sexual assault were meted out and notably how few students were expelled. The data also indicates that 237 sexual assault cases were dismissed for lack of evidence and 44 ended in acquittal. In 2014, the *Huffington Post* reviewed data from nearly three dozen colleges and universities and had similar findings. In less than one-third of the cases (30%), students found responsible for sexual assault were expelled. Students found responsible were suspended in 47 percent of the cases.

Sources

Anderson, Nick. (2014). Colleges Often Reluctant to Expel for Sexual Violence—with U. VA a Prime Example." *The Washington Post*. Retrieved May 20, 2016, from: http://apps.washingtonpost.com/g/page/local/how-colleges-resolve-sexual-assault-cases/1511/

Kingkade, Tyler. (2014). Fewer Than One-Third of Campus Sexual Assault Cases Result in Expulsion. *The Huffington Post*. Retrieved May 20, 2016, from: http://

www.huffingtonpost.com/2014/09/29/campus-sexual-assault_n_5888742.html

Lombardi, Kristen. (2010). A Lack of Consequences for Sexual Assault. The Center for Public Integrity. Retrieved May 20, 2016, from: https://www.publicintegrity .org/2010/02/24/4360/lack-consequences-sexual-assault

Colleges and Universities under Investigation by the Department of Education for Possible Title IX Violations for Mishandling Sexual Assault Cases

In May 2014, the Department of Education released a list of 55 colleges and universities under investigation for possible Title IX violations for mishandling sexual assault cases. The list of schools under investigation has grown considerably since. Thus far, there have been 367 Title IX investigations for the possible mishandling of sexual assault, of which 58 cases have been resolved and 309 remain open. The Chronicle of Higher Education operates a Title IX investigation tracker, and as of February, 2017, there were over 225 schools listed with active Title IX investigations for mishandling sexual assault cases (see Table 5.4).

Table 5.4   Colleges and Universities with Open Investigations for Possible Title IX Violations for Mishandling Sexual Assault Cases

Allegheny College

Alma College

American University

Amherst College

Arizona State University

Babson College

Bard College

Barnard College

Baylor University

Berklee College of Music

Bethany College (W.Va.)

Boston College

(continued)

Table 5.4   (*continued*)

Boston University

Brandeis University

Bringham Young University

Brown University

Buffalo State College

Butte College

California Institute of the Arts

California Polytechnic State University at San Luis Obispo

California State University at San Marcos

Canisius College

Carnegie Mellon University

Catholic University of America

Central Community College

Chadron State College

Cisco College

Clark University

Cleveland State University

College of Idaho

College of Saint Scholastica

College of William & Mary

College of Wooster (Ohio)

Colorado State University at Fort Collins

Columbia College Chicago

Columbia University

Cornell University

Corning Community College

Dartmouth College

Davis & Elkins College

Dawson Community College

Delaware State University

Denison University

Drake University

Duke University

Eastern Washington University

Edmonds Community College

Elizabethtown College

Emerson College

Emory University

Florida State University

Franklin & Marshall College

Full Sail University

Gannon University

George Mason University

Grace College and Seminary

Grand Valley State University

Grinnell College

Guilford College

Hamilton College (N.Y.)

Hampshire College

Hanover College

Harvard University

Harvey Mudd College

Hobart and William Smith Colleges

Idaho State University

Indiana University at Bloomington

Indiana University-Purdue University at Ft. Wayne

Iowa State University

Ithaca College

James Madison University

James Rumsey Technical Institute

John Carroll University

Johns Hopkins University

Judson University (Ill.)

Kansas State University

Kenyon College

Knox College

(*continued*)

Table 5.4   (*continued*)

La Sierra University

Langston University

Laramie County Community College

Lewis-Clark State College

Liberty University

Lincoln University (Pa.)

Louisiana State University system

Loyola Marymount University

Loyola University New Orleans

Marion Military Institute

Marlboro College

Marshall University

Massachusetts Institute of Technology

Medical College of Wisconsin

Methodist University

Miami University (Ohio)

Missouri University of Science and Technology

Monmouth College

Monmouth University

Monroe Community College

Morehouse College

Morgan State University

Mount St. Mary's University (Md.)

New York University

Northeastern University

Northwest College (Wy.)

Oberlin College

Oglethorpe University

Ohio State University

Oklahoma State University at Stillwater

Pace University

Paul Quinn College

Pennsylvania State University at University Park

Point Park University

Pomona College

Pratt Institute

Princeton University

Purdue University at West Lafayette

Regis College

Regis University

Rhodes College

Rider University

Rockefeller University

San Francisco State University

San Jose/Evergreen Community College District

Santa Clara University

Sarah Lawrence College

Seton Hall University

Skidmore College

Southern Illinois University at Carbondale

Southwest Tennessee Community College

Southwestern University (Tex.)

Spelman College

St. Cloud State University

St. John's University (N.Y.)

St. Mary's College of California

St. Mary's College of Maryland

St. Olaf College

St. Thomas Aquinas College

Stanford University

State University of New York College at Plattsburgh

State University of New York College at Potsdam

State University of New York College at Purchase

State University of New York at Stony Brook

State University of New York, The College at Brockport

Stetson University

(*continued*)

Table 5.4   (*continued*)

Stonehill College

Swarthmore College

Syracuse University

Temple University

Texas A&M University at College Station

Trinity University

Tufts University

Union College (N.Y.)

University at Albany, SUNY

University at Buffalo

University of Akron

University of Alabama at Birmingham

University of Alaska system

University of Arkansas at Fayetteville

University of California at Berkeley

University of California at Davis

University of California at Los Angeles

University of California at San Francisco

University of California at Santa Cruz

University of Chicago

University of Cincinnati

University of Colorado at Boulder

University of Colorado at Denver

University of Connecticut

University of Delaware

University of Denver

University of Florida

University of Hawaii-Manoa

University of Houston

University of Idaho

University of Illinois at Chicago

University of Illinois at Urbana-Champaign

University of Iowa

University of Kansas

University of Kentucky

University of Mary Washington

University of Maryland-Baltimore County

University of Maryland at College Park

University of Massachusetts at Amherst

University of Massachusetts at Dartmouth

University of Miami

University of Michigan at Ann Arbor

University of Nebraska at Kearney

University of Nebraska at Lincoln

University of North Carolina at Chapel Hill

University of North Texas

University of Notre Dame

University of Puerto Rico-Central Administration

University of Richmond

University of Rochester

University of San Diego

University of South Florida

University of Southern California

University of Southern Mississippi

University of Tennessee at Chattanooga

University of Tennessee at Knoxville

University of Texas Health Science Center at San Antonio

University of Texas-Pan American

University of Tulsa

University of Utah

University of Virginia

University of Washington

University of Wisconsin at Madison

University of Wisconsin at Whitewater

Valley Forge Military College

Valparaiso University

Vanderbilt University

Vincennes University

(continued)

Table 5.4   (*continued*)

Virginia Commonwealth University

Washburn University

Washington State University

Washington and Lee University

Wesley College (Del.)

West Virginia School of Osteopathic Medicine

Western New England University

Western Washington University

Westminster College (Utah)

Whitman College

Whitworth University

William Jewell College

Williston State College

Wittenberg University

Source: *The Chronicle of Higher Education.* Title IX: Tracking Sexual Assault Investigations. Retrieved February 23, 2017, from: http://projects.chronicle.com/titleix/#overview

Documents

Title IX (1972)

On June 23, 1972, President Nixon signed into law Title IX of the Education Amendments of 1972. This landmark federal law prohibits discrimination on the basis of sex in any federally funded education program or activity. If found in violation of Title IX, an elementary school, secondary school, college or university, or any federally funded education program or activity could lose federal funding. The impact of this law has been far reaching; it is credited for breaking down gender barriers in sports and for an overall reduction in gender discrimination in education. Sex discrimination includes sexual harassment and sexual assault. As discussed throughout this text, many survivors of college sexual assault have filed Title IX complaints against their colleges or universities for being in violation of the law.

In 2002, Title IX was renamed after the death of Patsy Mink, a former congresswoman and one of its primary authors and sponsors. The key language is below.

No person in the United States shall, on the basis of sex, be excluded from participation in, be denied the benefits of, or be subjected to discrimination under any education program or activity receiving Federal financial assistance.

Source: Title 20 U.S.C. Sections 1681–1688. *For the law in its entirety, including stated exceptions, visit* https://www.justice.gov/crt/title-ix-education-amendments-1972. *The implementing regulations for Title IX (34 CFR Part 106) can be found at* http://www2.ed.gov/policy/rights/reg/ocr/edlite-34cfr106.html.

The Clery Act (1990–2008)

Jeanne Clery was a college student who was raped and murdered in her dorm at Lehigh University in 1986. As there were numerous unpublicized violent crimes at Lehigh, her case drew national outrage about unreported crimes on college campuses. Passed in 1990, and renamed after Clery in 1998, the Jeanne Clery Disclosure of Campus Security Policy and Campus Crime Statistics Act requires schools that participate in federal financial aid programs to publicly disclose, on an annual basis, their campus security policies and crime statistics over the past three years. This includes forcible and non-forcible sex offenses and other crimes like arson, burglary, motor vehicle theft, aggravated assault, and robbery. The act requires schools to give timely warnings of crimes that represent a threat to the campus community. The act also imposes certain basic requirements on handling cases of sexual assault, stalking, and domestic and dating violence. Schools found in violation can be, and have been, fined by the U.S. Department of Education. Below is an excerpt of the act.

Each eligible institution participating in any program under this subchapter and part C of subchapter I of chapter 34 of title

42, other than a foreign institution of higher education, shall on August 1, 1991, begin to collect the following information with respect to campus crime statistics and campus security policies of that institution, and beginning September 1, 1992, and each year thereafter, prepare, publish, and distribute, through appropriate publications or mailings, to all current students and employees, and to any applicant for enrollment or employment upon request, an annual security report containing at least the following information with respect to the campus security policies and campus crime statistics of that institution:

(A) A statement of current campus policies regarding procedures and facilities for students and others to report criminal actions or other emergencies occurring on campus and policies concerning the institution's response to such reports.

(B) A statement of current policies concerning security and access to campus facilities, including campus residences, and security considerations used in the maintenance of campus facilities.

(C) A statement of current policies concerning campus law enforcement . . .

(D) A description of the type and frequency of programs designed to inform students and employees about campus security procedures and practices and to encourage students and employees to be responsible for their own security and the security of others.

(E) A description of programs designed to inform students and employees about the prevention of crimes.

(F) Statistics concerning the occurrence on campus, in or on noncampus buildings or property, and on public property during the most recent calendar year, and during the 2 preceding calendar years for which data are available—

   (i) of the following criminal offenses reported to campus security authorities or local police agencies:

(I)   murder;

(II)   sex offenses, forcible or nonforcible;

(III)   robbery;

(IV)   aggravated assault;

(V)   burglary;

(VI)   motor vehicle theft;

(VII)   manslaughter;

(VIII) arson;

(IX)   arrests or persons referred for campus disciplinary action for liquor law violations, drug-related violations, and weapons possession.

Source: Jeanne Clery Disclosure of Campus Security Policy and Campus Crime Statistics Act. 20 U.S.C. § 1092(f) (1990, amended in 1991, 1992, 1998, 2000, 2008). *Additional information about the Clery Act, including compliance resources and Clery Act statistics, can be found on the Jeanne Clery Act Information site: www.cleryact.info*

The Federal Campus Sexual Assault Victims Bill of Rights (1992)

The Clery Act has been amended and expanded upon numerous times. This includes the addition of the Federal Campus Sexual Assault Victims Bill of Rights (also referred to as the Ramstad Act) signed by President George H. W. Bush in 1992, which affords sexual assault victims certain basic rights, including their options to notify law enforcement and to be informed of counseling services. Congressman Jim Ramstad of Minnesota discussed the bill in the House in February 1992.

Mr. Speaker, last May I introduced H.R. 2363, the Campus Sexual Assault Victims' Bill of Rights Act. As of today, this measure has received the strong bipartisan support of 176 cosponsors.

This legislation is of vital importance to the thousands of women who are raped on our college and university campuses each year. Mr. Speaker, campus rape victims deserve to be informed of their legal rights. And whether the rape victim chooses to pursue the matter through campus proceedings or the court system, campus officials should provide them reasonable assistance in exercising their rights.

Mr. Speaker, knowing that one in four college women will be the victim of rape or attempted rape during her college career, Congress must take strong action to ensure victims their rights.

Last week, the Senate—without opposition—passed an amendment to the Higher Education Reauthorization Act which is based on the Campus Sexual Assault Victims' Bill of Rights Act.

Mr. Speaker, let us bring the higher education reauthorization bill to the floor as soon as possible so that we can join the Senate in taking this much needed action to protect campus sexual assault victims.

Source: *Congressional Record,* Vol. 138 (Pt. 3), Number 15. February 25, 1992. Washington, D.C.: Government Printing Office, 1992, 3336.

Dear Colleague Letter (2011)

In April 2011, the assistant secretary of civil rights to the U.S. Department of Education released a Dear Colleague letter to colleges, universities, and schools across the country. The primary intent of the letter was to reiterate that Title IX covers sexual violence. The letter served as a reminder to schools receiving federal funds that it was their responsibility to take immediate and effective steps to respond to sexual violence, and it was a signal that the Office for Civil Rights was cracking down on Title IX violations. The full 19-page message includes topics such as key Title IX requirements and obligations and proactive efforts the school can take to prevent sexual violence. While it did not create any new regulations per se, the letter elaborated on mandates that may have been unclear or misunderstood in the past. Many schools revisited their policies after the release of this letter, and some made significant changes to their policies and protocols. Additionally, as discussed earlier in this text, the letter's direction to schools to adapt a "preponderance of the evidence" standard is controversial, with some believing it fails to provide defendants adequate due process. Below is an excerpt from the letter.

Another related Dear Colleague letter was released by the assistant secretary of civil rights to the U.S. Department of Education in 2015 to remind school districts, colleges, and universities that receive federal funds that they must have a designated Title IX coordinator to ensure the school complies with the legal obligations outlined by Title IX. The letter can be found at http://www2 .ed.gov/about/offices/list/ocr/letters/colleague-201504-title-ix-coor dinators.pdf

April 4, 2011

Dear Colleague:

Education has long been recognized as the great equalizer in America. The U.S. Department of Education and its Office for Civil Rights (OCR) believe that providing all students with an educational environment free from discrimination is extremely important. The sexual harassment of students, including sexual violence, interferes with students' right to receive an education free from discrimination and, in the case of sexual violence, is a crime.

Title IX of the Education Amendments of 1972 (Title IX), 20 U.S.C. §§ 1681 *et seq.*, and its implementing regulations, 34 C.F.R. Part 106, prohibit discrimination on the basis of sex in education programs or activities operated by recipients of Federal financial assistance. Sexual harassment of students, which includes acts of sexual violence, is a form of sex discrimination prohibited by Title IX. In order to assist recipients, which include school districts, colleges, and universities (hereinafter "schools" or "recipients") in meeting these obligations, this letter explains that the requirements of Title IX pertaining to sexual harassment also cover sexual violence, and lays out the specific Title IX requirements applicable to sexual violence. Sexual violence, as that term is used in this letter, refers to physical sexual acts perpetrated against a person's will or where a person is incapable of giving consent due to the victim's use of drugs or alcohol. An individual also may be unable to give consent due to an intellectual or other disability. A number of different acts fall into the category of sexual violence, including rape, sexual assault, sexual battery, and sexual coercion. All such acts of sexual violence are forms of sexual harassment covered under Title IX.

The statistics on sexual violence are both deeply troubling and a call to action for the nation. A report prepared for the National Institute of Justice found that about 1 in 5 women are victims of completed or attempted sexual assault while in college. The report also found that approximately 6.1 percent of males were victims of completed or attempted sexual assault during college. According to data collected under the Jeanne Clery Disclosure of Campus Security and Campus Crime Statistics Act (Clery Act), 20 U.S.C. § 1092(f), in 2009, college campuses reported nearly 3,300 forcible sex offenses as defined by the Clery Act. This problem is not limited to college. During the 2007–2008 school year, there were 800 reported incidents of rape and attempted rape and 3,800 reported incidents of other sexual batteries at public high schools. Additionally, the likelihood that a woman with intellectual disabilities will be sexually assaulted is estimated to be significantly higher than the general population. The Department is deeply concerned about this problem and is committed to ensuring that all students feel safe in their school, so that they have the opportunity to benefit fully from the school's programs and activities.

This letter begins with a discussion of Title IX's requirements related to student-on-student sexual harassment, including sexual violence, and explains schools' responsibility to take immediate and effective steps to end sexual harassment and sexual violence. These requirements are discussed in detail in OCR's *Revised Sexual Harassment Guidance* issued in 2001 (*2001 Guidance*). This letter supplements the *2001 Guidance* by providing additional guidance and practical examples regarding the Title IX requirements as they relate to sexual violence. This letter concludes by discussing the proactive efforts schools can take to prevent sexual harassment and violence, and by providing examples of remedies that schools and OCR may use to end such conduct, prevent its recurrence, and address its effects. Although some examples contained in this letter are applicable only in the postsecondary context, sexual harassment and violence also are concerns for school districts. The Title IX obligations discussed in this letter apply equally to school districts unless otherwise noted.

Title IX Requirements Related to Sexual Harassment and Sexual Violence

Schools' Obligations to Respond to Sexual Harassment and Sexual Violence

Sexual harassment is unwelcome conduct of a sexual nature. It includes unwelcome sexual advances, requests for sexual favors, and other verbal, nonverbal, or physical conduct of a sexual nature. Sexual violence is a form of sexual harassment prohibited by Title IX.

As explained in OCR's *2001 Guidance*, when a student sexually harasses another student, the harassing conduct creates a hostile environment if the conduct is sufficiently serious that it interferes with or limits a student's ability to participate in or benefit from the school's program. The more severe the conduct, the less need there is to show a repetitive series of incidents to prove a hostile environment, particularly if the harassment is physical. Indeed, a single or isolated incident of sexual harassment may create a hostile environment if the incident is sufficiently severe. For instance, a single instance of rape is sufficiently severe to create a hostile environment.

Title IX protects students from sexual harassment in a school's education programs and activities. This means that Title IX protects students in connection with all the academic, educational, extracurricular, athletic, and other programs of the school, whether those programs take place in a school's facilities, on a school bus, at a class or training program sponsored by the school at another location, or elsewhere. For example, Title IX protects a student who is sexually assaulted by a fellow student during a school-sponsored field trip.

If a school knows or reasonably should know about student-on-student harassment that creates a hostile environment, Title IX requires the school to take immediate action to eliminate the harassment, prevent its recurrence, and address its effects. Schools also are required to publish a notice of nondiscrimination and to adopt and publish grievance procedures. Because of these requirements, which are discussed in greater detail in the following section, schools need to ensure that their employees are trained so that they know to report harassment to appropriate school officials, and so that employees with the authority to address harassment know how to respond properly. Training for employees should include practical information about how to identify and report sexual harassment and violence. OCR recommends that this training be provided to any employees likely to witness or receive reports of sexual harassment and violence, including teachers, school law enforcement unit employees, school administrators, school counselors, general counsels, health personnel, and resident advisors.

Schools may have an obligation to respond to student-on-student sexual harassment that initially occurred off school grounds, outside a school's education program or activity. If a student files a complaint with the school, regardless of where the conduct occurred, the school must process the complaint in accordance with its established procedures. Because students often experience the continuing effects of off-campus sexual harassment in the educational setting, schools should consider the effects of the off-campus conduct when evaluating whether there is a hostile environment on campus. For example, if a student alleges that he or she was sexually assaulted by another student off school grounds, and that upon returning to school he or she was taunted and harassed by other students who are the alleged perpetrator's friends, the school should take the earlier sexual assault into account in determining whether there is a sexually hostile environment. The school also should take steps to protect a student who was assaulted off campus from further sexual harassment or retaliation from the perpetrator and his or her associates . . .

Procedural Requirements Pertaining to Sexual Harassment and Sexual Violence

Recipients of Federal financial assistance must comply with the procedural requirements outlined in the Title IX implementing regulations. Specifically, a recipient must:

(A) Disseminate a notice of nondiscrimination;

(B) Designate at least one employee to coordinate its efforts to comply with and carry out its responsibilities under Title IX; and

(C) Adopt and publish grievance procedures providing for prompt and equitable resolution of student and employee sex discrimination complaints . . .

Prompt and Equitable Requirements

As stated in the *2001 Guidance*, OCR has identified a number of elements in evaluating whether a school's grievance procedures provide for prompt and equitable resolution of sexual harassment complaints. These elements also apply to sexual violence complaints because, as explained above, sexual violence is a form of sexual harassment. OCR will review all aspects of a school's grievance procedures, including the following elements that are critical to achieve compliance with Title IX:

• Notice to students, parents of elementary and secondary students, and employees of the grievance procedures, including where complaints may be filed;

- Application of the procedures to complaints alleging harassment carried out by employees, other students, or third parties;
- Adequate, reliable, and impartial investigation of complaints, including the opportunity for both parties to present witnesses and other evidence;
- Designated and reasonably prompt time frames for the major stages of the complaint process;
- Notice to parties of the outcome of the complaint; and
- An assurance that the school will take steps to prevent recurrence of any harassment and to correct its discriminatory effects on the complainant and others, if appropriate.

As noted in the *2001 Guidance*, procedures adopted by schools will vary in detail, specificity, and components, reflecting differences in the age of students, school sizes and administrative structures, State or local legal requirements, and past experiences. Although OCR examines whether all applicable elements are addressed when investigating sexual harassment complaints, this letter focuses on those elements where our work indicates that more clarification and explanation are needed, including:

(A) Notice of the Grievance Procedures

The procedures for resolving complaints of sex discrimination, including sexual harassment, should be written in language appropriate to the age of the school's students, easily understood, easily located, and widely distributed. OCR recommends that the grievance procedures be prominently posted on school Web sites; sent electronically to all members of the school community; available at various locations throughout the school or campus; and summarized in or attached to major publications issued by the school, such as handbooks, codes of conduct, and catalogs for students, parents of elementary and secondary students, faculty, and staff.

(B) ADEQUATE, RELIABLE, AND IMPARTIAL INVESTIGATION OF COMPLAINTS

OCR's work indicates that a number of issues related to an adequate, reliable, and impartial investigation arise in sexual harassment and violence complaints. In some cases, the conduct may constitute both sexual harassment under Title IX and criminal activity. Police investigations may be useful for fact-gathering; but because the standards for criminal investigations are different, police investigations or reports are not determinative of whether sexual harassment or violence violates Title IX. Conduct may constitute unlawful sexual harassment under Title IX even if the police do not have sufficient evidence of a criminal violation. In addition, a criminal investigation into allegations of sexual violence does not relieve the school of its duty under Title IX to resolve complaints promptly and equitably.

A school should notify a complainant of the right to file a criminal complaint, and should not dissuade a victim from doing so either during or after the school's internal Title IX investigation. For instance, if a complainant wants to file a police report, the school should not tell the complainant that it is working toward a solution and instruct, or ask, the complainant to wait to file the report.

Schools should not wait for the conclusion of a criminal investigation or criminal proceeding to begin their own Title IX investigation and, if needed, must take immediate steps to protect the student in the educational setting. For example, a school should not delay conducting its own investigation or taking steps to protect the complainant because it wants to see whether the alleged perpetrator will be found guilty of a crime. Any agreement or Memorandum of Understanding (MOU) with a local police department must allow the school to meet its Title IX obligation to resolve complaints promptly and equitably. Although a school may need to delay temporarily the fact-finding portion of a Title IX investigation while the police are gathering evidence, once notified that the police department has completed its gathering of evidence (not the ultimate outcome of the investigation or the filing of any charges), the school must promptly resume and complete its fact-finding for the Title IX investigation. Moreover, nothing in an MOU or the criminal investigation itself should prevent a school from notifying complainants of their Title IX rights and the school's grievance procedures, or from taking interim steps to ensure the safety and well-being of the complainant and the school community while the law enforcement agency's fact-gathering is in progress. OCR also recommends that a school's MOU include clear policies on when a school will refer a matter to local law enforcement.

As noted above, the Title IX regulation requires schools to provide equitable grievance procedures. As part of these procedures, schools generally conduct investigations and hearings to determine whether sexual harassment or violence occurred. In addressing complaints filed with OCR under Title IX, OCR reviews a school's procedures to determine whether the school is using a preponderance of the evidence standard to evaluate complaints. The Supreme Court has applied a preponderance of the evidence standard in civil litigation involving discrimination under Title VII of the Civil Rights Act of 1964 (Title VII), 42 U.S.C. §§ 2000e *et seq.* Like Title IX, Title VII prohibits discrimination on the basis of sex. OCR also uses a preponderance of the evidence standard when it resolves complaints against recipients. For instance, OCR's Case Processing Manual requires that a noncompliance determination be supported by the preponderance of the evidence when resolving allegations of discrimination under all the statutes enforced by OCR, including Title IX. OCR also uses a preponderance of the evidence standard in its fund termination administrative hearings. Thus, in order for a school's grievance procedures to be consistent with Title IX standards, the school must use a preponderance of the evidence standard (*i.e.*, it is more likely than not that sexual harassment or violence occurred). The "clear and convincing" standard (*i.e.*, it is highly probable or reasonably certain that the sexual harassment or violence occurred), currently used by some schools, is a higher standard of proof. Grievance procedures that use this higher standard are inconsistent with the standard of proof established for violations of the civil rights laws, and are thus not equitable under Title IX. Therefore, preponderance of the evidence is the appropriate standard for investigating allegations of sexual harassment or violence.

Throughout a school's Title IX investigation, including at any hearing, the parties must have an equal opportunity to present relevant witnesses and other evidence. The complainant and the alleged perpetrator must be afforded similar and timely access to any information that will be used at the hearing. For example, a school should not conduct a pre-hearing meeting during which only the alleged perpetrator is present and given an opportunity to present his or her side of the story, unless a similar meeting takes place with the complainant; a hearing officer or disciplinary board should not allow only the alleged perpetrator to present character witnesses at a hearing; and a school should not allow the alleged perpetrator to review the complainant's statement without also allowing the complainant to review the alleged perpetrator's statement.

While OCR does not require schools to permit parties to have lawyers at any stage of the proceedings, if a school chooses to allow the parties to have their lawyers participate in the proceedings, it must do so equally for both parties. Additionally, any school-imposed restrictions on the ability of lawyers to speak or otherwise participate in the proceedings should apply equally. OCR strongly discourages schools from allowing the parties personally to question or cross-examine each other during the hearing. Allowing an alleged perpetrator to question an alleged victim directly may be traumatic or intimidating, thereby possibly escalating or perpetuating a hostile environment. OCR also recommends that schools provide an appeals process. If a school provides for appeal of the findings or remedy, it must do so for both parties. Schools must maintain documentation of all proceedings, which may include written findings of facts, transcripts, or audio recordings.

All persons involved in implementing a recipient's grievance procedures (*e.g.*, Title IX coordinators, investigators, and adjudicators) must have training or experience in handling complaints of sexual harassment and sexual violence, and in the recipient's grievance procedures. The training also should include applicable confidentiality requirements. In sexual violence cases, the fact-finder and decision-maker also should have adequate training or knowledge regarding sexual violence. Additionally, a school's investigation and hearing processes cannot be equitable unless they are impartial. Therefore, any real or perceived conflicts of interest between the fact-finder or decision-maker and the parties should be disclosed.

Public and state-supported schools must provide due process to the alleged perpetrator. However, schools should ensure that steps taken to accord due process rights to the alleged perpetrator do not restrict or unnecessarily delay the Title IX protections for the complainant.

(C) Designated and Reasonably Prompt Time Frames

OCR will evaluate whether a school's grievance procedures specify the time frames for all major stages of the procedures, as well as the process for extending timelines. Grievance procedures should specify the time frame within which: (1) the school will conduct a full investigation of the complaint; (2) both parties receive a response regarding the outcome of the complaint; and (3) the parties may file an appeal, if applicable. Both parties should be given periodic status updates. Based on OCR experience, a typical investigation takes approximately 60 calendar days following receipt of the complaint. Whether OCR considers complaint resolutions to be timely, however, will vary depending on the complexity of the investigation and the severity and extent of the harassment. For example, the resolution of a complaint involving multiple incidents with multiple complainants likely would take longer than one involving a single incident that occurred in a classroom during school hours with a single complainant.

(D) Notice of Outcome

Both parties must be notified, in writing, about the outcome of both the complaint and any appeal, *i.e.*, whether harassment was found to have occurred. OCR recommends that schools provide the written determination of the final outcome to the complainant and the alleged perpetrator concurrently. Title IX does not require the school to notify the alleged perpetrator of the outcome before it notifies the complainant.

Due to the intersection of Title IX and FERPA requirements, OCR recognizes that there may be confusion regarding what information a school may disclose to the complainant. FERPA generally prohibits the nonconsensual disclosure of personally identifiable information from a student's "education record." However, as stated in the *2001 Guidance*, FERPA permits a school to disclose to the harassed student information about the sanction imposed upon a student who was found to have engaged in harassment when the sanction directly relates to the harassed student. This includes an order that the harasser stay away from the harassed student, or that the harasser is prohibited from attending school for a period of time, or transferred to other classes or another residence hall. Disclosure of other information in the student's "education record," including information about sanctions that do not relate to the harassed student, may result in a violation of FERPA . . .

Steps to Prevent Sexual Harassment and Sexual Violence and Correct Its Discriminatory Effects on the Complainant and Others

Education and Prevention

In addition to ensuring full compliance with Title IX, schools should take proactive measures to prevent sexual harassment and violence. OCR recommends that all schools implement preventive education programs and make victim resources, including comprehensive victim services, available. Schools may want to include these education programs in their (1) orientation programs for new students, faculty, staff, and employees; (2) training for students who serve as advisors in residence halls; (3) training for student athletes and coaches; and (4) school assemblies and "back to school nights." These programs should include a discussion of what constitutes sexual harassment and sexual violence, the school's policies and disciplinary procedures, and the consequences of violating these policies.

The education programs also should include information aimed at encouraging students to report incidents of sexual violence to the appropriate school and law enforcement authorities. Schools should be aware that victims or third parties may be deterred from reporting incidents if alcohol, drugs, or other violations of school or campus rules were involved. As a result, schools should consider whether their disciplinary policies have a chilling effect on victims' or other students' reporting of sexual violence offenses. For example, OCR recommends that schools inform students that the schools' primary concern is student safety, that any other rules violations will be addressed separately from the sexual violence allegation, and that use of alcohol or drugs never makes the victim at fault for sexual violence.

OCR also recommends that schools develop specific sexual violence materials that include the schools' policies, rules, and resources for students, faculty, coaches, and administrators. Schools also should include such information in their employee handbook and any handbooks that student athletes and members of student activity groups receive. These materials should include where and to whom students should go if they are victims of sexual violence. These materials also should tell students and school employees what to do if they learn of an incident of sexual violence. Schools also should assess student activities regularly to ensure that the practices and behavior of students do not violate the schools' policies against sexual harassment and sexual violence.

Remedies and Enforcement

As discussed above, if a school determines that sexual harassment that creates a hostile environment has occurred, it must take immediate action to eliminate the hostile environment, prevent its recurrence, and address its effects. In addition to counseling or taking disciplinary action against the harasser, effective corrective action may require remedies for the complainant, as well as changes to the school's overall services or policies. Examples of these actions are discussed in greater detail below.

Title IX requires a school to take steps to protect the complainant as necessary, including taking interim steps before the final outcome of the investigation. The school should undertake these steps promptly once it has notice of a sexual harassment or violence allegation. The school should notify the complainant of his or her options to avoid contact with the alleged perpetrator and allow students to change academic or living situations as appropriate. For instance, the school may prohibit the alleged perpetrator from having any contact with the complainant pending the results of the school's investigation. When taking steps to separate the complainant and alleged perpetrator, a school should minimize the burden on the complainant, and thus should not, as a matter of course, remove complainants from classes or housing while allowing alleged perpetrators to remain. In addition, schools should ensure that complainants are aware of their Title IX rights and any available resources, such as counseling, health, and mental health services, and their right to file a complaint with local law enforcement.

Schools should be aware that complaints of sexual harassment or violence may be followed by retaliation by the alleged perpetrator or his or her associates. For instance, friends of the alleged perpetrator may subject the complainant to name-calling and taunting. As part of their Title IX obligations, schools must have policies and procedures in place to protect against retaliatory harassment. At a minimum, schools must ensure that complainants and their parents, if appropriate, know how to report any subsequent problems, and should follow-up with complainants to determine whether any retaliation or new incidents of harassment have occurred.

When OCR finds that a school has not taken prompt and effective steps to respond to sexual harassment or violence, OCR will seek appropriate remedies for both the complainant and the broader student population. When conducting Title IX enforcement activities, OCR seeks to obtain voluntary compliance from recipients. When a recipient does not come into compliance voluntarily, OCR may initiate proceedings to withdraw Federal funding by the Department or refer the case to the U.S. Department of Justice for litigation.

Schools should proactively consider the following remedies when determining how to respond to sexual harassment or violence. These are the same types of remedies that OCR would seek in its cases.

Depending on the specific nature of the problem, remedies for the complainant might include, but are not limited to:

- providing an escort to ensure that the complainant can move safely between classes and activities;
- ensuring that the complainant and alleged perpetrator do not attend the same classes;
- moving the complainant or alleged perpetrator to a different residence hall or, in the case of an elementary or secondary school student, to another school within the district;
- providing counseling services;
- providing medical services;
- providing academic support services, such as tutoring;
- arranging for the complainant to re-take a course or withdraw from a class without penalty, including ensuring that any changes do not adversely affect the complainant's academic record; and
- reviewing any disciplinary actions taken against the complainant to see if there is a causal connection between the harassment and the misconduct that may have resulted in the complainant being disciplined.

Remedies for the broader student population might include, but are not limited to:

COUNSELING AND TRAINING

- offering counseling, health, mental health, or other holistic and comprehensive victim services to all students affected by sexual harassment or sexual violence, and notifying students of campus and community counseling, health, mental health, and other student services;
- designating an individual from the school's counseling center to be "on call" to assist victims of sexual harassment or violence whenever needed;
- training the Title IX coordinator and any other employees who are involved in processing, investigating, or resolving complaints of sexual harassment or sexual violence, including providing training on:
  - the school's Title IX responsibilities to address allegations of sexual harassment or violence
  - how to conduct Title IX investigations
  - information on the link between alcohol and drug abuse and sexual harassment or violence and best practices to address that link;
- training all school law enforcement unit personnel on the school's Title IX responsibilities and handling of sexual harassment or violence complaints;
- training all employees who interact with students regularly on recognizing and appropriately addressing allegations of sexual harassment or violence under Title IX; and
- informing students of their options to notify proper law enforcement authorities, including school and local police, and the option to be assisted by school employees in notifying those authorities.

Development of Materials and Implementation of Policies and Procedures

- developing materials on sexual harassment and violence, which should be distributed to students during orientation and upon receipt of complaints, as well as widely posted throughout school buildings and residence halls, and which should include:

  - what constitutes sexual harassment or violence
  - what to do if a student has been the victim of sexual harassment or violence
  - contact information for counseling and victim services on and off school grounds
  - how to file a complaint with the school
  - how to contact the school's Title IX coordinator
  - what the school will do to respond to allegations of sexual harassment or violence, including the interim measures that can be taken

- requiring the Title IX coordinator to communicate regularly with the school's law enforcement unit investigating cases and to provide information to law enforcement unit personnel regarding Title IX requirements;

- requiring the Title IX coordinator to review all evidence in a sexual harassment or sexual violence case brought before the school's disciplinary committee to determine whether the complainant is entitled to a remedy under Title IX that was not available through the disciplinary committee;

- requiring the school to create a committee of students and school officials to identify strategies for ensuring that students:

  - know the school's prohibition against sex discrimination, including sexual harassment and violence
  - recognize sex discrimination, sexual harassment, and sexual violence when they occur
  - understand how and to whom to report any incidents

- know the connection between alcohol and drug abuse and sexual harassment or violence
- feel comfortable that school officials will respond promptly and equitably to reports of sexual harassment or violence;

- issuing new policy statements or other steps that clearly communicate that the school does not tolerate sexual harassment and violence and will respond to any incidents and to any student who reports such incidents; and
- revising grievance procedures used to handle sexual harassment and violence complaints to ensure that they are prompt and equitable, as required by Title IX.

SCHOOL INVESTIGATIONS AND REPORTS TO OCR
- conducting periodic assessments of student activities to ensure that the practices and behavior of students do not violate the school's policies against sexual harassment and violence;
- investigating whether any other students also may have been subjected to sexual harassment or violence;
- investigating whether school employees with knowledge of allegations of sexual harassment or violence failed to carry out their duties in responding to those allegations;
- conducting, in conjunction with student leaders, a school or campus "climate check" to assess the effectiveness of efforts to ensure that the school is free from sexual harassment and violence, and using the resulting information to inform future proactive steps that will be taken by the school; and
- submitting to OCR copies of all grievances filed by students alleging sexual harassment or violence, and providing OCR with documentation related to the investigation of each complaint, such as witness interviews, investigator notes, evidence submitted by the parties, investigative reports and summaries, any final disposition letters, disciplinary records, and documentation regarding any appeals.

Conclusion

The Department is committed to ensuring that all students feel safe and have the opportunity to benefit fully from their schools' education programs and activities. As part of this commitment, OCR provides technical assistance to assist recipients in achieving voluntary compliance with Title IX.

If you need additional information about Title IX, have questions regarding OCR's policies, or seek technical assistance, please contact the OCR enforcement office that serves your state or territory. The list of offices is available at http://wdcrobcolp01 .ed.gov/CFAPPS/OCR/contactus.cfm. Additional information about addressing sexual violence, including victim resources and information for schools, is available from the U.S. Department of Justice's Office on Violence Against Women (OVW) at http://www.ovw.usdoj.gov/.

Thank you for your prompt attention to this matter. I look forward to continuing our work together to ensure that all students have an equal opportunity to learn in a safe and respectful school climate.

Sincerely,

/s/

Russlynn Ali

Assistant Secretary for Civil Rights

Source: U.S. Department of Education, http://www2.ed.gov/about/offices/list/ocr/letters/colleague-201104.html

The Campus Sexual Violence Elimination Act (2013)

The Campus Sexual Violence Elimination Act (The Campus SaVE Act), passed as part of the Violence against Women Reauthorization Act of 2013 and signed by President Barack Obama, is an update to the Clery Act. It encourages greater transparency by requiring campus crime statistics to also include and report instances of dating violence, domestic violence, and stalking.

Additionally, the SaVE Act requires campuses to guarantee the rights of victims of sexual assault and provide certain

accommodations, to provide sexual violence prevention education to enrolled students, and to have protocol and standards for disciplinary hearings. Representative Carolyn Maloney of New York introduced the Campus SaVE Act in the House of Representatives; her introduction follows.

Mr. Speaker, today, I am proud to introduce the Campus Sexual Violence Elimination (SaVE) Act. This bill will close a gap in current law by requiring universities and colleges to spell out their policies on sexual assault, stalking, dating violence, and domestic violence generally. By requiring transparency out of these institutions, this bill will increase awareness for the victimization students face every day on our college campuses.

Sexual and dating violence is a serious problem on our college campuses. Over 13 percent of female undergrads have reported being stalked while at school and one out of every five women in college have reported being sexually assaulted. While these statistics are shocking, what's even more shocking is that only a fraction of these incidents are reported. When these instances of abuse go unreported, our nation's female undergraduate victims never get the support they need.

The Campus SaVE Act would close the gap in current law by requiring institutions of higher education to clearly explain their policies on dating violence, sexual assault, stalking, and domestic violence. Institutions will be required to include in their annual security reports statistics on domestic violence, dating violence, and stalking that were reported to campus police or local police agencies. It will also promote prevention and bystander responsibility by requiring these institutions to develop clear statements of policy regarding domestic violence, dating violence, sexual assault, and stalking prevention programs. Campus SaVE ensures that victims get the help they need by requiring schools to provide clear statements regarding their procedures followed when a case of domestic violence, dating violence, sexual assault, or stalking is reported and provide victims an explanation of their rights in writing.

Young people should be able to focus on finding their intellectual passion during these years, not dealing with the mental and physical exhaustion of abuse. The Campus Sexual Violence Elimination Act will help ensure our college campuses and universities are safer and I urge my colleagues to support it.

Source: *Congressional Record,* Vol. 159, Number 26. February 25, 2013. Washington, D.C.: Government Printing Office, 2013, E179.

"Not Alone" Report (2014)

In January 2014, President Barack Obama called for the creation of a White House Task Force to Protect Students from Sexual Assault. Citing the alarming statistics on the prevalence of sexual assault on college campuses, Obama directed the Office of the Vice President and the White House Council on Women and Girls to lead an effort to develop a coordinated federal response to campus sexual assault through the creation of a task force.

Launched in connection with the Task Force to Protect Students from Sexual Assault, the website www.changingourcampus.org (formally www.notalone.gov) includes resources on how to respond to and prevent sexual assault. It includes data and resources for students and schools. Additionally, the task force released its first report in April 2014.

Executive Summary

Why We Need to Act

One in five women is sexually assaulted in college. Most often, it's by someone she knows—and also most often, she does not report what happened. Many survivors are left feeling isolated, ashamed or to blame. Although it happens less often, men, too, are victims of these crimes.

The President created the Task Force to Protect Students From Sexual Assault to turn this tide.

As the name of our new website—NotAlone.gov—indicates, we are here to tell sexual assault survivors that they are not alone. And we're also here to help schools live up to their obligation to protect students from sexual violence.

Over the last three months, we have had a national conversation with thousands of people who care about this issue. Today, we offer our first set of action steps and recommendations.

1. Identifying the Problem: Campus Climate Surveys

The first step in solving a problem is to name it and know the extent of it—and a campus climate survey is the best way to do that. We are providing schools with a toolkit to conduct a survey—and we urge schools to show they're serious about the problem by conducting the survey next year. The Justice Department, too, will partner with Rutgers University's Center on Violence Against Women and Children to pilot, evaluate and further refine the survey—and at the end of this trial period, we will explore legislative or administrative options to require schools to conduct a survey in 2016.

2. Preventing Sexual Assault—and Engaging Men

Prevention programs can change attitudes, behavior—and the culture. In addition to identifying a number of promising prevention strategies that schools can undertake now, we are also researching new ideas and solutions. But one thing we know for sure: we need to engage men as allies in this cause. Most men are not perpetrators—and when we empower men to step in when someone's in trouble, they become an important part of the solution.

As the President and Vice President's new Public Service Announcement puts it: if she doesn't consent—or can't consent—it's a crime. And if you see it happening, help her, don't blame her, speak up. We are also providing schools with links and information about how they can implement their own bystander intervention programs on campus.

3. Effectively Responding When a Student
Is Sexually Assaulted

When one of its students is sexually assaulted, a school needs to have all the pieces of a plan in place. And that should include:

Someone a survivor can talk to in confidence. While many victims of sexual assault are ready to file a formal (or even public) complaint against an alleged offender right away—many others want time and privacy to sort through their next steps. For some, having a confidential place to go can mean the difference between getting help and staying silent.

Today, we are providing schools with a model reporting and confidentiality protocol—which, at its heart, aims to give survivors more control over the process. Victims who want their school to fully investigate an incident must be taken seriously—and know where to report. But for those who aren't quite ready, they need to have—and know about—places to go for confidential advice and support.

That means a school should make it clear, up front, who on campus can maintain a victim's confidence and who can't—so a victim can make an informed decision about where best to turn. A school's policy should also explain when it may need to override a confidentiality request (and pursue an alleged perpetrator) in order to help provide a safe campus for everyone. Our sample policy provides recommendations for how a school can strike that often difficult balance, while also being ever mindful of a survivor's well-being.

New guidance from the Department of Education also makes clear that on-campus counselors and advocates—like those who work or volunteer in sexual assault centers, victim advocacy offices, women's and health centers, as well as licensed and pastoral counselors—can talk to a survivor in confidence. In recent years, some schools have indicated that some of these counselors and advocates cannot maintain confidentiality. This new guidance clarifies that they can.

A COMPREHENSIVE SEXUAL MISCONDUCT POLICY

We are also providing a checklist for schools to use in drafting (or reevaluating) their own sexual misconduct policies.

Although every school will need to tailor a policy to its own needs and circumstances, all schools should be sure to bring the key stakeholders—including students—to the table. Among other things, this checklist includes ideas a school could consider in deciding what is—or is not—consent to sexual activity. As we heard from many students, this can often be the essence of the matter—and a school community should work together to come up with a careful and considered understanding.

TRAUMA-INFORMED TRAINING FOR SCHOOL OFFICIALS

Sexual assault is a unique crime: unlike other crimes, victims often blame themselves; the associated trauma can leave their memories fragmented; and insensitive or judgmental questions can compound a victim's distress. Starting this year, the Justice Department, through both its Center for Campus Public Safety and its Office on Violence Against Women, will develop trauma-informed training programs for school officials and campus and local law enforcement.

The Department of Education's National Center on Safe and Supportive Learning Environments will do the same for campus health centers. This kind of training has multiple benefits: when survivors are treated with care and wisdom, they start trusting the system, and the strength of their accounts can better hold offenders accountable.

Better school disciplinary systems. Many sexual assault survivors are wary of their school's adjudication process—which can sometimes subject them to harsh and hurtful questioning (like about their prior sexual history) by students or staff unschooled in the dynamics of these crimes. Some schools are experimenting with new models—like having a single, trained investigator do the lion's share of the fact-finding—with very positive results. We need to learn more about these promising new ideas. And so starting this year, the Justice Department will begin assessing different models for investigating and adjudicating campus sexual assault cases with an eye toward identifying best practices.

The Department of Education's new guidance also urges some important improvements to many schools' current disciplinary

processes: questions about the survivor's sexual history with anyone other than the alleged perpetrator should not be permitted; adjudicators should know that the mere fact of a previous
consensual sexual relationship does not itself imply consent or
preclude a finding of sexual violence; and the parties should not
be allowed to personally cross-examine each other.

PARTNERSHIPS WITH THE COMMUNITY

Because students can be sexually assaulted at all hours of the
day or night, emergency services should be available 24 hours
a day, too. Other types of support can also be crucial—like
longer-term therapies and advocates who can accompany survivors to medical and legal appointments. Many schools cannot themselves provide all these services, but in partnership
with a local rape crisis center, they can. So, too, when both
the college and the local police are simultaneously investigating a case (a criminal investigation does not relieve a school of
its duty to itself investigate and respond), coordination can be
crucial. So we are providing schools with a sample agreement
they can use to partner with their local rape crisis center—and
by June, we will provide a similar sample for forging a partnership with local law enforcement.

4. Increasing Transparency and Improving Enforcement

MORE TRANSPARENCY AND INFORMATION

The government is committed to making our enforcement
efforts more transparent—and getting students and schools
more resources to help bring an end to this violence. As part
of this effort, we will post enforcement data on our new
website—NotAlone.gov—and give students a roadmap for filing a complaint if they think their school has not lived up to
its obligations.

Among many other things on the website, sexual assault survivors can also locate an array of services by typing in their zip
codes, learn about their legal rights, see which colleges have had
enforcement actions taken against them, get "plain English"

definitions of some complicated legal terms and concepts; and find their states' privacy laws. Schools and advocates can access federal guidance, learn about relevant legislation, and review the best available evidence and research. We invite everyone to take a look.

Improved Enforcement. Today, the Department of Education's Office for Civil Rights (OCR) is releasing a 52-point guidance document that answers many frequently asked questions about a student's rights, and a school's obligations, under Title IX. Among many other topics, the new guidance clarifies that Title IX protects all students, regardless of their sexual orientation or gender identity, immigration status, or whether they have a disability. It also makes clear that students who report sexual violence have a right to expect their school to take steps to protect and support them, including while a school investigation is pending. The guidance also clarifies that recent amendments to the Clery Act do not alter a school's responsibility under Title IX to respond to and prevent sexual violence. OCR is also strengthening its enforcement procedures in a number of ways—by, for example, instituting time limits on negotiating voluntary resolution agreements and making clear that schools should provide survivors with interim relief (like changing housing or class schedules) pending the outcome of an OCR investigation. And OCR will be more visible on campus during its investigations, so students can help give OCR a fuller picture about what's happening and how a school is responding.

The Departments of Education and Justice, which both enforce Title IX, have entered into an agreement to better coordinate their efforts—as have the two offices within the Department of Education charged with enforcing Title IX and the Clery Act.

NEXT STEPS

This report is the first step in the Task Force's work. We will continue to work toward solutions, clarity, and better coordination. We will also review the various laws and regulations that address sexual violence for possible regulatory or statutory improvements, and seek new resources to enhance enforcement. Also, campus law enforcement officials have special expertise to offer—and they should be tapped to play a more central role. We will also consider how our recommendations apply to public elementary and secondary schools—and what more we can do to help there.

* * *

The Task Force thanks everyone who has offered their wisdom, stories, expertise, and experiences over the past 90 days. Although the problem is daunting and much of what we heard was heartbreaking, we are more committed than ever to helping bring an end to this violence.

Source: White House Task Force to Protect Students from Sexual Assault. *Not Alone.* April 2014. https://www.notalone .gov/assets/report.pdf

Title IX Rights for Students Who Have Experienced Sexual Violence (2014)

Any college or university that receives federal funds must comply with Title IX. As such, individuals who have experienced campus sexual assault are provided with certain rights and protections. The Office for Civil Rights created the following document to clearly elucidate those rights.

Know Your Rights: Title IX Requires Your School to Address Sexual Violence

Title IX of the Education Amendments of 1972 prohibits sex discrimination—which includes sexual violence—in educational programs and activities. All public and private schools, school districts, colleges, and universities receiving federal funds must comply with Title IX. If you have experienced sexual violence, here are some things you should know about your Title IX rights:

Your School Must Respond Promptly and Effectively to Sexual Violence

- You have the right to report the incident to your school, have your school investigate what happened, and have your complaint resolved promptly and equitable.

- You have the right to choose to report an incident of sexual violence to campus or local law enforcement. But a criminal investigation does not relieve your school of its duty under Title IX to respond promptly and effectively.

- Your school must adopt and publish procedures for resolving complaints of sex discrimination, including sexual violence. Your school may use student disciplinary procedures, but any procedures for sexual violence complaints must afford you a prompt and equitable resolution.

- Your school should ensure that you are aware of your Title IX rights and any available resources, such as victim advocacy, housing assistance, academic support, counseling, disability services, health and mental health services, and legal assistance.

- Your school must designate a Title IX coordinator and make sure all students and employees know how to contact him or her. The Title IX coordinator should also be available to meet with you.

- All students are protected by Title IX, regardless of whether they have a disability, are international or undocumented, and regardless of their sexual orientation and gender identity.

Your School Must Provide Interim Measures as Necessary

- Your school must protect you as necessary, even before it completes any investigation. Your school should start doing this promptly once the incident is reported.

- Once you tell your school about an incident of sexual violence, you have the right to receive some immediate help, such as changing classes, dorms, or transportation. When taking these measures, your school should minimize the burden on you.
- You have the right to report any retaliation by school employees, the alleged perpetrator, and other students, and your school should take strong responsive action if it occurs.

Your School Should Make Known Where You Can Find Confidential Support Services

- Your school should clearly identify where you can go to talk to someone confidentially and who can provide services like advocacy, counseling, or academic support. Some people, such as counselors or victim advocates, can talk to you in confidence without triggering a school's investigation.
- Because different employees have different reporting obligations when they find out about sexual violence involving students, your school should clearly explain the reporting obligations of all school employees.
- Even if you do not specifically ask for confidentiality, your school should only disclose information to individuals who are responsible for handling the school's response to sexual violence. Your school should consult with you about how to best protect your safety and privacy.

Your School Must Conduct an Adequate, Reliable, and Impartial Investigation

- You have the right to be notified of the timeframes for all major stages of the investigation.
- You have the right to present witnesses and evidence.
- If the alleged perpetrator is allowed to have a lawyer, you have the right to have one too.
- Your school must resolve your complaint based on what they think is more likely than not to have happened (this is

called a preponderance-of-the-evidence standard of proof). Your school cannot use a higher standard of proof.

- You have the right to be notified in writing of the outcome of your complaint and any appeal, including any sanctions that directly relate to you.

- If your school provides for an appeal process, it must be equally available for both parties.

- You have the right to have any proceedings documented, which may include written findings of fact, transcripts, or audio recordings.

- You have the right not to "work it out" with the alleged perpetrator in mediation. Mediation is not appropriate in cases involving sexual assault.

Your School Must Provide Remedies as Necessary

- If an investigation reveals that sexual violence created a hostile environment, your school must take prompt and effective steps reasonably calculated to end the sexual violence, eliminate the hostile environment, prevent its recurrence, and, as appropriate, remedy its effects.

- Appropriate remedies will generally include disciplinary action against the perpetrator, but may also include remedies to help you get your education back on track (like academic support, retaking a class without penalty, and counseling). These remedies are in addition to any interim measures you received.

- Your school may also have to provide remedies for the broader student population (such as training) or change its services or policies to prevent such incidents from repeating.

If you want to learn more about your rights, or if you believe that your school is violating federal law, you may contact the U.S. Department of Education, Office for Civil Rights, at (800) 421–3481 or ocr@ed.gov. If you wish to fill out a complaint form online, you may do so at http://www.ed.gov/ocr/complaintintro.html.

Source: U.S. Department of Education, Office for Civil Rights. Available online at https://www2.ed.gov/about/offices/list/ocr/docs/know-rights-201404-title-ix.pdf

Victim's Impact Statement in Stanford Rape Sentencing (2016)

In January 2015, two witnesses saw Brock Turner, a varsity swimmer at Stanford University, sexually assaulting an unconscious woman behind a dumpster. Turner was found guilty of 3 counts of sexual assault and faced a maximum of 14 years in state prison. The judge in the case sentenced Turner to six months in county jail and three months of probation, sparking national outrage for the leniency in punishment. After the sentence was handed down in court, the survivor read a powerful 12-page letter outlining the profound impact the assault had on her life. A portion of the letter is below.

I thought there's no way this is going to trial; there were witnesses, there was dirt in my body, he ran but was caught. He's going to settle, formally apologize, and we will both move on. Instead, I was told he hired a powerful attorney, expert witnesses, private investigators who were going to try and find details about my personal life to use against me, find loopholes in my story to invalidate me and my sister, in order to show that this sexual assault was in fact a misunderstanding. That he was going to go to any length to convince the world he had simply been confused.

I was not only told that I was assaulted, I was told that because I couldn't remember, I technically could not prove it was unwanted. And that distorted me, damaged me, almost broke me. It is the saddest type of confusion to be told I was assaulted and nearly raped, blatantly out in the open, but we don't know if it counts as assault yet. I had to fight for an entire year to make it clear that there was something wrong with this situation . . .

I was pummeled with narrowed, pointed questions that dissected my personal life, love life, past life, family life, inane questions, accumulating trivial details to try and find an excuse for this guy who had me half naked before even bothering to ask for my name. After a physical assault, I was assaulted with questions designed to attack me, to say see, her facts don't line up, she's out of her mind, she's practically an alcoholic, she probably wanted to hook up, he's like an athlete right, they were both drunk, whatever, the hospital stuff she remembers is after the fact, why take it into account, Brock has a lot at stake so he's having a really hard time right now . . .

He has done irreversible damage to me and my family during the trial and we have sat silently, listening to him shape the evening. But in the end, his unsupported statements and his attorney's twisted logic fooled no one. The truth won, the truth spoke for itself.

You are guilty. Twelve jurors convicted you guilty of three felony counts beyond reasonable doubt, that's twelve votes per count, thirty six yeses confirming guilt, that's one hundred percent, unanimous guilt. And I thought finally it is over, finally he will own up to what he did, truly apologize, we will both move on and get better. Then I read your statement . . .

[Y]ou said, I want to show people that one night of drinking can ruin a life.

A life, one life, yours, you forgot about mine. Let me rephrase for you, I want to show people that one night of drinking can ruin two lives. You and me. You are the cause, I am the effect. You have dragged me through this hell with you, dipped me back into that night again and again. You knocked down both our towers, I collapsed at the same time you did. If you think I was spared, came out unscathed, that today I ride off into sunset, while you suffer the greatest blow, you are mistaken. Nobody wins. We have all been devastated, we have all been trying to find some meaning in all of this suffering. Your damage was concrete; stripped of titles, degrees, enrollment. My damage was internal, unseen, I carry it with me. You took away my worth, my privacy, my energy, my time, my safety, my intimacy, my confidence, my own voice, until today.

. . .

I used to pride myself on my independence, now I am afraid to go on walks in the evening, to attend social events with drinking among friends where I should be comfortable being. I have become a little barnacle always needing to be at someone's side, to have my boyfriend standing next to me, sleeping beside me, protecting me. It is embarrassing how feeble I feel, how timidly I move through life, always guarded, ready to defend myself, ready to be angry . . .

Your life is not over, you have decades of years ahead to rewrite your story. The world is huge, it is so much bigger than Palo Alto and Stanford, and you will make a space for yourself in it where you can be useful and happy. But right now, you do not get to shrug your shoulders and be confused anymore. You do not get to pretend that there were no red flags. You have been convicted of violating me, intentionally, forcibly, sexually, with malicious intent, and all you can admit to is consuming alcohol. Do not talk about the sad way your life was upturned because alcohol made you do bad things. Figure out how to take responsibility for your own conduct.

Source: *People of the State of California v. Brock Allen Turner* (2016). Available online at https://www.sccgov.org/sites/da/ newsroom/newsreleases/Documents/B-Turner%20VIS.pdf

Introduction

This chapter includes a selection of resources for readers interested in learning more about sexual assault in general and campus sexual assault specifically. The list of books is organized into five categories: sexual assault, campus sexual assault, campus crime, memoirs, and resources for healing. Following the book suggestions is a selection of recent (2010–2016) scholarly and peer-reviewed journals on the topic of sexual assault and campus sexual assault. Additionally, this chapter includes a list of relevant documentaries, sexual assault awareness campaigns, and recommended organizations, programs, and nonprofits.

Books

Sexual Assault

Allison, J., and Wrightsman, L., Jr. 1993. *Rape: The Misunderstood Crime*. Thousand Oaks, CA: Sage.

Anderson, I., and Doherty, K. 2007. *Accounting for Rape: Psychology, Feminism and Discourse Analysis in the Study of Sexual Violence*. Oxford: Routledge.

Recent Harvard graduate Alyssa Leader listens to her attorneys during a news conference in February 2016. Leader filed a Title IX lawsuit against Harvard, alleging the university failed to adequately protect her and failed to investigate her complaints of sexual assault, harassment, and retaliation. Leader is one of many students to file Title IX complaints against their colleges or universities for the mishandling of sexual assault cases. (AP Photo/ Elise Amendola)

Bevacqua, M. 2000. *Rape on the Public Agenda: Feminism and the Politics of Sexual Assault.* Boston, MA: Northeastern University Press.

Brownmiller, S. 1993. *Against Our Will: Men, Women, and Rape.* New York: Ballantine Books.

Buchwald, E., Fletcher, P., and Roth, M. 2005. *Transforming a Rape Culture.* Minneapolis, MN: Milkweed Editions.

Burns, S. 2011. *The Central Park Five: A Chronicle of a City Wilding.* New York: Knopf.

Cahill, A. 2001. *Rethinking Rape.* Ithaca, NY: Cornell University Press.

Corrigan, R. 2013. *Up against a Wall: Rape Reform and the Failure of Success.* New York: New York University Press.

Cuklanz, L. 1995. *Rape on Trial: How the Mass Media Construct Legal Reform and Social Change.* Philadelphia, PA: University of Pennsylvania Press.

Cuklanz, L. 1999. *Rape on Prime Time: Television, Masculinity, and Sexual Violence.* Philadelphia, PA: University of Pennsylvania Press.

Deer, S. 2015. *The Beginning and End of Rape: Confronting Sexual Violence in Native America.* Minneapolis, MN: University of Minnesota Press.

Estrich, S. 1987. *Real Rape: How the Legal System Victimizes Women Who Say No.* Cambridge, MA: Harvard University Press.

Estrich, S. 2003. *Representing Rape: Language and Sexual Consent.* Oxford: Routledge.

Finley, L. 2016. *Domestic Abuse and Sexual Assault in Popular Culture.* Westport, CT: Praeger.

Freedman, E. 2013. *Redefining Rape: Sexual Violence in the Era of Suffrage and Segregation.* Cambridge, MA: Harvard University Press.

Freidman, J., and Valenti, J. 2008. *Yes Means Yes! Visions of Female Power and a World without Rape.* New York: Seal Press.

Gavey, N. 1998. *Just Sex? The Cultural Scaffolding of Rape.* Hove, East Sussex: Routledge.

Girschik, L. 2002. *Woman-to-Woman Sexual Violence: Does She Call It Rape?* Boston, MA: Northeastern University Press.

Harding, K. 2015. *Asking for It: The Alarming Rise of Rape Culture—and What We Can Do about It.* Boston, MA: De Capo Press.

Henry, N., and A. Powell (eds.). 2014. *Preventing Sexual Violence: Interdisciplinary Approaches to Overcoming a Rape Culture.* London: Palgrave Macmillan.

Horek, T. 2003. *Public Rape: Representing Violation in Fiction and Film.* London: Routledge.

Katz, J. 2006. *The Macho Paradox: Why Some Men Hurt Women and How All Men Can Help.* Naperville, IL: Sourcebooks.

Lefkowtiz, B. 1997. *Our Guys: The Glen Ridge Rape and the Secret Life of the Perfect Suburb.* Berkeley: University of California Press.

Lueders, Bill. 2006. *Cry Rape: The True Story of One Woman's Harrowing Quest for Justice.* Madison, WI: Terrace Books.

Mardorossian, C. 2014. *Framing the Rape Victim: Gender and Agency Reconsidered.* Brunswick, NJ: Rutgers University Press.

Mulla, S. 2014. *The Violence of Care: Rape Victims, Forensic Nurses and Sexual Assault Intervention.* New York: New York University Press.

Patterson, J. (ed.). 2016. *Queering Sexual Violence: Radical Voices from within the Anti-Violence Movement.* New York: Riverdale Avenue Books.

Projanksy, S. 2001. *Watching Rape: Film and Television in Postfeminist Culture.* New York: New York University Press.

Raphael, J. 2013. *Rape Is Rape: How Denial, Distortion, and Victim-Blaming Are Fueling a Hidden Acquaintance Rape Crisis.* Chicago: Chicago Review Press.

Richards, T., and C. Marcum (eds.). 2014. *Sexual Victimization: Then and Now*. Thousand Oaks, CA: Sage.

Sanday, P.R., 2011. *A Woman Scorned: Acquaintance Rape on Trial*. New York: Anchor.

Scarce, M. 2001. *Male on Male Rape: The Hidden Toll of Stigma and Shame*. New York: Basic Books.

Schulhofer, S. 2000. *Unwanted Sex: The Culture of Intimidation and the Failure of the Law*. Cambridge, MA: Harvard University Press.

Skaine, R. 2015. *Sexual Assault in the US Military: The Battle within America's Armed Forces*. Westport, CT: Praeger.

Smith, A. 2015. *Conquest: Sexual Violence and American Indian Genocide*. Durham, NC: Duke University Press.

Tazlitz, A. 1999. *Rape and the Culture of the Courtroom*. New York: New York University Press.

Ullman, S. 2010. *Talking about Sexual Assault: Society's Response to Survivors*. Washington, DC: American Psychological Association.

Campus Sexual Assault

Bohmer, C. 1993. *Sexual Assault on Campus: The Problem and the Solution*. Lanham, MD: Lexington Books.

Clark, A. and Pino, A. 2016. *We Believe You: Survivors of Campus Sexual Assault Speak Out*. New York: Henry Holt & Company.

Dick, K., and Ziering, A. 2016. *The Hunting Ground: The Inside Story of Sexual Assault on American College Campuses*. New York: Skyhorse Publishing.

Fisher, B., Daigle, L., and Cullen, F. 2010. *Unsafe in the Ivory Tower: The Sexual Victimization of College Women*. Thousand Oaks, CA: Sage.

German, L. 2016. *Campus Sexual Assault: College Women Respond*. Baltimore, MD: Johns Hopkins Press.

Gold, J., and Villari, S. 1999. *Just Sex: Students Rewrite the Rules on Sex, Violence, Equality and Activism*. Lanham, MD: Rowman & Littlefield Publishers.

James, V. 2015. *Campus Rape Victims: How They See the Police*. El Paso, TX: LFB Scholarly Publishing.

Krakauer, J. 2015. *Missoula: Rape and the Justice System in a College Town*. New York: Doubleday.

Maiuro, R. (ed.). 2015. *Perspectives on College Sexual Assault*. New York: Springer Publishing Company.

Oliver, K. 2016. *Hunting Girls: Sexual Violence from the Hunger Games to Campus Rape*. New York: Columbia University Press.

Ottens, A., and K. Hotelling (eds.). 2000. *Sexual Violence on Campus: Policies, Programs, and Perspectives*. New York: Springer Publishing Company.

Paludi, M. (ed.). 2016. *Campus Action against Sexual Assault: Needs, Policies, Procedures, and Training Programs*. Westport, CT: Praeger.

Sanday, P.R. 2007. *Fraternity Gang Rape: Sex, Brotherhood, and Privilege on Campus*. New York: New York University Press.

Schwartz, M., and DeKeseredy, W. 1997. *Sexual Assault on the College Campus: The Role of Male Peer Support*. Thousand Oaks, CA: Sage.

Searles, P., and R.J. Berger (eds.). 1995. *Rape & Society: Readings on the Problem of Sexual Assault*. Boulder, CO: Westview Press.

Warshaw, Robin. 1988. *I Never Called It Rape: The Ms. Report on Recognizing, Fighting, and Surviving Date and Acquaintance Rape*. New York: Harper & Row.

Wooton, S., and R. Mitchell (eds.). 2015. *The Crisis of Campus Sexual Violence: Critical Perspectives on Prevention and Response*. New York: Routledge.

Campus Crime

Fisher, B., and J. Sloan III (eds.). 2013. *Campus Crime: Legal, Social and Policy Perspectives, 3rd edition.* Springfield, IL: Charles C. Thomas Publishers.

Flowers, B.R. 2009. *College Crime: A Statistical Study of Offenses on American Campuses.* Jefferson: NC: McFarland & Company, Inc.

Fox, J., and Burstein, H. 2010. *Violence and Security on Campus: From Preschool to College.* Westport, CT: Praeger.

Paludi, M. 2008. *Understanding and Preventing Campus Violence.* Westport, CT: Praeger.

Sloan, J., III. 2010. *The Dark Side of the Ivory Tower: Campus Crime as a Social Problem.* New York: Cambridge University Press.

Van Brunt, B. 2012. *Ending Campus Violence: New Approaches to Prevention.* New York: Routledge.

Memoirs

Arter, N. 2015. *Controlled.* New York: Heliotrope Books.

Brison, S. 2003. *Aftermath: Violence and the Remaking of a Self.* Princeton, NJ: Princeton University Press.

Conners, J. 2016. *I Will Find You: A Reporter Investigates the Life of a Man Who Raped Her.* New York: Atlantic Monthly Press.

Douglas, R. 2016. *On Being Raped.* Boston, MA: Beacon Press.

Factora-Borchers, L. (ed.) and A.S. Simmons. 2014. *Dear Sister: Letters from Survivors of Sexual Violence.* Oakland, CA: AK Press.

Francisco, P.W. 2000. *Telling: A Memoir of Rape and Recovery.* New York: Harper Perennial.

Freedman, K. 2014. *One Hour in Paris: A True Story of Rape and Recovery.* Chicago, IL: University of Chicago Press.

Gray-Rosendale, L. 2014. *College Girl: A Memoir*. New York: Excelsior Editions.

Leo, J. 2011. *Rape New York*. New York: Feminist Press.

Matis, A. 2015. *Girl in the Woods*. New York: HarperCollins Publishers.

Meili, T. 2004. *I Am the Central Park Jogger: A Story of Hope and Possibility*. New York: Scribner.

Pierce-Baker, C. 2000. *Surviving the Silence: Black Women's Stories of Rape*. New York: W.W. Norton & Company.

Raine, N.V. 1999. *After Silence: Rape and My Journey Back*. New York: Crown Publishers.

Sebold, A. 2002. *Lucky*. New York: Back Bay Books.

Seccuro, L. 2011. *Crash into Me: A Survivor's Search for Justice*. New York: Bloomsbury USA.

Uttaro, R. 2013. *To The Survivor's: One Man's Journey as a Rape Crisis Counselor with True Stories of Sexual Violence*. Charleston, NC: Create Space.

Resources for Healing

Atkinson, M. 2008/2015. *Resurrection after Rape: A Guide to Transforming from Victim to Survivor*. Oklahoma, OK: R.A.R. Publishing.

Carpenter, E. 2013. *Life, Reinvented: A Guide to Healing from Sexual Trauma for Survivors and Loved Ones*. Denver, CO: Quantam Publishing Group.

Herman, J. 1992/2015. *Trauma and Recovery: The Aftermath of Violence—From Domestic Abuse to Political Terror*. New York: Basic Books.

Maltz, W. 2012. *The Sexual Healing Journey: A Guide for Survivors of Sexual Abuse, 3rd edition*. New York: William Morrow Paperbacks.

Matsakis, A. 2003. *The Rape Recovery Handbook: Step-by-Step Help for Survivors of Sexual Assault*. Oakland, CA: New Harbinger Publications.

van der Kolk, B. 2015. *The Body Keeps Score: Brain, Mind and Body in the Healing of Trauma*. New York: Penguin Books.

Journal Articles and Research Reports (2010–Present)

Amar, A.F., Strout, T.D., Simpson, S. Cardiello, M., and Beckford, S. 2014. Administrators' Perceptions of College Campus Protocols, Response, and Student Prevention Efforts of Sexual Assault. *Violence & Victims, 29*(4): 579–593.

American Association of University Professors. 2012. Campus Sexual Assault: Suggested Policies and Procedures. https://www.aaup.org/file/Sexual_Assault_Policies.pdf

Association of American Universities. 2015. Campus Climate Survey on Sexual Assault and Sexual Misconduct. https://www.aau.edu/Climate-Survey.aspx?id=16525

Black, M.C., Basile, K.C., Breiding, M.J. Smith, S.G., Walters, M.L., Merrick, M.T., Chen, J., and Stevens, M.R. 2011. *The National Intimate Partner and Sexual Violence Survey (NISVS): 2010 Summary Report*. Atlanta, GA: National Center for Injury Prevention and Control, Centers for Disease Control and Prevention.

Buchholz, L. 2015. The Role of University Health Centers in Intervention and Prevention of Campus Sexual Assault. *Journal of the American Medical Association, 314* (5): 438–440.

Burgess-Proctor, A., Pickett, S.M., Parkill, M.R., Hamill, T.S., Kirwan, M., and Kozak, A.T. 2016. College Women's Perceptions of and Inclination to Use Campus Sexual Assault Resources: Comparing the Views of Students with and without Sexual Victimization Histories. *Criminal Justice Review, 41* (2): 204–218.

Cantalupo, N.C. 2011. Burying Our Heads in the Sand: Lack of Knowledge, Knowledge Avoidance and the Persistent

Problem of Campus Peer Sexual Violence. *Loyola University Chicago Law Journal, 43*: 205–266.

Carey, K.B., Durney, S.E., Shepardson, R.L., and Carey, M.P. 2015. Incapacitated and Forcible Rape of College Women: Prevalence across the First Year. *Journal of Adolescent Health 56*: 678–680.

Chang, E., Jilani, Z., Yu, T., Lin, J., Muyan, M., and Hirsch, J. 2015. Relationship between Sexual Assault and Negative Affective Conditions in Female College Students: Does Loss of Hope Account for the Association? *Journal of Interpersonal Violence*. Advance online publication. doi: 10.1177/0886260515588534

Cleere, C., and Lynn, S.J. 2013. Acknowledged versus Unacknowledged Sexual Assault among College Women. *Journal of Interpersonal Violence, 28*(12): 2593–2611.

Decker, J.F., and Baroni, P.G. 2011. "No" Still Means "Yes": The Failure of the "Non-Consent" Reform Movement in American Rape and Sexual Assault Law. *The Journal of Criminal Law and Criminology, 101*(4): 1081–1169.

DeMatteo, D., Galloway, M., Arnold, S., and Patel, U. 2015. Sexual Assault on College Campuses: A 50-State Survey of Criminal Sexual Assault Statutes and Their Relevance to Campus Sexual Assault. *Psychology, Public Policy, and Law, 21*(3): 227–238.

Donde, S. 2015. College Women's Attributions of Blame for Experiences of Sexual Assault. *Journal of Interpersonal Violence*. Advance online publication. doi:10.1177/0886260515599659

Dupain, M., and Lombardi, J.A. 2014. Developing and Implementing a Sexual Assault Violence Prevention and Awareness Campaign at a State-Supported Regional University. *American Journal of Health Studies, 29*(4): 264–270.

Eisenberg, M., Lust, K., Hannan, P., and Porta, C. 2016. Campus Sexual Violence Resources and Emotional Health of College Women Who Have Experienced Sexual Assault. *Violence and Victims, 31*(2): 274–284.

Fedina, L., Holmes, J.L., and Backes, B. 2016. Campus Sexual Assault: A Systematic Review of Prevalence Research from 2000 to 2015. *Trauma, Violence, and Abuse.* doi:10.1177/1524838016631129

Flack, W.F., Hansen, B.E., Hopper, A.B, Bryant, L.A., Lang, K.W., Massa, A.A., and Whalen, J.E. 2015. Some Types of Hookups May Be Riskier Than Others for Campus Sexual Assault. *Psychological Trauma: Theory, Research, Practice, and Policy, 8*(4): 413–420.

Flack, W.F., Jr., Kimble, M.O., Campbell, B.E., Hopper, A.B., Petercă O., and Heller, E.J. 2014. Sexual Assault Victimization among Female Undergraduates during Study Abroad: A Single Campus Survey Study. *Journal of Interpersonal Violence, 30*(20): 3453–3466.

Foubert, J.D., Brosi, M.W., and Bannon, R.S. 2011. Pornography Viewing among Fraternity Men: Effects on Bystander Intervention, Rape Myth Acceptance and Behavioral Intent to Commit Sexual Assault. *Sexual Addiction & Compulsivity: The Journal of Treatment & Prevention, 18*(4): 212–231.

Franklin, C.A. 2015. Sorority Affiliation and Sexual Assault Victimization: Assessing Vulnerability Using Path Analysis. *Violence against Women,* 22(8): 895–922.

Franklin, C.A., Bouffard, L.A., and Pratt, T.C. 2012. Sexual Assault on the College Campus: Fraternity Affiliation, Male Peer Support, and Low Self-Control. *Criminal Justice and Behavior, 30*: 1457–1480.

Garrity, S.E. 2011. Sexual Assault Prevention Programs for College-Aged Men: A Critical Evaluation. *Journal of Forensic Nursing, 7*(1): 40–48.

Hayes, R.M., Abbott, R.L., and Cook, S. 2016. It's Her Fault: Student Acceptance of Rape Myths on Two College Campuses. *Violence against Women,* 13: 1540–1555.

Hayes-Smith, R.M., and Levett, L.M. 2010. Student Perceptions of Sexual Assault Resources and Prevalence of Rape Myth Attitudes. *Feminist Criminology, 5*(4): 335–354.

Hines, D., Armstrong, J.L., Reed, K.P., and Cameron, A.Y. 2012. Gender Differences in Sexual Assault Victimization among College Students. *Violence and Victims, 27*(6): 922–940.

Hust, S.T., Marett, E.G., Ren, C., Adams, P., Willoughby, J., Lei, M., Ran, W., and Norman, C. 2014. Establishing and Adhering to Sexual Consent: The Association between Reading Magazines and College Students' Sexual Consent Negotiation. *Journal of Sex Research, 51*(3): 280–290.

Jordan, C.E. 2014. The Safety of Women on College Campuses: Implications of Evolving Paradigms in Postsecondary Education. *Trauma Violence & Abuse,15*(3): 143–148.

Jozkowski, K., Peterson, Z.D., Sanders, S.A., Dennis, B., and Reece, M. 2014.Gender Differences in Heterosexual College Students' Conceptualizations and Indicators of Sexual Consent: Implications for Contemporary Sexual Assault Prevention Education. *The Journal of Sex Research, 51*(8): 904–916.

Katz, J. 2015. Effects of Group Status and Victim Sex on Male Bystanders' Responses to a Potential Party Rape. *Journal of Aggression, Maltreatment & Trauma, 24*(5): 588–602.

Katz, J., May, P., Sörensen, S., and DelTosta, J. 2010. Sexual Revictimization during Women's First Year of College: Self-Blame and Sexual Refusal Assertiveness and Possible Mechanisms. *Journal of Interpersonal Violence, 25(11):* 2113–2126.

Katz, J., and Moore, J. 2013. Bystander Education Training for Campus Sexual Assault Prevention: An Initial Meta-analysis. *Violence and Victims, 28*(6): 1054–1067.

Koelsch, L.E., Brown, A., and Boisen, L. 2012. Bystander Perceptions: Implications for University Sexual Assault

Prevention Programs. *Violence and Victims, 27*(4): 563–579.

Koss, M.P., Wilgus, J.K., and Williamsen, K.M. 2014. Campus Sexual Misconduct Restorative Justice Approaches to Enhance Compliance with Title IX Guidance. *Trauma, Violence, & Abuse, 15*(3): 242–257.

Krebs, C., Barrick, K., Lindquist, C.H., Crosby, C.M., Boyd, C., and Bogan, Y. 2011. The Sexual Assault of Undergraduate Women at Historically Black Colleges and Universities (HBCUs). *Journal of Interpersonal Violence, 26*(18): 3640–3666.

Krebs, C., Lindquist, C., Berzofsky, M., Shook-Sa, B., and Peterson, K. 2016. Campus Climate Survey Validation Study Final Technical Report. *National Institute of Justice, Bureau of Justice Statistics*. http://www.bjs.gov/content/pub/pdf/ccsvsftr.pdf

Lawyer, S., Resnick, H., Bakanic, V., Burkett, T., and Kilpatrick, D. 2010. Forcible, Drug-Facilitated, and Incapacitated Rape and Sexual Assault among Undergraduate Women. *Journal of American College Health, 58*(5): 453–460.

Lombardi, Kristen. 2009–2015. Sexual Assault on Campus: A Frustrating Search for Justice. Investigative Project. *The Center for Public Integrity*. https://www.publicintegrity.org/accountability/education/sexual-assault-campus

Lund, E.M., and Thomas, K. 2015. Necessary but Not Sufficient: Sexual Assault Information on College and University Websites. *Psychology of Women Quarterly, 39*(4): 530–538.

Martin, S.L., Fisher, B.S., Warner, T.D., Krebs, C.P., and Lindquist, C.H. 2011. Women's Sexual Orientations and Their Experiences of Sexual Assault before and during University. *Women's Health Issues, 21*(3): 199–205.

McGregor, K.M. 2015. Raped a Second Time: The Mental Health Impact of Campus Sexual Assault Investigation and Adjudication. *Quinnipiac Health Law Journal,*18: 401–.

McMahon, S. 2010. Rape Myth Beliefs and Bystander Intervention Attitudes among Incoming College Students. *Journal of American College Health, 59*: 3–11.

Orchowski, L.M., and Gidycz, C.A. 2012. To Whom Do College Women Confide Following Sexual Assault? A Prospective Study of Predictors of Sexual Assault Disclosure and Social Reactions. *Violence against Women, 18*(3): 264–288.

Orchowski, L.M., Untied, A.S., and Gidycz, C.A. 2013. Factors Associated with College Women's Labeling of Sexual Victimization. *Violence & Victims, 28*(6): 940–958.

Palmer, R.S., McMahon, T.J., Rounsaville, B.J., and Ball, S.A. 2010. Coercive Sexual Experiences, Protective Behavioral Strategies, Alcohol Expectancies and Consumption among Male and Female College Students. *Journal of Interpersonal Violence, 25*(9): 1563–1578.

Paul, L.A., and Gray, M.J. 2011. Sexual Assault Programming on College Campuses: Using Social Psychological Belief and Behavior Change Principles to Improve Outcomes. *Trauma, Violence & Abuse, 12*(2): 99–109.

Piccigallo, J.R., Lilley, T.G., and Miller, S.L. 2012. "It's Cool to Care about Sexual Violence": Men's Experiences with Sexual Assault Prevention. *Men and Masculinities, 15*(5): 507–525.

Porter, J., and Williams, L.M. 2011. Intimate Violence among Underrepresented Groups on a College Campus. *Journal of Interpersonal Violence, 26*(16): 3210–3224.

Potter, S.J. 2016. Reducing Sexual Assault on Campus: Lessons from the Movement to Prevent Drunk Driving. *American Journal of Public Health, 106*(5):822–829.

Pryor, D.W., and Hughes, M.R. 2013. Fear of Rape among College Women: A Social Psychological Analysis. *Violence and Victims, 28*(3): 443–465.

Reingold, R., and Gostin, L.O. 2015. Sexual Assaults among University Students: Prevention, Support, and Justice. *Journal of the American Medical Association, 314*(5): 447–448.

Sabina, C., and Ho, L.Y. 2014. Campus and College Victim Responses to Sexual Assault and Dating Violence: Disclosure, Service Utilization, and Service Provision. *Trauma, Violence, & Abuse, 15*(3): 201–226.

Senn, C., Eliasziw, M., Barata, P.C., Thurston, W.E., Newby-Clark, I., Radtke, L., and Hobden, K. 2015. Efficacy of a Sexual Assault Resistance Program for University Women. *New England Journal of Medicine, 372*: 2326–2335.

Smith, C.P., and Freyd, J. 2013. Dangerous Safe Havens: Institutional Betrayal Exacerbates Sexual Trauma. *Journal of Traumatic Stress, 26*(1): 119–124.

Sorenson, S.B., Joshi, M., and Sivitz, E. 2014. Knowing a Sexual Assault Victim or Perpetrator: A Stratified Random Sample of Undergraduates at One University. *Journal of Interpersonal Violence, 29*(3): 394–416.

Streng, T.K., and Kamimura, A. 2015. Sexual Assault Prevention and Reporting on College Campuses in the U.S.: A Review of Policies and Recommendations. *Journal of Education and Practices, 6*(3): 65–71.

Strozer, R.L., and McCartney, D. 2015. The Role of Institutional Factors on On-Campus Reported Rape Prevalence. *Journal of Interpersonal Violence, 31*(16): 2687–2707.

Sweeney, B.N. 2011. The Allure of the Freshman Girl: Peers, Partying, and the Sexual Assault of First-Year College Women. *Journal of College and Character, 12*(4). doi: 10.2202/1940–1639.1790

Veidlinger, R.L. 2016. Title IX: Role of Sexual Assault Nurse Examiners in Campus Sexual Assault Proceedings. *The Journal for Nurse Practitioners, 12*(2): 113–119.

Vladutiu, C.J., Martin, S.L., and Macy, R.J. 2011. College- or University-Based Sexual Assault Prevention Programs: A Review of Program Outcomes, Characteristics, and Recommendations. *Trauma, Violence, & Abuse, 12*(2): 67–86.

Walsh, W.A., Banyard, V.L., Moynihan, M., Ward, S., and Cohn, E.S. 2010. Disclosure and Service Use on a College Campus after an Unwanted Sexual Experience. *Journal of Trauma and Dissociation, 11*(2): 134–151.

Washington Post–Kaiser Family Foundation Poll. 2015. *Survey on Current and Recent College Students on Sexual Assault.* http://kff.org/other/poll-finding/survey-of-current-and-recent-college-students-on-sexual-assault

Weiss, K.G. 2010. Male Sexual Victimization: Examining Men's Experiences of Rape and Sexual Assault. *Men and Masculinities, 12*(3): 275–298.

White House Council on Women and Girls. 2014. Rape and Sexual Assault: A Renewed Call to Action. Washington, DC: Office of the Vice President. https://www.whitehouse.gov/sites/default/files/docs/sexual_assault_report_1–21–14.pdf

White House Task Force to Protect Students from Sexual Assault. 2014. Not Alone: Together against Sexual Assault. www.notalone.gov

Wies, J.R. 2015. Title IX and the State of Campus Sexual Violence in the United States: Power, Policy, and Local Bodies. *Human Organization, 74*(3): 276–286.

Yung, C.R. 2015. Concealing Campus Sexual Assault: An Empirical Examination. *Psychology, Public Policy, and Law, 21*(1): 1–9.

Zinzow, H.M., and Thompson, M. 2011. Barriers to Reporting Sexual Victimization: Prevalence and Correlates among Undergraduate Women. *Journal of Aggression, Maltreatment & Trauma, 20*(7): 711–725.

Documentaries

After the Rape: The Mukhtar Mai Story (2008)
> In Pakistan in 2002, Mukhtar Mai survived a gang rape by order of her tribal council as punishment for her younger brother's alleged relationship with a woman from another clan. Afterward, Mai spoke out and started two schools for girls and a crisis center for abused women.

Asking for It: The Ethics & Erotics of Sexual Consent (2010)
> Utilizing the lens of law and ethics, this film clarifies that consent must always be explicitly granted.

Audrie & Daisy (2016)
> This documentary chronicles two separate high-profile sexual assault cases of high school girls by their male peers. Audrie committed suicide within a week of her attack, and Daisy was subsequently driven out of town. Additionally, despite public outrage, the perpetrators did not receive serious punishment. See the film's website for information on the #SurvivorLoveLetter digital gallery (www.audrieanddaisy.com).

The Brandon Teena Story (1998)
> The true story behind the Academy Award winning film *Boys Don't Cry*. Brandon Teena was a trans-man raped and murdered in Nebraska. His story, and Matthew Shepard's, spurred increased lobbying for hate crime laws.

Brave Miss World (2013)
> Miss Israel, Linor Abargil, was abducted, stabbed, and raped by her travel agent in Milan, Italy, at age 18. Just six weeks later, she won the Miss World competition. Fulfilling her vow to do something about rape, this film follows her mission to fight for justice and break the silence. The film's website has a forum for survivors (www.bravemissworld.com).

The Central Park Five (2012)

In 1989, five black and Latino teenagers were wrongfully convicted of raping a white woman who was jogging in Central Park. Years later, a serial rapist confessed to the crime. This film provides the perspective of the five teenagers and their experience with racism and a miscarriage of justice.

Date Rape Backlash: Media and the Denial of Rape (1994)

Media portrayal in the early 1990s of date rape spanned from discussing date rape as an epidemic to the belief that women "cry rape." Noted scholars, journalists, and authors critique the media's reliance upon Katie Roiphe's beliefs that college women are typically partially to blame for their assaults.

Dissolve: A Documentary on Drug Facilitated Sexual Assault (2009)

This documentary discusses the use of date rape drugs to render women unconscious or semi-unconscious in order to sexually assault them.

Every Two Minutes (2014)

Created by a group of Michigan State University students, this documentary profiles sexual assault testimonials from a diverse group of women and men. Their stories are interspersed with interviews with police, nurses, therapists, and sexual assault advocates. Visit the film's website to find a forum for sexual assault survivors (everytwo minutesfilm.com).

Flirting with Danger: Power & Choice in Heterosexual Relationships (2012)

Based on interviews conducted by social psychologist Lynn Phillips with hundreds of young women, this film explores the line between consent and coercion and the ways women and girls navigate relationships and hook-ups.

The Greatest Silence: Rape in the Congo (2007)
> Lisa F. Jackson, a survivor of gang rape, travels to the war zones in the Democratic Republic of Congo to investigate the plight of women and girls kidnapped, raped, mutilated, and tortured by soldiers. Jackson interviews survivors, law officials, and self-confessed rapists.

Half the Sky (2012)
> Inspired by Nicholas D. Kristoff and Sheryl WuDunn's book, *Half the Sky: Turning Oppression into Opportunity for Women Worldwide*, this four-hour series filmed in ten countries exposes global oppression against women and girls (including sexual assault). The book, the film, and the website (www.halftheskymovement.org) all highlight grassroots activism and provide suggestions on ways to help.

The Hunting Ground (2015)
> Written and directed by Kirby Dirk and produced by Amy Ziering, this film presents the stories of students sexually assaulted on their college campuses and the failure of their institutions to handle the cases adequately. An edited version was screened on CNN in 2015. For further information about campus sexual assault, and for ways to get involved, visit the websites associated with the film (www.thehuntinggroundfilm.com and www.seeactstop.org).

India's Daughter (2015)
> In 2012, Jyoti Singh was brutally gang raped on a bus in New Delhi. The attack was reported worldwide, and she received emergency treatment and several surgeries. Singh subsequently died due to the serious injuries she sustained in the assault. This documentary covers the tragic event, including profiling the six perpetrators. Visit the film's website for information about the #StoptheShame movement (http://indiasdaughter.com).

The Invisible War: Rape and Sexual Assault in the Military (2012)
Written and directed by Kirby Dirk and produced by
Amy Ziering, this investigative documentary exposes the
epidemic of rape and sexual assault in the U.S. military.
Since its release, the film has influenced government poli-
cies to reduce the instances of sexual assault in the military.

It Happened Here (2014)
Through the stories of five student survivors, this film
documents the pervasiveness of campus sexual assault, the
institutional cover-ups, and the students' fight for change
and accountability.

It Was Rape (2013)
In this film by feminist Jennifer Baumgardner, eight
women with different backgrounds, ages, and ethnicities
share their stories surviving sexual assault.

Justice Denied: Military Sexual Trauma, the Men's Stories (2013)
Focusing on male sexual assault within the armed forces,
this documentary incorporates interviews with victims,
their families, and professionals. The film looks at the
difficulties for men to report their assaults in the current
culture of the military.

The Line (2009)
Nancy Schwartzman confronts the man who raped her in
this short documentary and discusses the contested line
between consensual and nonconsensual sex through conversations with sex workers, survivors, and activists.

No! The Rape Documentary (2004)
A labor of love for filmmaker, feminist, and rape and
incest survivor Aishah Shahidah Simmons, this film high-
lights rape, sexual violence, and healing in African American communities.

Rape in the Fields (2013)

Frontline and Univision partner to tell the story of rampant sexual assault and harassment of migrant women working in America's fields and packing plants. For news updates and additional information about this crisis, visit the Center for Investigative Reporting: http://cironline .org/rapeinthefields.

Rape Is . . . (2003)

This short documentary explores the meaning and consequences of rape from a global and historical perspective.

Rape Myths on Trial: Naming the Unnamed Conspirator (2012)

This illustrated lecture with a career prosecutor explains how cultural myths and sexism often shape jurors' decision making in sexual assault cases.

Spitting Game: The College Hookup Culture (2008)

In this concise documentary, students, parents, and experts examine hook-up culture, sexual assault, and binge drinking on college campuses.

Tapestries of Hope (2009)

Filmed in Zimbabwe, Africa, this is the story of human rights activist Betty Makoni and the Child Girl Network. The documentary aims to bring awareness about the abuse of women and girls by exposing the myth that if a man rapes a virgin he will be cured of HIV/AIDS.

Turned Out: Sexual Assault behind Bars (2004)

An investigation into prison rape and the social structure that enables it to occur.

Uniform Betrayal: Rape in the Military (2012)

Produced for PBS, this documentary discusses the problem of sexual assault in the U.S. military from the viewpoint of survivors and experts.

Yeah Maybe No: A Documentary about Consent (2016)

This documentary tells the story of a male sexual assault survivor and his difficulties with gaps in the legal system and in finding support from his peers.

Campus Activism

The following list outlines selected opportunities for sexual assault awareness campaigns and activism. While some campuses have their own school-specific campaigns, this is a selection of programs that can be adopted by any interested individual, group, or institution. The websites provide information and directions on how to bring the project, campaign, or event to a specific campus or community.

Bandana Project (www.thebandanaproject.org)

This Bandana Project is aimed at raising awareness about sexual violence against migrant farm worker women in the United States. Participants decorate and wear white bandanas to show support for survivors who have come forward to confront their abusers and hold their employers responsible.

Clothesline Project (www.clotheslineproject.org)

For over 25 years, this project bears witness to violence against women. Participants put their personal experiences, thoughts, or statements on a t-shirt that is hung on display on a clothesline. The t-shirts are color coded to represent various forms of violence, including battering, sexual assault, and incest.

Denim Day in LA and USA (http://denimdayinfo.org)

Denim Day encourages participants to wear denim on a set date in April to raise awareness about sexual violence, spurred by a ruling of the Italian Supreme Court, where a rape conviction was overturned because the justices believed that the victim's jeans were so tight that she must have helped remove them, which, in their view, implied consent. The following day, women in the Italian Parliament came to work wearing jeans in solidarity with the victim.

Hands and Words Are Not for Hurting Project (http://hands project.org/)

The goal of the Hands and Words Are Not for Hurting Project is to end abuse and violence in homes, schools, and communities by raising awareness and encouraging people to take the pledge "I will not use my hands or words for hurting myself or others." Schools and communities who participate often create pieces of art or murals using handprints.

It Happens Here Project (www.ihhproject.org)

Developed by sexual assault survivors and allies at Middlebury College, the It Happens Here Project is based on the belief that recognition and discussion is the first step toward change. The project empowers survivors to anonymously post their personal stories with sexual violence and have them read by other students at public events.

It's on Us (www.itsonus.org)

Launched by President Obama, It's on Us is an awareness campaign to end sexual assault on college campuses. The campaign asks everyone to be a part of the solution and encourages people to take the pledge to help keep women and men safe from sexual assault.

Monument Quilt (www.themonumentquilt.org)

Sponsored by the art activist effort Force: Upsetting Rape Culture, survivors of rape and abuse write, stitch, or paint their stories on red fabric to be displayed as part of the Monument Quilt. To date, the quilt has been displayed in a variety of cities, with the ultimate goal to blanket over a mile of the National Mall in Washington, D.C., spelling "Not Alone."

NoMore (www.nomore.org)

No More is both a symbol and a campaign to raise awareness and engage bystanders in ending domestic violence and sexual assault. Comprised of a coalition of advocacy groups, service providers, the U.S. Department of Justice, corporations, individuals, and others, No More suggests a variety of ways to get involved. For example, groups and organizations can adopt the No More Week of Action, a preplanned week with a variety of activities, including media screenings, fundraising, and bystander intervention training.

RAINN Day (https://rainn.org/rainnday)

Created by the Rape, Abuse, and Incest National Network (RAINN), RAINN Day is an annual day of action in September to educate and raise awareness about sexual violence on college campuses. RAIIN Day events are tailored by the hosting individual, department, student group, or organization to fit the needs of the campus.

Red Flag Campaign (www.theredflagcampaign.org)

The Red Flag Campaign encourages people to speak out when they see warning signs (red flags) for sexual assault, stalking, or dating violence in their peer's relationships. The campaign includes placing red flags on campus to raise awareness.

Ribbon Campaigns

White Ribbon (www.whiteribbon.ca): This is an awareness campaign that involves men in working to end violence against women. Male participants wear a white ribbon and sign a pledge stating they will never commit, condone, or remain silent about violence.

Teal Ribbon (http://www.nsvrc.org/saam): Teal is the official color for Sexual Assault Awareness Month (SAAM) held in the United States every April. The National Sexual Violence Resource Center provides resources and graphics for SAAM events.

SlutWalk (https://www.facebook.com/SlutWalk)
The first SlutWalk occurred in Toronto after a Toronto police officer stated that "women should avoid dressing like sluts in order not to be victimized." Now a global phenomenon, SlutWalks are protest marches that raise awareness about slut shaming and victim blaming and call for the end of rape culture. A complementary online event is the International Day Against Victim-Blaming (#EndVictimBlaming) scheduled for April 3 each year.

Take Back the Night (http://takebackthenight.org)
Take Back the Night events have occurred in the United States since the 1970s with the aim to eliminating sexual and domestic violence in all forms. Now a nonprofit, the Take Back the Night Foundation supports events throughout the world, typically in the form of rallies, runs, walks, vigils, performances, and/or speak-outs.

V-Day (http://www.vday.org)
Created by Eve Ensler, a playwright, performer, and activist, V-Day is a global movement to end violence against women and girls. Campuses and community organizations can produce benefit performances that raise money for grassroots, national, and international organizations that work to stop gender violence. The performances include artistic works such as *The Vagina Monologues*, which addresses women's sexuality; *A Memory, a Monologue, a Rant and a Prayer: Writings to End Violence against Women and Girls*, a collection of monologues by authors and playwrights; and the documentary *What I Want My*

Words to Do to You, about a writing group Ensler led at a women's correctional facility. Additionally, in 2012, Ensler launched the One Billion Rising Campaign (www .onebillionrising.org), a global mass action where people come together to express outrage and rise in defiance against violence against women.

Walk a Mile in Her Shoes: The International Men's March to Stop Rape, Sexual Assault, and Gender Violence (www.walka mileinhershoes.org)

Walk a Mile in Her Shoes events are designed to raise awareness about men's sexualized violence against women. The fundraising event is open to everyone, but men are encouraged to wear women's high-heel shoes for the mile-long walk.

Nonprofits, Organizations, Programs, and Campaigns

The following list includes selected nonprofits, organizations, programs, and campaigns that work to end, and raise awareness about, sexual assault and violence against women. Additionally, many of the following provide guidance on combating sexual assault on campus, including some programs that can be brought to campus to provide prevention training. Note that colleges and universities, in addition to local and state rape crisis or antiviolence centers and organizations, also have their own programs and informational websites.

American Association of University Women (www.aauw.org)

Since 1881, the AAUW has promoted equity and education for women in girls. Included in their many online resources is the Ending Campus Sexual Assault Toolkit for students and faculty.

American College Health Association (www.acha.org)

ACHA is a leadership organization for advancing the health of college students and campus communities.

Their resources on campus sexual violence include a primary prevention toolkit and a campus safety and violence coalition.

Arte Sana (www.arte-sana.com)
Arte Sana (art heals) is a Latina-led nonprofit committed to ending sexual violence and other forms of gender-based aggressions. By engaging marginalized communities as agents of change, the organization promotes awareness, healing, and empowerment through bilingual professional training, community education, and the arts.

Association of Title IX Administrators (https://atixa.org)
ATIXA is a professional organization for school and college Title IX administrators and coordinators. It provides resources and professional development.

Breakthrough (http://us.breakthrough.tv)
Fueled by their mission to prevent violence against women by transforming the norms and cultures that enable it, this organization encourages a *breakthrough generation* to step up and make change. One of their available programs is campus leadership training to prevent campus sexual violence.

Circle of 6 (www.circleof6app.com)
Winner of the White House Apps against Abuse technology challenge, the Circle of 6 app allows users to let friends know of their location and if they need an interruption or help getting home.

Clery Center for Security on Campus (www.clerycenter.org)
The Clery Center works with colleges and universities to create safer campuses, including offering Clery Act compliance training and information for sexual assault victims and their families.

Culture of Respect (www.cultureofrespect.org)
> Officially part of NASPA-Student Affairs Administrators in Higher Education, this site provides tools and resources for students and administrators to assess and improve efforts to eliminate sexual assault from their campuses.

Date Safe Project (www.datesafeproject.org)
> Through workshops, books, and videos, the Date Safe Project provides skills for addressing verbal consent, respecting boundaries, sexual decision making, bystander intervention, and supporting survivors.

Define Your Line (www.defineyourline.org)
> Started by college students at Texas Tech, this campaign is "unblurring the lines" by promoting clear communication between sexual partners. Their site has a forum for discussion and advice from sexual health experts.

End Rape on Campus (www.endrapeoncampus.org)
> Cofounded by women highlighted in the film *The Hunting Ground* for their campus activism following sexual assaults on them, EROC works to end campus sexual assault through education, advocacy, and direct support for survivors and their communities.

End the Backlog (www.endthebacklog.org)
> A program of the Joyful Heart Foundation (see later), End the Backlog shines a light on the accumulation of untested rape kits and aims to end injustice by raising awareness, advocating for comprehensive reform legislation, and engaging in research to identify the extent of the backlog and best practices for eliminating it.

End Violence against Women International (www.evawintl.org)
> EVAWI is dedicated to improving the criminal justice response to sexual assault. Their campaign, *Start by Believing*,

wishes to change the way we respond to sexual assault in our communities.

Equality Now (www.equalitynow.org)
> Equality Now works for the protection and promotion of the human rights of women and girls around the world. With the help of activists and grassroots and human rights organizations, Equality Now documents violence and discrimination against women and mobilizes international action to stop the abuses. Sexual violence is one of their four main program areas.

Everfi (www.everfi.com)
> This company offers a variety of online education platforms, including *Haven*, which addresses sexual assault and relationship violence.

Faculty against Rape (www.facultyagainstrape.net)
> A collective dedicated to getting faculty involved in confronting campus sexual assault.

FaithTrust Institute (www.faithtrustinstitute.org)
> FaithTrust Institute provides faith communities and advocates with the tools and knowledge they need to address faith and cultural issues related to sexual assault and domestic violence.

Feminist Campus (www.feministcampus.org)
> A project of the Feminist Majority Foundation, Feminist Campus helps students start new groups or assists those who wish to align themselves with the Feminist Majority Leadership Alliance. The group has many campaigns, including one to end sexual violence on campus.

FORCE: Upsetting Rape Culture (http://upsettingrapeculture .tumblr.com)
> FORCE is an "art activist effort" with the goal of upsetting the dominant culture of rape and promoting a

counter-culture of consent. They are currently sponsoring the Monument Quilt for survivors of rape and abuse, discussed earlier as a possibility for campus activism.

Futures without Violence (www.futureswithoutviolence.org)
Working to prevent gender-based violence on college campuses, Futures has a range of resources, including guidelines for campus administrators, a leadership program to reinforce the intersection of health and gender-based violence prevention, a conference to facilitate grassroots change, and an awareness-building effort to increase visibility of the issue during the first 15 weeks of school.

Green Dot, etc. (www.livethegreendot.com)
The non-profit Green Dot, etc. provides bystander training on reducing violence. The curriculum centers on the premise that green dots are behaviors, choices, words, or attitudes that promote safety and communicates zero tolerance for violence.

Hollaback (www.ihollaback.org)
Hollaback is a movement to end street harassment by encouraging individuals to use their phones or computers to document, map, and share incidents of harassment.

Joyful Heart Foundation (www.joyfulheartfoundation.org)
Founded by actress Mariska Hargitay, the Joyful Heart Foundation aspires to transform society's response to sexual assault, domestic violence, and child abuse; support survivors' healing; and end violence. The foundation raises money to send survivors to therapeutic programs.

Know Your IX: Empowering Students to Stop Sexual Violence (www.knowyourix.org)
A survivor- and youth-led organization, Know Your IX, aims to empower students to end sexual and dating

violence in their schools. Drawing on Title IX as an alternative to the criminal justice system, the organization provides education on legal rights and training for student activists and advocates for policy change.

MaleSurvivor (www.malesurvivor.org)
MaleSurvivor provides support and resources for male survivors of sexual abuse, including healing retreats and a therapist directory.

Man Up (https://manupcampaign.org)
Man Up is a nonprofit that aims to activate youth to stop violence against women and girls. Through sport, music, the arts, and technology, the campaign partners with young men and women to give them a voice in developing models of change.

Men Can Stop Rape (www.mencanstoprape.org)
With the goal to promote healthy and nonviolent masculinity, this organization mentors male youth to prevent men's violence against women and other men. MCSR provides direct services, public service messages, and leadership training for schools, agencies, and organizations.

Mentors in Violence Prevention (www.mvpnational.org)
Founded by author, filmmaker, and cultural theorist, Jackson Katz, MVP is a sexual and relationship abuse prevention program offered in high schools, colleges, the military, and sports culture. Led by former athletes, the MVP program trainings raise awareness about men's violence against women and challenge participants to develop bystander intervention strategies.

National Alliance to End Sexual Violence (www.endsexualviolence.org)
NAESV's mission is to be the voice in Washington, D.C., for advocating and organizing against sexual violence and for survivors. The alliance educates the policy community

about federal laws, legislation, and appropriations impact-
ing the fight to end sexual violence.

National Coalition of Anti-Violence Programs (www.avp.org)
NCAVP works to prevent, respond to, and end all forms
of violence against and within LGBTQ communities,
including a crisis hotline (212–714–1141), community
organizing, and legal services.

National Online Resource Center on Violence against Women
(www.vawnet.org)
A project of the National Recourse Center on Domestic
Violence, VAWnet offers an online collection of full-text
and searchable materials and resources on domestic and
sexual violence.

National Organization of Asians and Pacific Islanders Ending
Sexual Violence (www.napiesv.org)
NAPIESV provides technical assistance and support to
community programs and government organizations in
enhancing their services to victims of sexual violence from
Asian and Pacific Islander communities.

National Organization of Sisters of Color Ending Sexual Assault
(www.sisterslead.org)
SCESA is an antiviolence advocacy organization. They
provide community awareness and education, policy advocacy, and support and training for leaders in the anti–sexual
assault movement. In partnership with the Black Wom-
en's Blueprint Project (www.blackwomensblueprint.org)
and the Office on Violence against Women, SCESA provides culturally specific technical assistance, training, and
support to address gender violence on historically black
college and university campuses.

National Sexual Violence Resource Center (www.nsvrc.org)
NSVRC is a national information and resource center for
all aspects of sexual violence. The site includes statistics,

relevant research, prevention initiatives, training curricula, and information about Sexual Assault Awareness Month.

Not Alone (www.changingourcampus.org)
The White House Task Force to Protect Students from Sexual Assault, created by President Obama, released their first report Not Alone, along with the original website notalone.gov. The website provides information, resources, and data for students and schools on how to prevent campus sexual assault. See information earlier under Campus Activism for President Obama's related awareness campaign Its on Us.

One in Four (www.oneinfourusa.org)
One in Four offers trainings and other materials for the prevention of sexual assault and serves as an umbrella organization for collegiate chapters.

Only with Consent (www.onlywithconsent.org)
Dedicated to stopping sexual violence through consent and health education, Only with Consent offers age-appropriate workshops and presentations.

Pact5 (www.pact5.org)
Students at five universities created short documentaries on rape and sexual assault. The films and the documentary guides are available on their website.

PreventConnect (www.preventconnect.org)
A national online community for violence prevention practitioners, the PreventConnect Campus is a national community of campus prevention practitioners. Their website offers web conferences, eLearning programs, and podcasts.

Prevention Innovations Research Center (http://cola.unh.edu/prevention-innovations-research-center)
Housed at the University of New Hampshire, Prevention Innovations helps campus communities with

policies, procedures, and programs on issues relating to violence against women on campus. They provide consultations, workshop presentations, technical assistance, and offer an in-person prevention program Bringing in the Bystander and a social marketing campaign Know Your Power.

Project UnBreakable (http://projectunbreakable.tumblr.com/)
   With the aim of giving survivors of sexual assault, domestic violence, and child abuse a voice, participants in this photography project hold posters with quotes from their abusers. Created in 2011 by a 19-year-old photographer, Grace Brown, the project has grown to include over 4,000 pictures, including photos taken by Brown and submissions from around the world. While the images are still available online, the project is no longer accepting new submissions.

Promoting Awareness, Victim Empowerment (www.pavingthe way.net)
   Founded by Angela Rose after being kidnapped and sexually assaulted as a teenager, PAVE works to prevent sexual assault and heal survivors through social advocacy, prevention education, and survivor support. PAVE provides educational speakers and workshops on sexual assault prevention and survivor empowerment; additionally, campuses can start PAVE chapters.

Rape, Abuse, & Incest National Network (www.rainn.org)
   The largest anti–sexual assault organization in the United States, RAINN operates the National Sexual Assault Hotline (1–800–656–HOPE and online.rainn.org), operates a safe hotline for the Department of Defense, and provides programming on preventing sexual violence, helping victims, and ensuring rapists are brought to justice. See Campus Activism earlier for information on RAINN Day.

Sex Signals (www.catharsisproductions.com)
> Sex Signals is a sexual assault prevention program that utilizes a humor-facilitated approach to teaching about bystander intervention.

Step Up! Bystander Intervention Program (http://stepuppro gram.org)
> Developed by the University of Arizona, Step Up! is a bystander intervention program. They offer facilitator materials for the program and national facilitator trainings.

Stop Sexual Assault in Schools (http://stopsexualassaultinschools .org)
> SSAIS is the only organization that specifically addresses sexual harassment and violence at the K-12 level. They offer resources, prevention programs, trainings, and youth engagement programs.

Stop Street Harassment (www.stopstreetharassment.org)
> SSH is a nonprofit dedicated to documenting and ending gender-based street harassment. They provide a street harassment hotline, information about applicable laws, and tips on how to deal with harassers. Additionally, they host a blog where people share their experiences and sponsor an international anti–street harassment week.

Student Coalition against Rape (http://studentcoalitionagain strape.org)
> SCAR provides a network to connect students in order to work together to expose and eradicate campus administrative failures regarding student-on-student crime, specifically sexual violence and sexual assault.

Students Active for Ending Rape (www.safercampus.org)
> SAFER strengthens student-led movements to combat sexual and interpersonal violence in campus communities.

The organization provides resources on policy and activism, in addition to offering campus-specific mentoring for student activists interested in bolstering their campaign efforts for sexual assault policy reform.

Student Success (http://public.studentsuccess.org)
The organization Student Success offers an online interactive sexual assault program for campuses called Not Anymore and, in partnership with Green Dot, etc., a bystander intervention program called Every Choice.

SurvJustice (www.survjustice.org)
Founded by Laura Dunn, campus sexual assault survivor turned victim's rights attorney, SurvJustice aims to increase the prospect of justice for survivors by holding both perpetrators and enablers of sexual violence accountable. SurvJustice provides resources and legal assistance to survivors to enforce their rights in campus, criminal, and civil systems of justice in addition to providing trainings to institutes to prevent and address sexual violence.

Ultraviolet (https://weareultraviolet.org)
This women's rights advocacy organization works on a full range of issues. One of their campaigns calls for the removal of a judge from the bench after he gave a lenient sentence to a Stanford student found guilty of sexual assault.

Unacceptable Acceptance Letters (www.dontacceptrape.com)
This campaign includes videotaped stories of sexual violence survivors in the form of "acceptance letters" detailing the event as if it were coming from the college itself. The goal is to raise awareness and demand accountability from colleges and universities.

Victim Rights Law Center (www.victimrights.org)
Founded as the first law center in the nation dedicated solely to serving the legal needs of sexual assault victims,

VRLC offers legal services in select areas and training for attorneys and advocates nationally.

We End Violence (www.weendviolence.com)
This company offers educational campaigns, workshops, trainings, lectures, performances, and consulting on the topic of violence prevention.

This timeline includes a select list of key events concerning campus sexual assault. This includes the publication of key research, relevant legislation, examples of campus activism and activist organizations, and numerous high-profile campus sexual assaults and/or related hearings, court cases, or federal complaints. Due to the high rate of sexual assault on college and university campuses, the increasing numbers of Title IX complaints, and the widespread campus activism that is occurring across the nation, it would be challenging to list all known incidents and events here. Instead, what is included is a selection of cases that received a fair amount of public attention, because of the assault itself, because of the way the university or college (mis)handled it, or because of the survivor's ensuing actions. Additionally, the timeline has more entries in recent years. As discussed previously, this is not because campus sexual assault is a new phenomenon; rather, it is because as a culture, we have only recently started paying attention.

February 1957   The journal *American Sociological Review* publishes Clifford Kirkpatrick and Eugene Kanin's ground-breaking article "Male Sex Aggression on a University Campus."

A college student demonstrates the use of a campus emergency call box. Colleges and universities across the nation have experimented with various security measures in the effort to reduce the likelihood of sexual assaults. (iStockPhoto)

1971 The first rape crisis center is established by Bay Area Women against Rape in response to the rape of a Berkeley High School student.

September Susan Griffin's classic essay "Rape: The All American Crime" appears in *Ramparts* magazine. Griffin discusses rape in terms of domination, departing from commonly held beliefs of rape as a sexual act.

1972 In response to a series of gang rapes and abductions, students lobby for one of the first campus-based rape crisis centers, at the University of Maryland.

June 23 President Nixon signs into law Title IX of the Education Amendments of 1972. This landmark federal law prohibits discrimination on the basis of sex in any federally funded education program or activity. If found in violation of Title IX, any federally funded school, education program, or activity could lose federal funding.

1973 A four-day sit-in as a reaction to rapes at the University of Pennsylvania leads to rape crisis services, a women's studies program, and increased campus security.

1974 Six University of Notre Dame football players are accused of the gang rape of a local woman. A top school administrator refers to her as "a queen of the slums with a mattress tied to her back." The men are suspended for one year for violating campus rules, and no criminal charges are filed.

August 21 President Gerald Ford signs into law the Family Education Rights and Privacy Act, also known as the Buckley Amendment. FERPA protects the privacy of student education records.

1975 Susan Brownmiller publishes the classic *Against Our Will: Men, Women and Rape*. Brownmiller is widely credited with being the first to use the phrase *date rape*.

The first Take Back the Night marches occur in Philadelphia in response to violent crimes against women, later becoming a college staple.

1976   University of California–Berkeley leads the way for campus-wide sexual assault programming to be adopted at all schools in the University of California system.

1977   In *Alexander vs. Yale*, a group of female Yale students bring a landmark Title IX suit against the school, arguing that sexual harassment and violence constitute discrimination. While the case is thrown out on technical grounds in 1980, the court upheld the legal argument that sexual harassment is discrimination.

1981   Therapist Claire Walsh creates Sexual Assault Recovery Service (SARS) and, a year later, Campus Organized against Rape (COAR) at the University of Florida. COAR is a peer education group that becomes one of the earliest nationally recognized antirape education programs, serving as a model for similar programs across the country.

October 5, 1984   Liz Seccuro is gang raped at the Phi Kappa Psi fraternity house at the University of Virginia. Campus authorities take no action. Over 20 years later, she receives an apology from one of her attackers, spurring her desire to pursue justice. Seccuro chronicles her story in a 2011 memoir.

1985   *Ms.* magazine publishes "Date Rape: The Story of an Epidemic and Those Who Deny It" based on the research of Mary Koss. Koss's research shows most perpetrators of sexual assault are known to the victim.

January   In response to perceived insensitive comments about sexual assault made by the vice president of Student Services, University of Michigan students hold a sit-in protest. The protest prompts the creation of an assault prevention program.

April 5, 1986   Jeanne Clery, a student at Lehigh University is raped and murdered in her dorm room. The Clery Act (1990) is spurred by her tragedy.

April 1987   Princeton University holds its first Take Back the Night vigil. Some fraternity members respond with misogynistic threats. The event is filmed and covered by national media.

1988   Robin Warsaw publishes the classic *I Never Called It Rape* on the then hidden topic of acquaintance and date rape.

March 1, 1989   A mentally challenged girl is gang raped by football players at Glen Ridge High School. The case draws national attention, sharply splits residents of the town, and is adapted into a book and movie.

1990   Students at Brown University create "rape lists," naming "men who won't take 'no' for an answer" on bathroom walls. The lists, and the controversy surrounding them, gain national attention.

Peggy Reeves Sanday publishes *Fraternity Gang Rape: Sex, Brotherhood, and Privilege on Campus*. The widely acclaimed book draws on interviews with victims and fraternity members to analyze the existence of rape culture in all-male groups.

October   The first Clothesline Project occurs in Hyannis, Massachusetts, as part of annual Take Back the Night march.

November 8   President George H.W. Bush signs into law the Crime Awareness and Campus Security Act. The federal statute requires schools that participate in federal financial aid programs to publicly disclose, on an annual basis, their campus security policies and crime statistics over the past three years. The act is subsequently amended several times, and renamed the Clery Act after Jeanne Clery in 1998.

1991   Four student sexual assault survivors file a landmark lawsuit against Carleton College for failing to protect them against known assailants and mishandling their complaints.

Three white St. John's lacrosse players charged with the gang rape of an African American woman are acquitted. The case involved six men accused of raping the intoxicated student after she had been pressured to drink.

SpeakOut: The North American Student Coalition against Campus Sexual Violence, and the Coalition of Campuses against Rape (CCOAR) are formed. Over the years, SpeakOut holds held national conferences, and CCOAR maintains a network committed to advocacy and resource development.

March   Katie Koestner calls local newspapers telling her experience of being raped by a date in her freshman year while attending the College of William and Mary. Her assault results in the first sexual misconduct hearing at a university. Later, a cover of *Time* magazine features Koestner, and an HBO docudrama is loosely based on the incident. Koestner's story is credited with starting a nationwide conversation about date rape, and she later serves as the executive director of the Take Back the Night Foundation.

February 26, 1992   In *Franklin v. Gwinnett County Public Schools*, the U.S. Supreme Court upholds the award of monetary damages under Title IX.

June 1992   Antioch College adopts a Sexual Offense Prevention Policy that requires on-going verbal consent at every step of a sexual encounter. Nationally, the precedent-setting policy is ridiculed.

July 1992   The Federal Campus Sexual Assault Victims Bill of Rights, also referred to as the Ramstad Act, is signed into law by President George H.W. Bush. The bill exists as part of the Clery Act and affords sexual assault victims certain basic rights, including their options to notify law enforcement and to be informed of counseling services.

1993   Journalist Katie Roiphe publishes a book chronicling her personal thoughts on date rape and contemporary feminism, entitled *The Morning After: Sex, Fear and Feminism*. In it, Roiphe questions the notion of an epidemic of campus sexual assault and argues that in cases of campus date rape, women are at least partially responsible for their actions.

1994   Congress enacts the Violence against Women Act. The act improves federal, state, and local responses to sexual assault, domestic violence, and stalking and provides various grants, including those for campus sexual violence. VAWA was reauthorized in

2000, 2005, and 2013 with modifications and additions. The 2013 reauthorization includes the Campus SaVE Act.

March 1998   Hundreds of students at Bates College stage a protest over the college's mishandling of sexual assaults, spurring changes to campus policy.

June 22, 1998   In *Gebser v. Lago Vista Independent School District*, the Supreme Court argued that school administrators are not liable under Title IX for civil damages if they are unaware of instances of sexual discrimination.

June 24, 1998   Brenda Tracy asserts she is gang raped by four men, two of whom are Oregon State football players. The players are suspended for one game and the coach said they made "a bad choice." Tracy came public with her experience in 2014 and met with the coach, Mike Riley, in 2016.

May 24, 1999   The Supreme Court in *Davis v. Monroe County Board of Education* rules that schools can be held liable under Title IX for failing to address known student-on-student harassment, including assault.

2000   With funding from the Bureau of Justice Statistics and the National Institute of Justice, Bonnie S. Fisher, Francis T. Cullen, and Michael G. Turner publish results from the National College Women Sexual Victimization Survey.

Columbia University students start SAFER (Students Active for Ending Rape). The organization empowers student-led campaigns to reform campus sexual assault policies.

December 7, 2001   Lisa Simpson and Anne Gilmore allege they are gang raped by University of Colorado–Boulder football players and high school recruits. The incident sets off a long-running scandal that cost many university officials their jobs and called into question recruiting tactics. The university settles with the women in the court case *Simpson vs. University of Colorado* in 2007.

February 2002   The journal *Violence and Victims* publishes David Lisak and Paul M. Miller's oft-cited article "Repeat Rape and Multiple Offending among Undetected Rapists." Based on research of male college students, they find most rapes are committed by a small number of undetected and repeat offenders.

January 23, 2004   *Sports Illustrated* publishes a story breaking the silence of Katie Hnida, the first female placekicker on the University of Colorado football team. Hnida discloses that in 2000, she was raped by a football player and sexually harassed by fellow teammates.

April 2004   Laura Dunn, a student at the University of Wisconsin–Madison, alleges she is sexually assaulted by two men from her crew team. She argues she was denied justice from campus and police officials. Currently a victim's rights attorney, she is the founder and executive director of the nonprofit SurvJustice.

May 2006   Megan Wright reports being gang raped at Dominican College; the school did little in response. Wright subsequently dropped out of college for fear of seeing her attackers on campus and committed suicide in December.

December 13, 2006   Laura Dickinson is raped and murdered in her dorm room at Eastern Michigan University. Afterward, the school says there was no foul play. Ultimately, school authorities are found to have withheld information, deceived the public, and violated the Clery Act.

2007   In a report prepared for the National Institute of Justice, Christopher P. Krebs, Christine H. Lindquist, Tara D. Warner, Bonnie S. Fisher, and Sandra L. Martin publish their findings from the Campus Sexual Assault Survey.

April 11   The North Carolina attorney general drops charges against three Duke University lacrosse players who were charged with first-degree sexual offense and the kidnapping of an exotic dancer they had hired to perform. What is later believed to be a false allegation, the scandal results in the firing of the lacrosse coach, the disbarring of the district attorney, and civil suits lodged against the city and the school by lacrosse players.

2009–2010   The Center for Public Integrity, in collaboration with National Public Radio, releases a series of landmark investigative reports on sexual assault on campus entitled Sexual Assault on Campus: A Frustrating Search for Justice.

April 1, 2009   President Barack Obama declares April Sexual Assault Awareness Month.

October 24, 2009   A sophomore at Richmond High School leaves a homecoming dance and is robbed, beaten, and gang raped by six boys and men over the span of two hours. The case draws national attention for the "mob mentality" of the attackers and for the presence of ten or more bystanders who failed to intervene.

September 10, 2010   Elizabeth "Lizzy" Seeberg, a 19-year-old freshman at St. Mary's College commits suicide ten days after accusing a Notre Dame football player of sexual assault. Many are troubled by Notre Dame's slow response to Seeberg's report and their ultimate decision to find the accused "not responsible."

October 13, 2010   Pledges to the Yale fraternity Delta Kappa Epsilon chant "No means yes, yes means anal" and other similar phrases through an area of campus with a concentration of student housing Yale suspends the fraternity for five years.

April 4, 2011   The U.S. Department of Education's Office for Civil Rights releases a Dear Colleague letter to colleges, universities, and schools across the country. The primary intent of the letter is to reiterate that Title IX covers sexual violence and includes topics such as key Title IX requirements and obligations and proactive efforts the school can take to prevent sexual violence.

June 2012   Thomas Francis "Trey" Malone III commits suicide nine months after reporting surviving sexual assault at Amherst College. His suicide note alleges institutional callousness.

June 22, 2012   A jury finds former Pennsylvania State assistant football coach Jerry Sandusky guilty on 45 out of 48 counts of sexual abuse, stemming from the sexual assault of ten young boys, culled from a charity he created, over the course of over a decade. The scandal results in the termination of the school president and head football coach. Sandusky is later sentenced to at least 30 years in prison.

August 11, 2012 A 16-year-old girl attends parties with Steubenville High School students and is sexually assaulted by two football players over the course of several hours. The assaults were captured and widely disseminated on social media.

October 2012 Flyers that list Top Ten Ways to Get Away with Rape are found at Miami University of Ohio.

October 10, 2012 *The Amherst Student,* a student newspaper at Amherst College, publishes an essay by Angie Epifano that discusses her sexual assault by a male acquaintance and subsequent institutional callousness. Her widely read essay spurs changes at the school.

December 2012 The Sigma Phi Epsilon fraternity at the University of Vermont sends out a questionnaire asking "who would you rape?" National leadership closes the chapter.

December 7, 2012 Florida State University student Erica Kinsman reports she is sexually assaulted to the Tallahassee Police Department. Kinsman later identifies her alleged assailant as football player Jameis Winston. Winston is cleared of wrongdoing by the school in 2013, and the school settles with Kinsman in 2016. Kinsman is profiled in the documentary *The Hunting Ground.*

2013 The Campus Sexual Violence Elimination (SaVE) Act, an amendment to the Violence against Women Reauthorization Act, is signed into law by President Barack Obama. The act expands upon the Clery Act and includes a provision requiring specialized training to those who investigate and decide sexual assault cases.

A group of students, survivors, and professors cofound the advocacy group End Rape on Campus to formalize and centralize work around campus sexual assault. Three of the original student survivor cofounders, Annie Clark, Andrea Pino, and Sofie Karasek, are predominately featured in the film *The Hunting Ground.*

Know Your IX is cofounded by sexual assault survivors Dana Bolger and Alexandra Brodskey to empower students to end sexual violence at their schools. The student-led campaign informs students of their rights under Title IX.

Three mothers of sons accused of campus sexual assault cofound FACE (Families Advocating Campus Equality), which provides resources and support for wrongly accused college students and their families.

March   Sexual assault survivor and political analyst Zerlina Maxwell appears on Fox News to address the possibility of arming women to prevent rape. Maxwell says the responsibility should be on men instead, unleashing a fury of racially fueled threats against her on social media.

April   Thirty-seven former and current Occidental College sexual assault survivors file two federal complaints against the college for violation of the Clery Act and Title IX.

They hold a press conference to voice experiences and concerns about the school's policies and mishandling of the reports. Allegations that the school retaliates against those who speak out against sexual assault are part of the complaint.

April 24   Carolyn Luby, a University of Connecticut student, publishes an open letter to the campus president drawing attention to violence on campus and questioning aggressive logo rebranding. In response, Luby is harassed and receives rape threats. Luby is one of five women who file a federal lawsuit saying the university responded to their sexual assault complaints with indifference and is featured in the film *It Happened Here.*

June 23   Brandon Vandenburg, a Vanderbilt football player, organizes some of his teammates to sexually assault a woman he has been dating. After protracted legal proceedings, some argue the sentences the perpetrators ultimately receive are too lenient.

July 15   Activists from the Know Your IX ED ACT NOW campaign travel to Washington, D.C., to protest outside the Department of Education and deliver a petition calling on the Office for Civil Rights to conduct timely and transparent investigations and issue meaningful sanctions for schools found to be in violation of Title IX.

August 2   Lena Sclove, a student at Brown University, is choked and sexually assaulted by fellow student Daniel Kopin. While found responsible in the disciplinary hearing for four counts of misconduct, Kopin was suspended for one year and was able to return while Sclove was still a student.

October   A member of the Phi Kappa Tau fraternity at Georgia Tech sends an instructional email to members titled "Luring Your Rapebait" encouraging members to ply women with a lot of alcohol. As a result, the chapter is suspended by the university for three years.

2014   Male students at North Carolina State University create Undercover Colors, a nail polish that detects the presence of date-rape drugs in a drink, sparking a debate about whose responsibility it is to prevent sexual violence.

January 10   A Dartmouth student-run website publishes a student's "rape guide" encouraging the rape of a freshman student. The named student was sexually assaulted weeks later at a fraternity.

January 22   President Barack Obama creates the White House Task Force to Protect Students from Sexual Assault.

March 31   The *Harvard Crimson*, Harvard's school newspaper, publishes an anonymous editorial entitled "Dear Harvard: You Win," chronicling a student's sexual assault and failure of the institution to take action. The column went viral. In a follow-up essay after her graduation, the author identifies herself as Ariane Litalien. Her original essay spurs campus change.

April 2   James Madison University punishes three fraternity members found guilty of sexual assault and sexual harassment with "expulsion after graduation." The men filmed the assault of Sarah Butters and distributed it around campus. Butters filed a Title IX complaint, and the sentence drew national outrage and a petition for reform at the university.

April 29   The Department of Education's Office for Civil Rights releases a 53-page FAQ to address and clarify the 2011 Dear Colleague letter.

The White House Task Force to Protect Students from Sexual Assault releases its first report titled Not Alone.

May 12   Release of the documentary *It Happened Here*, which through the portraits of campus sexual assault survivors, discusses campus sexual assault and institutional cover-ups.

June 6   Conservative political pundit George Will pens an article for *The Washington Post* about campus sexual assault, arguing that victims have a "coveted status that confers privileges." One newspaper drops his syndicated column, Scripps College rescinds its invitation for him to speak, students protest his speech at Ohio's Miami University, and many advocacy groups are outraged.

July 12   *The New York Times* publishes "Reporting Rape, and Wishing She Hadn't," chronicling a woman's experience being gang raped by football players at Hobart and William Smith College and illustrating the inadequacies of the school's adjudication system.

August 25   Faculty against Rape is formed to get faculty more involved in preventing campus sexual assault and improving campus responses.

September   Emma Sulkowicz begins carrying a 50-pound dorm mattress around Columbia University as part of her senior art thesis entitled Carry That Weight. Vowing to cease carrying the mattress only after the accused perpetrator of her 2012 sexual assault is expelled or leaves the university, she ends up carrying it to her graduation ceremony. Her activism inspires similar protests across the nation and globe.

Nearly 200 students at the University of Chicago march in protest of a campus hacking group that threatened sexual assault to students. The threat was made in retaliation for a list posted to Tumblr with names of students accused of varying degrees of sexual assault.

September 19   The Phi Delta Theta fraternity at Texas Tech holds a party with a banner that reads "No Means Yes, Yes Means Anal," sparking campus protests. The fraternity's charter was revoked.

September 28   California becomes the first state to enact legislation that college students get "affirmative consent" before engaging in sexual activity.

October 23   California Institute of the Arts students walk out of their classes and hold a peaceful occupation of the school's administrative offices to protest the handling of rape allegations.

November 19   *Rolling Stone* publishes an article chronicling a gang rape at a fraternity party at the University of Virginia. The main informant's story is found to be fabricated, and the magazine retracts the story.

2015   The American Association of Universities releases the findings from their Campus Climate Survey on Sexual Assault and Sexual Misconduct.

The Washington Post–Kaiser Family Foundation Poll releases the findings from their Survey on Current and Recent College Students on Sexual Assault.

January 18   Brock Turner, a Stanford freshman, sexually assaults an unconscious woman behind a dumpster. Turner later receives a punishment of six months in county jail and three months' probation, sparking national outrage for the leniency in punishment.

February 27   Release of *The Hunting Ground*, a critically acclaimed documentary about campus sexual assault and institutional mishandling. An edited version is later screened on CNN.

April 21   Best-selling author Jon Krakauer releases his book *Missoula: Rape and the Justice System in a College Town*. The book chronicles several sexual assaults that occurred at the University of Montana and illustrates the difficulties the survivors endured after their assaults.

April 24   The assistant secretary of civil rights to the U.S. Department of Education releases a Dear Colleague letter to remind school districts, colleges, and universities that receive federal funds that they must have a designated Title IX coordinator to ensure the school complies with the legal obligations outlined by Title IX.

October 9   Harvard's school newspaper, *The Harvard Crimson*, publishes Vivian Maymi's essay chronicling her rape by a date in her sophomore year.

November 15   Cherelle Locklear commits suicide less than two months after she was raped at the Sigma Pi fraternity house at William Paterson University.

2016   The 114th Congress is scheduled to consider several pending federal bills, including The Safe Campus Act, The Fair Campus Act, The Campus Accountability and Safety Act, The Hold Accountable and Lend Transparency Campus Sexual Violence Act, and the Survivor Outreach and Support Campus Act.

January 20   The National Institute of Justice releases the results of the Campus Climate Survey, a key deliverable of the White House Task Force to Protect Students From Sexual Assault.

February   Eight female students file a Title IX civil suit against the University of Tennessee, stating that the university creates a hostile environment for women by ignoring sexual assaults committed by athletes, in addition to condoning an athletic culture that encourages underage drinking, drug use, and sexual violence. Avoiding trial, the schools settles with the plaintiffs in July 2016.

February 28   At the 88th Academy Awards, Vice President Joe Biden urges people to take the It's on Us pledge to intervene in potentially dangerous situations. Lady Gaga follows with a performance of the Oscar nominated song "Til It Happens to You" from the documentary *The Hunting Ground*. She is joined on stage with 50 sexual assault survivors.

March 2   Jesse Matthew accepts a plea deal for the murder and kidnapping of University of Virginia student Hannah Graham and Virginia Tech student Morgan Harrington. The murders, which occurred five years apart, add four life sentences to the three life sentences he was serving for sexual assault, abduction, and attempted murder from an incident that occurred in 2005. Matthew is accused of raping students at both Liberty University in 2002 and Christopher Newport University in 2003.

April   Students accuse Brigham Young University, operated by the Church of Jesus Christ of Latter-day Saints, of charging sexual assault victims who come forward with breaking the rigid student honor code that prohibits premarital sex. The accusations result in the filing of a Title IX complaint and the creation of an online petition calling for the university to give immunity to sexual assault victims so that they can come forward without fear. BYU eventually changed its policy and no longer investigates sexual assault victims for honor code violations.

April 2   *The Harvard Law Record* publishes an editorial written by Kamilah Willingham, in which she defends her rape allegation to 19 faculty of the law school who published an open letter discrediting her account. The story of her assault, and Harvard's reaction to it, is predominantly featured in the film *The Hunting Ground*.

May 26   Baylor campus president Kenneth Starr is removed from his position in the wake of a campus scandal and findings that Baylor mishandled sexual assault cases. He is transitioned to a chancellor role and resigns a week later.

June   Former Indiana University student and fraternity member John P. Enochs accepts a plea deal dismissing two felony charges of sexual assault stemming from 2013 and 2015. He is sentenced to a year's probation with no prison time. His punishment is widely criticized for being too lenient.

June 2   The victim ("Emily Doe") in the Stanford Brock Turner sexual assault case reads a powerful 12-page letter outlining the profound impact the assault had on her life during Turner's sentencing hearing. The letter is widely circulated and read on the floor by members of Congress. Vice President Joe Biden writes the victim a letter of support in response to her statement, and *Glamour Magazine* names her the "2016 Woman of the Year."

December 17   The University of Minnesota's football team ends their short-lived boycott of all football-related activities. The team initiated the boycott to protest the suspension of ten players from the team for sexual assault.

Glossary

This glossary defines some of those terms that have been used in this book, along with some terms that one may encounter in additional research on the topic.

acquaintance rape   Rape committed by someone known to the victim. Although often referred to as "date rape," the assailant can be anyone the victim knows (a friend, neighbor, coworker, peer, date, etc.) Perpetrators of rape are acquaintances to the victim in approximately 75 percent of cases.

advocate   In general, victim advocates are trained to help victims of crime by offering them information, resources, and support. With regard to sexual assault, an advocate typically works with or for a campus, the police, or an organization to help survivors navigate services, resources, the legal system, and campus policies and procedures.

affirmative consent or affirmative consent standard   Requires parties to get affirmative and continuous consent in a sexual encounter. The standard is often referred to as "yes means yes," as opposed to the popular slogan "no means no," which is argued to place an undue burden on victims. While some maintain consent can only be in the form of a verbal "yes," others argue the consent can be verbal or in the form of unambiguous body language. Affirmative consent policies are part of state law in various states and have been adopted by numerous colleges and universities.

attempted rape   A crime in which rape was the motivation for assault, though no nonconsensual sexual penetration occurred. The violence of an attempted rape can have the same impact on a victim as a completed rape. Legal definitions vary by state.

binge drinking   The Centers for Disease Control and Prevention relies upon the National Institute on Alcohol Abuse and Alcoholism's definition of binge drinking as a pattern of drinking that brings a person's blood alcohol concentration to 0.08 gram percent or above. Typically, for men this is achieved by consuming five or more drinks and for women four or more drinks in the course of about two hours.

bystander intervention   Bystanders who witness problematic incidents or behaviors often fail to get involved. To counteract this common phenomenon (referred to as *bystander apathy* or the *bystander effect*), bystander intervention training teaches participants to help others in situations of need. On college campuses, bystander intervention training teaches students to feel a sense of responsibility for others and have the confidence and skills to intervene if they see someone who needs help.

clear and convincing standard of proof   With regards to campus sexual assault, the clear and convincing standard of proof requires that a hearing determine that sex discrimination is highly and more substantially likely to have occurred than not. This standard was most commonly employed by colleges and universities before the Department of Education changed the standard to "preponderance of the evidence" in the Dear Colleague letter of 2011. The clear and convincing standard requires roughly 75 percent chance that the accused is responsible and therefore requires a higher burden of proof than the preponderance of the evidence standard.

consent   A voluntary agreement between participants to engage in sexual activity. Consent cannot be given if a person is intoxicated, unconscious, under threat, under age of consent, or mentally or physically unable to give consent. While there is no single legal definition of consent, each state sets its own definition through either law or court cases. States typically analyze consent based on whether it was offered by a person's free will (without violence or coercion), whether a person expressed overt actions or words indicating agreement, and whether the individual had capacity and legal ability to agree to sexual activity. *See also* affirmative consent or affirmative consent standard.

date rape drugs   Used as tools to aid in drug-facilitated sexual assault. Often referred to as "party" or "club drugs" due to their use in dance club settings, these odorless, colorless, and tasteless drugs can be consumed in an alcoholic drink without knowledge. The most common include gamma-hydroxybutyric acid (GHB), which is a central nervous system depressant. Victims who have consumed GHB (street names include Liquid X, Liquid Ecstasy, "Georgia Home Boy) become incapacitated and unable to resist assault; some suffer amnesia. Rohypnol (street names include Roofies, Roach, Ruffles) is a strong sedative that causes partial amnesia. Katamine (street names include Special K, Kitkat, Cat Valium) is a dissociative anesthetic that creates a dreamlike state and makes it difficult for the user to move. It is worth noting that alcohol is the drug most commonly used as a tool in facilitating sexual assault.

drug- or alcohol-facilitated sexual assault   Also known as predator rape, this occurs when alcohol or drugs are used as a tool to incapacitate or compromise someone's ability to consent to sex. This includes intentionally forcing a victim to use drugs. *See* date rape drugs.

feminism   A movement for social, political, and economic equality of men and women fueled by the belief that men and women should have equal rights and opportunities.

feminist   Someone who believes that men and women should have equal rights and opportunities.

FERPA, or Family Educational Rights and Privacy Act   Signed into law in 1974, FERPA protects the privacy of student education records for parents and eligible students (over the age of 18 or attending a school beyond the high school level). In general, with some exceptions, schools must have written permission from the parent or eligible student before releasing information about a student's education records.

forcible sexual assault   Includes unwanted sexual contact or intercourse that occurs due to force or threat of force.

hearing   With regard to sexual assault cases on college or university campuses, a hearing gives the survivor and the accused the opportunity to give statements to a group of people affiliated with the school and who are charged with making decisions about the case, typically about whether there were violations of the student code of conduct.

heteronormative   A world view that promotes heterosexuality as the preferred or normal sexual orientation.

hook-up culture   Refers to brief uncommitted sexual encounters between individuals who are not dating each other. Hooking up has largely replaced traditional dating on college campuses as the primary means of forming romantic and/or sexual relationships.

incapacitated sexual assault   Unwanted sexual acts that occur after a victim voluntarily consumes alcohol or drugs, or a combination of both, that renders him or her physically and/or cognitively impaired.

IPV or intimate partner violence   Physical, sexual, or psychological violence by a current or former intimate partner or spouse. Also referred to as *domestic violence.*

LGBTQIA, LGBT, or LBGTQ   An umbrella acronym for people who identify as lesbian, gay, bisexual, transgender, queer, questioning, intersex, or asexual.

misogyny   Hatred, dislike, or mistrust of women.

multiple perpetrator sexual assault   When two or more perpetrators act together to sexually assault the same victim, commonly referred to as *gang rape.*

panic attack   A sudden onset of fear that can be brought about by extensive stress or a negative life condition. Panic attacks typically reach their peak within minutes and can include some of the following symptoms: pounding heart, sweating, shaking, shortness of breath, feelings of choking, chest pain, nausea, feeling dizzy, chills, heat sensations, numbness, fear of losing control, fear of dying, and feelings of being detached from oneself.

patriarchy   A system in which men dominate women. A patriarchal society is one in which men hold the positions of power.

posttraumatic stress disorder (PTSD)   An anxiety disorder that can result from a traumatic event, including sexual violence. PTSD is marked by extreme and persistent feelings of stress, fear, anxiety, and nervousness. Symptoms include re-experiencing (through flashbacks, dreams); avoidance (changing behaviors to avoid scenarios associated with the event); hyper-arousal (feeling "on edge," being easily startled); and difficulties with cognition and mood (distorted feelings of guilt or blame, failure to remember key details of the traumatic event). A psychologist or psychiatrist diagnoses PTSD if the patient exhibits the aforementioned symptoms over a period of time and has difficulty with daily functioning.

preponderance of the evidence standard of proof   The Department of Education's Dear Colleague letter (2011) set forth the requirement that schools and universities use preponderance of the evidence as a standard of proof for complaints of sex discrimination, including sexual harassment and violence. The standard requires that a hearing determine that discrimination is "more likely than not" or 50.1 percent likely to have occurred. This is a lower burden of proof than is required in the "clear and convincing" standard commonly used before the Department of Education's letter.

psychological theories   As applied to sexual assault, psychological theories explore potential factors including the personality and/or psychological disorders of perpetrators and abusive backgrounds of perpetrators.

rape Sexual penetration of vagina, anus, or mouth with any body part or object without consent of the victim. Rape is achieved by physical force, by emotional or psychological coercion, by deception, by threat, or against a person incapable of giving consent. Legal definitions vary by state.

rape culture Societal attitudes and cultural practices in which male violence against women is encouraged and normalized and where victims are blamed for their own abuse.

rape kit The kit used in a sexual assault forensic exam. It includes checklists, instructions, and materials. The contents vary by state, but include various materials for evidence collection that can aid a criminal rape investigation. Common items include combs, bags, paper sheets, swabs, sterile containers, glass slides, nail picks, labels, and envelopes.

rape schedule An element of rape culture. Refers to women living their day-to-day lives assuming they could be sexually assaulted and consequently altering their lifestyle and behavior in attempts to try to prevent the anticipated assault.

rape trauma syndrome Common emotional, behavioral, and physical reactions to experiencing rape or attempted rape exhibited in the months or years after an assault.

red zone Typically defined as the period of time between the beginning of fall semester and Thanksgiving in which college students, especially freshmen women, are at the highest risk of experiencing sexual assault.

sexual assault Any type of sexual contact or behavior that occurs without consent. Behaviors include penetration, attempted rape, forcing a victim to perform sexual acts, incest, child molestation, fondling, or unwanted sexual touching. Legal definitions vary by state. *See* rape.

sexual assault nurse examiner A registered nurse who has received special training and clinical preparation to be able to provide care to victims of sexual assault. She or he can perform forensic medical examinations and gather evidence utilizing a rape kit and may provide expert testimony if a case goes to trial.

sexual coercion The use of pressure, force, or alcohol and drugs to get someone to do something sexual against their will. Best understood as existing on a continuum, it includes subtle persuasion, verbal and/or emotional coercion, and physical force.

sexual harassment Unwelcome sexual advances, requests for sexual favors, and other verbal or physical conduct of a sexual nature that creates a hostile or offensive environment.

sexual violence An umbrella term that encompasses sexual assault, rape, sexual harassment, and stalking.

sodomy With regard to sexual assault, forcible sodomy refers to oral or anal sex in which the victim does not consent or is legally unable to consent. The generic classification also includes intercourse with an animal, commonly referred to as bestiality. The legal definition of sodomy varies by state.

stalking Repeated following, watching, and/or harassing of another person.

statutory rape A general term referring to sexual relations with someone below the *age of consent* that is defined by state law (typically set at age 16, 17, or 18).

stranger rape Rape in which the perpetrator is not known by the victim. Stranger rape is less common than acquaintance rape, occurring in approximately 25 percent of cases.

street harassment A form of sexual harassment, it includes unwanted comments, whistles, gestures, "catcalls," and other actions by strangers in a public environment.

trigger Situations or stimuli that set off a flashback or memory to the original traumatic event.

Index

About the Author

Alison E. Hatch received her Ph.D. in Sociology at the University of Colorado–Boulder. She is an associate professor of Sociology and Gender Studies at Armstrong State University in Savannah, Georgia. Dr. Hatch teaches classes on gender, sexuality, family, service learning, and gender violence. In addition to researching and presenting on various topics related to campus sexual assault, she developed a Bystander Intervention and Sexual Assault Awareness Program for college students. Over the span of her career, Dr. Hatch has received awards for her activism, campus involvement, and teaching excellence. She currently serves as the president for the Georgia Sociological Association.